M000281943

Growing up Asian in Australia

Growing up Asian
in Australia

Edited by
Alice Pung

Published by Black Inc.,
an imprint of Schwartz Publishing Pty Ltd
37–39 Langridge Street
Collingwood VIC 3066 Australia
email: enquiries@blackincbooks.com
http://www.blackincbooks.com

Photo of Hoa Pham (p.263) by Alister Air. Photo of Joy Hopwood (p.277)
by Yanna Black.

The National Library of Australia Cataloguing-in-Publication entry:

Pung, Alice (ed.)
Growing up Asian in Australia.
ISBN 9781863951913

1. Pung, Alice. 2. Asians – Australia – Social life and customs.
3. Immigrants' writings – Australia. 4. Asians – Australia –
Literary collections. 5. Race relations – Australia. 6. Australia –
Social conditions.

A820.80355

Book design: Thomas Deverall
Typeset by J&M Typesetting

Printed in Australia by Griffin Press. The paper this book is printed on
is certified against the Forest Stewardship Council® Standards. Griffin
Press holds FSC chain of custody certification SGS-COC-005088. FSC
promotes environmentally responsible, socially beneficial and economically
viable management of the world's forests.

FSC
www.fsc.org
MIX
Paper from
responsible sources
FSC® C009448

*Dedicated to all Asian-Australians, whose struggles,
aspirations and hopes across the generations have
helped make this an ace country in which to grow up.*

*For Alexander, Alison and Alina, who make life
wonderful, because they are.*

Contents

UnAustralian?

Tall Poppies

Leaving Home

Homecoming

Introduction

When I was growing up, we were called Power-Points. I thought it was because we were so smart and dweeby in a dynamic Micro-soft-magnate sort of way. All that untapped potential! All that electrifying brain power! Then someone pointed to an Australian power socket, and told me to take a closer look. Imagine that if it was a face, they said, think about what kind of face it would be. They saw two sloping lines and one straight down the middle, and thought it was hilarious. I didn't get it, because the power socket was white.

In fact, if there was any kind of 'face' on it, it looked vacuously cute, like most of the lead characters in the teen fiction I was reading at the time. After a while – with the exception of Claudia from the Babysitters Club, who was Asian *and* funny, good at art *and* bad at maths – most teen fiction gave me the idea that I needed extensive plastic surgery. So I stopped reading those books and turned to John Marsden and Robert Cormier instead, who wrote with raw honesty and real feeling about coming of age.

Growing up is a funny time. During no other period will we experience so many 'firsts': first day at school, first friend, first love, first fear, first heartbreak, first loss, first epiphany. This anthology is a book of firsts – all from a uniquely Asian-Australian perspective. Whether growing up in the 1950s with ancestry from the gold-rush days, or arriving more recently and attempting to find solidarity in schoolyard friendship, our authors show us what it is like behind the stereotypes. Asian-Australians have often been written about by outsiders, as outsiders. Here, they tell their own stories. They are not distant observers, plucking the most garish fruit from the lowest-hanging branches of an exotic cultural tree. These writers *are* the tree, and they write from its roots.

The poet Horace said *Mutato nomine de te fabula narratur*: 'Change only the name and this story is also about you.' I felt this way when reading many of these stories. Compiling this anthology also made me more aware of the difficulties faced by earlier generations of immigrants – parents, grandparents and great-grandparents. Even with our mastery of 'Strine,' those born in Australia in the past four decades find it difficult to be Asian-Australian. Imagine what it must be like for Asian-Australians who didn't and still don't have the language. Usually, it is the second generation that accumulates enough cultural capital to be able to put their parents' experiences into words. They also have their own stories to tell about mediating between two cultures. Stories such as Thao Nguyen's 'Water Buffalo' and Pauline Nguyen's 'The Courage of Soldiers' explore the generational divide with compassion, while Mia Francis's ode to her adopted son and Blossom Beeby's acceptance of her adopted heritage move us with their unassuming love.

This collection also reveals that there is more than one voice within any given culture – from Tom Cho's brilliant satirical surrealism to Vanessa Woods's wonderful self-deprecating humour, from Paul Nguyen's aching account of adolescent loneliness to Chi Vu's bewildered young lovers, from Hoa Pham's painful personal journey towards acceptance to Francis Lee's arrival in the 'Upside-Down Year' of 1961, and from Jenny Kee's jubilant adolescent sexual awakening to Quan Yeoman's insightful meditation on art and family. As Benjamin Law tentatively steps towards manhood with Mariah Carey's *Music Box* blaring in his ears, as Shalini Akhil works towards becoming Indian Wonder Woman, as Annette Shun Wah helps run her family chicken farm, and as HaiHa Le leaves Jehovah to become an actress – these stories show us what it is like beyond the stereotypes.

I have arranged the anthology around loose themes selected with a certain irony, picking out traits that have been worthy of collective national pride – the Battler, the Pioneer, the Legend – to show that these heroic characteristics are not confined to those with white faces and First-Fleet heritage.

Strine explores the difficulties of navigating a different language: Ivy Tseng receives careful Chinese lessons from her father, Sunil Badami tries to change his name, and Amy Choi reminisces about her late grandfather. *Pioneers* includes Ken Chau's personally political poems, their impact like a punch to the gut, while Simon Tong surmounts a loss of words through sheer will and quiet observation, and Christopher Cyrill shows that a sense of home can be tied to, but can also transcend, the physical landscape. *Battlers* features Hop Dac's charming carnivorous pigs, Kevin Lai's nostalgic supermarket through Matt Huynh's incredible artistry, and Lily Chan's deftly humorous observations of the characters who turn up in her family's country-town restaurant.

Mates explores stories of school, from the warm humour of Oliver Phommavanh, Tanveer Ahmed and Aditi Gourvernel, to Ray Wing-Lun's poignant insights, gleaned from his struggles with institutional learning. *The Folks* includes Oanh Thi Tran's charmingly stilted conversations with her parents, Rudi Soman's affection for his Acha and Amma, and Simone Lazaroo and Bon-Wai Chou's sensitive reflections on the death of a parent. *The Clan* features stories as diverse as Diem Vo's 'Family Life,' with its gentle sense of security and place, Ken Chan's beautifully narrated account of feuding grandparents and Benjamin Law's hilarious yet heartbreaking look at parental separation. In *Legends*, Phillip Tang and his father find a connection through the death of screen icon Leslie Cheung, Chin Shen's 'Papa Bear' paves the way for his progeny, Glenn Lieu inadvertently becomes the 'New Challenger,' and Cindy Pan's father dreams of her winning every single category of Nobel Prize. *The Hots* explores love and sexuality: we meet Xerxes Matsa's amazingly virile family, and Lian Low recounts coming to terms with her 'forbidden' obsession with KD Lang.

UnAustralian deals with issues of identity and race, from Mei-Yen Chua's special menu of cultural secrets to Uyen Loewald's ironic poem about being 'good little migrants,' from Tony Ayres's unsettling encounter with homophobic racism to Leanne Hall's fear of serial Asian fetishists, from Michelle Law's 'call to arms' to Joo-Inn Chew's whimsical childhood with her hippy parents.

I have also subverted the term *Tall Poppies*, a term often used disparagingly, but in this instance used to cast a new light on inspirational Asian-Australians: artists, film directors, writers, rock musicians, actors, lawyers, politicians, journalists, comedians, radio DJs, even the first Asian presenter on *Play School*. The diversity of our authors shows that Asian-Australians have flourished in almost every occupational field. Sociologists have sometimes described us as a 'model minority' – working hard, studying hard, conforming to the expectations and ideals of the dominant culture. This can be a burden for young Asian-Australians growing up. It implies that external indicators of success – money, education, fame, career – define the value of our contribution to society. Our Tall Poppies are included here not because they are 'model minorities,' but because they express, with great depth and generosity, what it is like to persist in pursuing one's passion, to surmount racism and overcome adversity.

Leaving Home explores the painful journeys we make in order to reconcile our internal and external struggles, including Diana Nguyen's achingly funny instructions on 'how to disappoint your Vietnamese mother' and Emily J. Sun's haunting tale of frustrated ambition and love. Finally, *Homecoming* is all about recovering a feeling of home, whether it is an actual physical journey like Kylie Kwong's return to her family's ancestral home in China, Jacqui Larkin's sweet tale of a return to childhood, or Sim Shen's reflections on having his first child and 'returning' to South-East Asia.

I hope that these loose themes will help bring to the forefront questions of identity, place and perspective. Because the stories deal so insightfully with the challenges of coming to terms with multiple identities, they move beyond crude labels such as 'bananas' and 'coconuts.' We are not fruit (or power sockets!), we are people. These are not sociological essays, but deeply personal stories told with great literary skill. These stories show us not only what it is like to grow up Asian in Australia, but also what it means to be Asian-Australian. And this is exactly the sort of book I wish I had read when I was growing up.

Alice Pung

Strine

The Relative Advantages of Learning My Language

Amy Choi

I was never particularly kind to my grandfather. He was my mother's father, and he lived with us when I was a teenager. I remember him coming into the lounge room one night, and when he went to sit down, I said to my brother, 'I hope he doesn't sit down.' I didn't think my grandfather understood much English, but he understood enough, and as I watched, he straightened up again, and without a word, returned to his room. I was twelve years old.

My grandfather wrote poetry on great rolls of thin white paper with a paintbrush. He offered to read and explain his poems to me several times over the years, but I only let him do it once. I'd let my Chinese go by then, which made listening to him too much of an effort. Though I was raised speaking Chinese, it wasn't long before I lost my language skills. I spoke English all day at school, listened to English all night on TV. I didn't see the point of speaking Chinese. We lived in Australia.

Monday to Friday, Grandad went to the city, dressed in a suit with a waistcoat, a hat, and carrying his walking stick. He would take the bus to the station, the train to the city, the tram to Little Bourke Street. On Mondays, he'd be sitting at a large round table at Dragon Boat Restaurant with other old Chinese men. Tuesdays to Fridays, he was at a small square table by himself with a pot of tea and the Chinese newspaper. I watched him leave in the morning and come back in the afternoon, as punctual and as purposeful as any school kid or office worker, for years.

One afternoon, he didn't come home until well after dark. We assumed he'd got off the bus at the wrong stop or had turned into the wrong street at some point, forcing him to wander around for a bit before finding his way home.

A month after that, he tried to let himself into a stranger's house. It looked just like our house. The yellow rose bush, the painted timber mailbox, even the Ford Falcon parked out the front were the same. But it was the home of a gentle Pakistani couple who let him use the phone to call us.

Two months after that, he fell and hit his head on something. When he didn't come home, Mum and I drove around looking for him. We finally found him stumbling along in the dark, two kilometres from the house. There was a trickle of blood down the side of his face.

From that day forward, Grandad was only allowed to go to the city if someone accompanied him. Once or twice during the school holidays that task fell to me.

After rinsing out his milk glass, Grandad would pick up his walking stick and head out into the street. I'd follow, a few steps behind. He wasn't aware of me. He wasn't aware of the milk on his lip, the upside-down watch on his wrist, the scrape of branches against his coat. He had a blank, goofy, content expression on his face, and turned instinctively into platform five when he was at the train station and into Dragon Boat Restaurant when he was on Little Bourke Street.

When he was about to board the wrong tram or turn round the wrong corner, I'd step forward to take him by the elbow and steer him back on course. He'd smile innocently and seem glad to see me. 'Hello there, Amy. Finished school already?' Then he'd look away and forget I was ever there.

He'd been diagnosed with a brain tumour and, three months later, he died.

At the funeral, my sadness was overshadowed by a sense of regret. I'd denied my grandfather the commonest of kindnesses. I was sixteen years old.

I am now twenty-six. A few weeks ago, during a family dinner at a Chinese restaurant, the waiter complimented my mum on the fact that I was speaking to her in Chinese. The waiter told Mum with a sigh that his own kids could barely string a sentence together in Chinese. Mum told the waiter I had stopped speaking Chinese a few years into primary school, but that I had suddenly started up again in my late teens.

I have often wondered how aware my mum is of the connection between Grandad's death and my ever-improving Chinese. Whenever I am stuck for a word, I ask her. Whenever I am with her, or relatives, or a waiter at a Chinese restaurant, or a sales assistant at a Chinese department store, I practise. I am constantly adding new words to my Chinese vocabulary, and memorising phrases I can throw into a conversation at will. It is an organic way of relearning a language. Textbooks and teachers are not necessary, since I am only interested in mastering the spoken word. I am not interested in the written word or in the many elements of Chinese culture of which I am ignorant. I am not trying to 'discover my roots.' I am simply trying to ensure that the next time an elderly relative wants me to listen to them, I am not only willing, I am able.

Sticks and Stones and Such-like

Sunil Badami

I've been called a lot of things. Especially growing up, being one of only three Indian kids at school, the others being my brother and a squeaky-voiced boy whose name escapes me now. Curry-muncher, towel-head, abo, coon, boong, darkie, nig-nog, golli-wog. 'Black' followed by any suitable or just thunk-up epithet. Often all at once, accompanied by a Chinese burn or dead-leg.

My mother would always say, 'Stones and sticks and such-like can only shake your skeletons. Just rise over it!' Which was even more irritating than if it had been said correctly. She was right, though – after being called anything and everything enough times, I stopped wincing. Even for dead-legs. 'Ya black bastard,' kids would say affectionately, and I'd take it good-naturedly. Didn't want to appear a bad sport – especially when I wasn't any good at any sport at all.

But the one thing that always got under my skin was my own name. *Sunil.* My mother and Indian relatives pronounce it '*Soo*-neel'; my own broad accent makes it '*Sir*-neil.'

SUN-ill, SOON-ull, SAN-eel, I've heard 'em all. 'Sunil? Like *senile?*' Or that old playground favourite: 'Sunil? Like banana *peel?*' If I had a dollar for every time, how many rupees would that make?

Naturally, growing up, I didn't want to be a nigger, a coon, a darkie. I didn't feel 'black' anything. I just wanted to fit in.

'Why dontcha wash the black off, ya dirty black bastard?' playground wits would yell. And sometimes their parents too, although always with an *affectionate* chuckle. 'Perhaps if you wash hard enough, it'll come orf?'

And I did once, too: scrubbing my right arm with the floor brush till tiny spots of blood started weeping into the sink, discovering nothing but angry blooming red underneath. 'We're all pink on the inside, aren't we?' the day nurse at my mother's surgery said kindly afterwards, as though it were some kind of consolation, despite rubbing me with stingy alcohol. I wondered how Michael Jackson had managed it.

My father, who'd run off with one of the nurses at his hospital, *hated* Indians. He thought they were vulgar and ill mannered, unlike him and his new wife, who'd never been to India. 'Uncle-uncles and aunty-aunties,' he called them, laughing at the way we called them Uncle or Aunty, laughing even harder at their flared trousers and flat feet spilling out of sandals after his new wife had thrown out his flares and sandals and bought him a fashionable new Western wardrobe.

Still, he had to have rice and my stepmother's watery Clive of Indian dhal once a week – but only once a week, because according to her, curry stank the house out. She was a formidable house-keeper – probably more pathological than formidable – and their house always seemed too neat to be alive: the magazines at right angles to the coffee-table edges, the paintings all a similarly blurry pastel, everything reeking of furniture spray and air freshener.

My mother's house, on the other hand, was always messy, always redolent of the trinity that jostles you when you enter an Indian home: not Brahma, Vishnu or Shiva, but asafoetida, cumin and incense. And there was always a crowd in our house after my father left, all part of the same little South Indian clique who'd known each other since medical school, bearing saris, curries, sympathy and gossip. (Until we finally went back to India, I was convinced all grown-up Indians were general practitioners with degrees from Kasturba Medical College, Manipal University, Mangalore, Karnataka).

On hot, interminable Sunday afternoons everyone would gather in our house: the uncles setting up with their cards, little buckets full of change and plastic bankers' visors in the dining room, smoking fat, acrid cigars, telling bawdy jokes in Kannada – which, even if I could speak it, I wouldn't have understood anyway.

And the aunties in the kitchen, rolling puri atta into little balls with deft hands, their bangles jangling, before flinging them into hot woks, pushing children out of the way as those little nuggets bloomed and swelled into crisp balloons. All talking frantically and loudly in English, Hindi, Kannada, Konkani: every sentence a masala of different vocabularies. And all talking about the one thing that interested them most: their children. 'Rahul is come first in his class, *hunh*! He has state rank.' 'Sangeetha is champion of tennis club, *nah*!' 'Preeti has finished her internship, and now only she's deciding between ortho or cardio.' 'When's she getting married, *nah*? I know a boy ...'

When they weren't clucking over their children, they'd analyse their names' meanings. *Abhay* meant fearless. *Gourangi*, wheatish complexion. *Rajesh*, King of the Gods – or God of Kings. *Anant*, truth. *Padma*, lotus. As too *Rajiv*, *Padma*, *Pushpa* and *Arvind*. 'Flower-power babies,' my mother joked.

We, the above-discussed children, would try our luck near the wok, stealing puri flakes fallen out of the oil while dodging the aunties' grinding fingers as they tried to pinch our cheeks. Or taking pappadums or chaklis – crunchy wheel-shaped chickpea snacks – to our friends in the backyard (with an extra one for our troubles, of course). We'd loll about, wishing for it to end: this endless unintelligible chatter, wishing we were somewhere else, wishing we were someone else. All our Aussie friends would probably be having barbecues – something unimaginable for us and our strictly vegetarian parents. And they wouldn't have to translate everything into English in their heads, then back again before answering.

There were two boys, the Balgis, whose names were Jason and Andrew. I couldn't believe their luck. Sure, they looked Indian, but nobody ever got *their* names wrong. Even my little brother had a Western name: *Monty*. His real name was Sumant, but when he was born, I was too young to say it properly. Mont became Monty. I stayed Senile.

I couldn't stand it: it was hard enough not being able to catch, let alone being a darkie. If I couldn't *be* less black, surely I could get a name that made me *feel* less black? If Sumant was Monty, why couldn't I be – well, *Neil*?

Neil. I liked it: it sounded like an astronaut's name. It sounded grown-up. We'd just started cursive writing at school, and I'd practise my new name for hours. Neil. Neil Badami. My name's Badami. Neil Badami. *The Neilster.* I told people to call me Neil, and nobody laughed like they did when I told them my real – I mean, my other – name. Neil seemed to fit their mouths better, and I could feel their approval at the effort I was making to fit in. Still couldn't catch a cricket ball, though I was working on it.

At home, I was Sunil, trying not to eat my dhal with my left hand, trying to get my mouth around tongue-twisting Venkateshwara bhajjans at morning puja. In the real world, in the brilliant universe of my imagination, I was Neil. I fitted in. I scored a double century in the Ashes. I could fly, dropping water bombs on playground bullies called Wesley and Boyd. Neil, like *unreal*!

Which would've been fine, until the afternoon my best friend, Kieran ('It's Indian name, no?' said my mother, thinking of *Kiran*, meaning ray of light), started laughing about Neil trying to catch the ball Mark Keary'd belted for six past the shelter sheds at lunch, coming a cropper on the handball courts. Despite Neil frantically trying to shoosh him in the back seat.

'Who's this Neil?' my mother asked. Then, seeing everything from the rear-view mirror, saying nothing. Even Kieran got it, as the car swelled with a hot puri silence. 'See ya, Ne – um, *mate*,' he said, scrambling out of the car. That silence bubbled all the way home, the steam threatening to burst, and I knew, as all children do, that it's when your mother *doesn't* shout that you're in really big trouble.

When we got home, my mother sent Monty out to play, then sat me down in the kitchen. 'What is this?' she said, handing me a bowl of curds and sugar that somehow didn't taste quite as sweet as usual. 'Changing your name? Being a *Neil*?' She spat my unreal new name out like something bitter and stringy, too difficult to swallow.

'It's just that – I – um, I hate it. Sunil. It's too hard to say. It's too – it's too *Indian*!'

My mother looked out the window, at the bare backyard, the yellow tips of the grass, unmowed since Dad left, barely flickering in the yellow heat, the shy tops of the mango tree she'd planted peeking out over the weedy ruins. 'But Sunil is a beautiful name,' she said quietly, distantly.

'What's it mean, then?' I asked. In all the times I'd snuck into the kitchen and heard snatches of the name game, I'd never heard my name being explained. I knew heaps of Rajes, loads of Madhus, but nobody else with my name (apart, of course, from Sunil Gavaskar, the cricket player).

Something lit up in her eyes, faint but fierce. She took both my arms, holding them tight with her pinchy fingers. 'Sunil – beautiful name! You know Lord Shiva, God of Destruction?'

I nodded, a little afraid. Like fearful black Kali, Shiva frightened me, with his unkempt hair, draped in leopard skins, a snake writhing round his neck, his turbulent temper reminding me of my father. Why couldn't our family worship Krishna, always laughing, always up to mischief?

But my mother was warming up to it, the explanation of my name. 'And where does Lord Shiva live?'

'On top of Mount Everest,' I muttered.

'Yes, highest mountain in the world – the world! – in India. Indian mountain,' she said proudly. 'And Sunil is breeze that blows at sunset on Shiva's birthday once every thousand years, blowing snow from his head-top into ice cave below, where the snow melts and flows down mountain and becomes what?'

'I dunno.'

She looked at me witheringly. 'Holy Ganga only, *poda*!' She slapped my thigh, looking triumphant. 'And you want to change this name to be a – a *Neil*?' She flicked her wrist in that contemptuous way only Indians can. 'Neil is what you do in temple to gods. You want to Neil for everyone else, too? Sunil is best name ever! Sunil is name I always wanted my first-born son to have. And you? Who are you? *What* are you? You should be proud!' She smiled and sat back, her logic as round and delectable as a hot chakli.

I shifted a little under the weight of that, but it seemed to fit. As did my name, even though it might take some growing into.

'So?' my mother said after I'd finished my curds.

'It's a good name, I guess,' I said, smiling a little.

'*Best* name!' she cried. 'First-class name!'

'Sure.' I didn't want to concede too much: if I allowed she was right this time, I'd hear about it for a long time to come. Like most Indian mothers, she had an elephantine memory for recipes, relations, festivals – and for being right. I could be living this down for years.

Even if I still found it hard to tie my Indian appearance to my Australian feeling (eventually settling for an awkwardly knotted hyphen to make me Indian-Australian or Australian-Indian, depending on the day), I didn't worry so much about my name anymore. No matter how people said it, I didn't wince: I knew what it meant. And when someone kindly said, 'SUN-el, that's an interesting name! What's that mean, then?' I'd usually proudly oblige (although I did once reply, 'Only if you tell me what Barbara means.').

And, although I hated to admit it then, my mother was right: I *was* proud. Even when, after finding out where I was *really* from, people tried their terrible Peter Sellers birdy-num-num impersonations; even when they made snide comments about immigrants on the train, loud enough for us to hear; even though no matter how deliberately I said my name, they still mangled it, it didn't matter: I knew what it meant, and what it meant to my mother. All those Kylies and Brents and Kimbaleahs could keep their ordinary, unimaginative monikers: I had a name that had its own story, its own place: a name I shared with nobody, apart from the Little Master. Every roll call, I felt sorry for Matthews B, C and H; everyone knew who *I* was. Every time someone mispronounced my singular name, I saw Shiva, serene and powerful on his distant peak, flesh-coloured breeze blowing the Ganges out of his hair.

Years later, in a Bangalore bookshop, my future wife came across a book of Indian children's names.

'Do you think you're in here?' she asked.

'Are you joking?' I replied. 'I bet there's like a whole chapter or something – what with Mount Everest, the ice cave, Shiva's birthday, the Ganges and all that ...'

It was a thick book with lots of names – many of which meant lotus. Past *Sudesha*, through *Sunam* and *Sujat, Sujit, Sukhwant, Sumitr, Sunay*, we finally got to *Sunil*.

It wasn't a paragraph, let alone a chapter. Just two little words: *dark one*.

Learning English

Tom Cho

When I first arrived in Australia, I did not know a word of English. I began English lessons through a migrant settlement program soon after I arrived, but I found it all very difficult. But things did improve a little once I learnt the trick of replacing words I did not know with phrases like 'bla bla bla,' 'yada yada yada,' 'whatever,' or the name of a celebrity. Australia is very different from my homeland. I was born and raised in a town called Rod Stewart. Back in those days, Rod Stewart was a very busy town. The major industries were David Hasselhoff and coal. I think it is hard for a non-migrant to understand just how difficult it is to learn a new language while adapting to life in a new country. Every single day presented me with new frustrations. This was why I ended up hiring the actor Bruce Willis to talk for me. I was inspired by his work as the voice of the baby in the films *Look Who's Talking* and *Look Who's Talking Too* and so I decided that Bruce Willis should do my voice. Bruce Willis took on the job. He was very bla bla bla. He ordered for me at restaurants, answered the telephone for me, spoke to salespeople for me, made prank telephone calls on my behalf, and Cher. Like the character of baby Mikey in the *Look Who's Talking* films, Bruce Willis gave me an adorable, wisecracking personality. Thus, it actually became very useful for me to have Bruce Willis's voice and I soon became quite popular. But, in the end, I learnt to speak English for myself and so I eventually became independent of Bruce Willis. Like numerous migrants, I picked up a lot of English by watching television. I especially liked watching television shows that featured lawyers, and I used to pay particular attention to plea-bargaining scenes. As a result, my day-to-day speech was soon filled with sentences like, 'Murder in the second, twenty to thirty-five years, and we'll drop the conspiracy charge. We have a witness who can place your client at the scene.' Some people were impressed by my apparent knowledge of the US legal system. Gomer Pyle. Last year, I decided to commemorate the twentieth anniversary of my arrival in Australia by adopting an anglicised name. I turned once again to television for inspiration and began watching repeats of *Fantasy Island* and this is why I now answer to the name 'Ricardo Montalban.' However, this morning, my friend Chuck told me that 'Ricardo Montalban' is not quite the right name for me. He said that this is because I am more like 'a Chinese version of Heather Locklear.' Chuck told me that I am like Heather Locklear in every respect – looks, lifestyle, love-life, family, worldview, etc – except that I am Chinese. Part of me really wanted to believe that Chuck was right but, the thing is, only earlier that day someone else had told me that I am 'the Korean equivalent of Oprah Winfrey.' I guess I wanted to believe the Oprah thing more. So I just looked at Chuck and said: 'Yada yada yada. Whatever.'

Chinese Lessons

Ivy Tseng

I always dreaded eleven o'clock on Saturday mornings.

Eleven o'clock meant the end of *Video Hits*.

Eleven o'clock meant the end of the Mandarin program on SBS radio.

Eleven o'clock was Mum washing the floors.

Eleven o'clock meant Chinese lessons.

At the stroke of eleven, Dad would round up my sisters and me. We'd troop half-heartedly to the cheap pine shelf in the living room that held the battered Chinese readers, with their colourful images of happy children playing games. After collecting pencils, notebooks, rubbers, each of us sat in a different room. Jona would be in the living room, Lin in the small bedroom she shared with Jona. I would be at the dining-room table, at which we really only ever ate breakfast.

As we struggled with each character, sounding out slowly the pinyin next to it, prompted and corrected by Dad, we'd finally reach the bottom of a sentence. Then we would repeat the laborious experience on the next line.

Each reader was divided into sixteen or so passages covering various subjects, such as grocery shopping, family trips, traditional fables and proverbs. For each passage there were comprehension exercises: sentence construction, new vocabulary, cloze passages. Dad would move from room to room, checking our progress, marking the exercises we had done, listening to us reading out the passages in what I now recognise to be sloppy Australian-accented Mandarin.

There'd be a break in the middle of the lesson. 'Five minutes only,' Dad would say, although it sometimes stretched to ten. My sisters and I would escape into the sun-drenched backyard, walking around, kicking tufts of dried grass, clutching the plastic mugs of water that Mum always pressed on us as we passed through the kitchen.

Those breaks were always too short. We were soon back in the house, bent over the Chinese books, messily copying out new characters. All the while, Dad would be telling us to sit up straight. I was always thinking about lunch or what would be on TV or what library book I could be reading.

*

For me, the lessons started when I was in Year One. They ended at different times for each of my sisters and me.

For my Taiwanese father, these lessons probably started as soon as Jona was born. They were a way of ensuring he would still be able to connect to his past. Rather than simply being an Asian migrant who couldn't speak English well, something of the Taiwanese country boy could remain. In the man remained the boy who didn't have any shoes till halfway through primary school, didn't have electricity till high school and had to help his parents every day, early in the morning before school and in the evening after, with their small plot of land.

Maybe these lessons were also a way to ensure that his three Australian-born and bred daughters recognised that their Chineseness was not restricted to their black hair, small round noses and consumption of rice. Theirs was deeper, a heavier inheritance of over 4000 years of history, language and values. The best way to hang on to these things was to teach his three daughters the Mandarin language.

Unfortunately, I didn't quite grasp the significance of these lessons as a bratty kid who just wanted to muck around on weekends.

While I was supposed to be committing to memory the intricate characters and sounds for words such as 'snow' and 'blood,' I'd be staring out the kitchen window, looking at the gum trees swaying around the tiled rooftops, wishing I was white or Aussie (the two were interchangeable to me) and doing Little Athletics or watching TV; anything other than Chinese lessons on a lazy Saturday morning. Many lessons I spent sulking, glaring at Dad, the readers, the faded blue grid-lines of the exercise books. I fantasised about having parents who spoke perfect English, who knew what was really going on during the confusing montage of images on the six o'clock news, who would be able to talk to teachers and other parents instead of always standing awkwardly to one side, smiling, at school functions.

As a student progressed, she could change to different coloured books, in which the squares would correspondingly shrink, until she could write small and neat characters. I never graduated beyond the huge boxes, which barely contained my scratchy, stubbornly clumsy characters. I couldn't understand why I had to learn Chinese when everyone around us seemed to speak, think, dream, *do* in English. Why did I have to waste my time? And why, I wondered as I grew older, did Dad waste his time on us?

I always envied my two older sisters and was always trailing after them. I couldn't wait to grow up and be just like them: to go to high school on a bus, to wear their cool clothes, to have braces. This burning desire to be just like my sisters extended to Chinese lessons. I'd seen glimpses of *their* readers. They always seemed to get exciting and impressive passages – the story of the frog in the well, or the old man and the mountain – while I had to read about children going to school, to parks, to the sea. But slowly I reached those hallowed passages. And they weren't as great as I expected them to be. The frog in the well was a stupid, tiny amphibian with a gargantuan superiority complex. The old man turned out to be an equally stupid peasant who thought he could make the journey to a market on the other side of the mountains easier by literally digging down the mountain.

As I moved through school, I slowly moved through the readers. But I never fully absorbed the characters, the phrases, the essence. By the time I was in Year Ten and studying from a Grade Seven reader the only characters I knew (as in, could read *and* write) were elementary ones such as 'I,' 'you,' 'them.' I learnt the character for 'male' from a glossy Giorgio Armani perfume ad in *Marie Claire*. The only sentence I could write entirely was: 'My name is Ivy Tseng.' I could speak more, but even then I stumbled and stopped, trying to fill the gaps in my sentences from my near-empty cache of words.

I think Dad realised it wasn't working. Getting an education, preferably at university level, was another thing close to Dad's heart. It was a compromise. Jona had to study. Lin stopped in Year Eleven. As usual, I had to wait a little longer. I learnt a few more characters and a bit about Chinese culture. I came to understand its constancy or inflexibility, the passive strength that is the key to its longevity. I became familiar with the emperors and poets and stories. I came to appreciate how a four-character phrase, and even a single character itself, embodies thousands of years of development and knowledge.

*

But then a change occurred.

The lessons began to start later – ten, twenty, even thirty minutes past eleven. Mum was now listening to the SBS Mandarin broadcast on her walkman as she wiped the floors. As the weeks went by without a lesson, I watched *Video Hits*, sprawled on the creased leather couch, one eye on the clock, the other on the gyrating bodies of scantily clad dancers in a Nelly video clip, relaxing as the clock hands moved away from eleven and towards noon without Dad calling out, 'IVY!'

Chinese lessons on a Saturday morning became an anomaly, a special event when Dad was in the mood.

'Do you want to learn Chinese?' Dad would ask.

Sometimes I said, 'Yes.'

Most times I played the school card.

'Maybe next week ... I have a lot of homework,' I'd reply, before going to my room to draw or read or do something that was categorically not homework.

*

I regret not paying closer attention during those Chinese lessons. At my school, there are people from many different cultural and language backgrounds. They shift confidently between English and their parents' first language, equally fluent in both. If I'd paid more attention, maybe I wouldn't feel, as I sometimes do during those long silences in the car or at dinner when we're all watching *Neighbours*, a tinge of regret. Regret that if only I could speak just a tiny bit more Mandarin ...

There are also selfish reasons to be regretful. I could, if I'd been more diligent in my lessons, write on my resume: 'Speaks fluent Mandarin.' I could work in a glamorous job, have a career as an interpreter, or a diplomat, jet-setting to countries all over the world. Chinese people are, after all, everywhere. I could eat at a Chinese restaurant, one of those bustling, raucous ones that line the boulevard of Chinatown in Sydney, and order in Mandarin, eavesdropping on Mandarin conversations all around me as I slurp up soft, squidgy noodles, slick from a hot, salty broth. Maybe I'd feel more authentic in some way.

Because every time I look in the mirror to brush my hair, a Chinese face looks back at me. The skin is tanned from the Australian sun. But the blood comes from Taiwan and China. The thick black hair and eyebrows are from a foreign gene pool. Most times, I don't care. I really don't. But sometimes there's a sense of shame, a vague unease. When I open my mouth, I wish streams of Mandarin would tumble out. When I write, I wish neat blocks of characters, with their careful strokes and ordered shapes, would appear on the paper.

I know that there's more to a person then their cultural background, how they look on the outside – more to me than being Taiwanese-Chinese-Australian. Do I even need those hyphenated, cut-and-paste identities? There are other parts of me.

But …

Maybe I'd feel more authentic?

*

Now, at eleven o'clock on a Saturday morning, I'm bent over exercise books, sheets with black print covering the dining table, scribbling away with a smudgy blue pen.

At eleven o'clock on a Saturday morning, the TV is off. It's usually only on during mealtimes.

At eleven o'clock on a Saturday morning, the house is quiet. Mum might be washing the floors.

At eleven o'clock on a Saturday morning, the driveway is empty. Dad's out buying the weekend papers – the *Sydney Morning Herald* and *Sing Tao Daily*.

Sometimes, when Dad reads *Sing Tao Daily*, the paper spread wide over the table, his glasses discarded and his nose centimetres away from the print, I'll point at a picture. 'What's that? What are you looking at?' I'll say in Mandarin. Or I'll read out the single character I can recognise – a simple character for 'island' or 'life.' These characters float about in my mind, without the other characters and sounds that could join them into a cohesive, glittering sentence, something intelligible to Dad or Mum. Dad will squint at it, and then put his glasses on, straightening up. He'll answer me, jumping from Mandarin to English to Mandarin. I'll listen, nodding. I might reply in kind, shifting awkwardly between English and Mandarin, a unique pidgin language called Chinglish.

I'm not interested in what it's actually about.

I just want to understand my father.

Pioneers

The Early Settlers

Great-Grandfather arrived

in 1897 to grow corn
cabbage tobacco in Wahgunyah

the early settlers
already entrenched

each a foreign devil
a potential terrorist

the first terrorist
he called a fucking bastard

in his own language.

—KEN CHAU

The Terrorists

They are everywhere

I wear paranoia
like armour

like stone

like a raincoat
when it rains

when it doesn't

when smothered
by their attacks

I want to die

I want to kill
the fucking bastards

for making me feel that

being born in Australia
and being an Australian

are not the same.

—KEN CHAU

The Upside-Down Year

Francis Lee

1961: The radios in Hong Kong named it the Upside-Down Year, in reference to the peculiar shape of the numerals, which could be turned on their heads and still read the same. The previous Upside-Down Year had been 1881, a mere eighty years ago, but the next Upside-Down Year would not be until 6009 – a very long time to wait.

To me, a sixteen-year-old Hong Kong schoolboy, the Upside-Down Year seemed nothing out of the ordinary. The second semester had begun after the Chinese New Year holidays and all appeared normal. The boys' school I attended belonged to the Italian Salesian order of the Catholic Church. We had an earthen soccer field and soccer became our primary love affair. In the mornings, we would throw down our bags and dash over to join one of the many games that were already in progress, provided we could escape the grabbing hands of the duty priest, who wanted to drag us into the chapel. During recess, after lunch and in any few minutes we could spare, we would play soccer. The field was packed with players and balls flew everywhere. We pushed and ducked and yelled and tunnelled our way through, enjoying every moment.

The Salesian boys had a reputation: we would end up as either soccer brutes or atonement monks. I was neither (I preferred the soccer-brute option, but my talent did not match my enthusiasm). That year, thankfully, my studies showed a little improvement. This lessened the pressure at home and I was content to continue my love affair with soccer. However, the Upside-Down Year would not leave me alone.

All of a sudden, a new craze took hold of the families of my father's friends: their children were heading overseas to study. Australia was one of the favourite destinations.

Australia, we had learned at school, had a high standard of living on account of its rich mineral resources and abundant primary produce. A teacher who had recently returned from a visit to Australia was given the nickname 'Australian Beef' for no reason other than his raving about how good Australian meat was on the first day of class.

We had also learned that Australia was an intriguing world of opposites. There, winter became summer. People walked at an oblique, upside-down angle. They kicked a ball in the shape of an olive and threw a stick that came back. Children answered back their parents, whom they addressed by their first names – a real upside-down world. All this sounded both exciting and scary, and I wasn't sure it was worth trading my soccer games for.

But an Uncle Lam, whom I had never met before (Chinese children address all seniors as Uncle or Aunt) was very persuasive. He explained to Dad and Mum the advantages of studying in Australia: there was a better chance of getting into university; I could find a part-time job to help pay my way; even if I did not make a success at study, I would surely find a better paid job than if I had stayed in Hong Kong.

Uncle Lam had a good relationship with some of the Australian immigration officials and many locals went to him for assistance. He had a son called Ah Sing, who lived in Sydney and who obtained for me an acceptance letter from a registered college. With that, and with Uncle Lam's connections, my application passed the test.

One day Uncle Lam came to our house with a stack of forms for my parents and me to sign. The four of us sat around the small square multipurpose table in the lounge room. Dad gave him money for all the associated expenses, and an additional two thousand dollars, said to be 'tea money' for the immigration officials. Dad and Mum kept thanking Uncle for his assistance, while I sat there quietly. Uncle Lam had a large frame and his hair was loose and thinning. He had a dark complexion and deep eye-sockets, and a pair of golden-framed glasses rested near the tip of his nose. When he spoke, he tilted his head downwards to look over the top of his glasses, and he spoke slowly and croakily. His coat must have had cavernous inner pockets, for he was able to put all the documents and cash into them.

When all was completed, and after Dad and Mum had walked away, Uncle Lam suddenly turned to me and rumbled:

'Fai (my Chinese name), your opportunity has come. When you get to Australia you must study hard. You understand?'

'Understand.' I replied.

'After you settle in, find yourself some work. Send some money back to your parents and brothers and sisters for their yum cha.'

'Umm ...'

'And don't fool around with Aussie girls!'

'Why not?' I was curious.

Uncle Lam opened his eyes wide and stared at me intensely. His voice sharpened. *'What did you say?'*

'I mean, what's the difference between Aussie girls and Chinese girls?' I scrambled to clarify my question.

'Go ask Ah Sing!' Uncle Lam bellowed impatiently, 'He will meet you at the Sydney wharf.'

*

At that time, nearly all Hong Kong students came to Australia by ship. It was cheaper than air travel, and the luggage limit was more generous. People heading overseas would ensure they were well stocked with provisions, down to items such as soap and electric irons. There was a general belief that everything was much dearer in the Western world – or not available at all. The direct journey took thirteen days. I was booked on a Dutch ship, the *Tjiluwah*.

I left Hong Kong on 15 April 1961, a fine day. Dad was full of energy. He got up early and saw to it that a wooden crate containing the bulk of my luggage was safely transferred to the ship. Mother, however, seemed a bit lost and uncharacteristically lethargic. In the morning she sat on the sofa and gazed at the large bag which contained my immediate needs. Our radio was turned off, which added to the silence, in spite of the inescapable background noise of Hong Kong.

Mum turned to me as we were ready to leave home. 'You will write home often, won't you?'

'Yes, I will! I will!' I replied.

Mum took me to a small restaurant near the wharf for lunch and ordered sweet corn, fish fillet and rice, a dish I had not eaten many times before. She said, 'Eat a bit more, for we don't know when you will eat your dinner.'

To be sure, I did not know when I would have such a nice meal again. Going overseas was a major and expensive event. Some people we knew had gone for over ten years and never returned. Moreover, my board and lodging plans in Australia were still a bit vague. Dad had a distant cousin in Sydney whom I called Uncle Tat. He was about thirty years old, not married, and had just completed a wireless course. When we had last met him, I was still in primary school. Uncle Tat had agreed to be named as my guardian in my visa application. He was renting a room and had written to tell us that I could rent a room next to his for a few days before making other plans.

Mum was reticent throughout the whole meal, saying only, 'Go for three or five years, then make a trip back to see us! Okay?'

After lunch, we walked to the wharf. Friends and relatives had already gathered there, as well as several of my schoolmates. All of them followed me onto the ship. To most of us, whose experience of ships went no further than the harbour ferries, the *Tjilwah* was big. We made our way through the maze of passages and located my cabin, which housed two double-decker beds and a small, round, sealed window. Then we ventured into the dining room and back onto the upper deck, which was fitted with deck chairs, a ping-pong table and a small swimming pool. From there we could see a large chimney and some suspended lifeboats, and there were ducts and fastenings in inexplicable places. My two small brothers were especially excited at the novel experience, while their two older sisters tried hard to keep them in check.

We continued to look around and take photos until a siren rang out. Then all the visitors were ushered to the wharf below to await the ship's departure. I jammed in amid the crowd of passengers by the ship's railing, clutching a number of paper streamers in my hands. The other ends of the streamers were held by people standing on the wharf, not necessarily people I knew. I spotted my friends and relatives. My family were gazing at me, all except Mum, who was staring at the floor. I held back tears and put on a cheerful smile.

I don't recall anything more until long after the ship had left the wharf. I was sitting on something on a deserted deck and could no longer control my tears. I don't remember ever crying harder than that before, and I have hardly cried again since, even to this day.

Years later, on those rare occasions when we met again, Mum would tell me that every time she heard the siren of a ship her heart would jerk. In quiet moments she would ask herself whether she had done the right thing letting me go overseas at such a young age.

*

Like most of the ship's passengers, I travelled in second class. There were Chinese people, Australian people and people of other nationalities, including some South Africans who were on their way home via Australia. Apart from the children who travelled with their families, all the passengers were older than I. I did not know who travelled in first class, which was out of bounds for us. We were allowed to wander into the third-class area but we seldom did. There, tent-like structures housed Russian refugees from China. This was the first time I had come into contact with such a diverse group of people. Everyone treated me with courtesy and I felt as if I was suddenly thrust into adulthood.

The ocean put on a different mask everyday. In the first two days it seemed to boil over and I became very sick. Then it merely simmered. I struggled up to the deck and watched the froth left in the ship's wake. I sensed the enormity of the transformation in my life. The sea reminded me of the scene from the rear balcony of our rented apartment in Hong Kong, only now I was lost in the scene somewhere, drifting further and further away, not knowing when I would see my family again.

There was a day or two when the ocean took off its mask and was as smooth as velvet. Never before had I seen a mass of water so calm. I wished I could share the scene with my family, and the scene of stars at night, too – a sight rarely enjoyed by residents of Hong Kong.

At sea, it felt as though the world was endless. I sat on a deck chair and rested my chin on the ship's rail, like I did from the rear balcony at home, and gazed into the horizon. I contemplated my future, but my mind was blank. On some days we passed islands

– some of them deserted. When we crossed the equator, every passenger was presented with a certificate by the captain.

Before I left Hong Kong, my older sister had told me to look out for the famous Great Barrier Reef. Our ship would surely pass through it, she said. However, I did not quite know what to look for and could not see anything resembling coral. Instead I saw flying fish trying to escape the path of our ship. A day before we reached Sydney, I watched four dolphins leading our ship for a good half-hour. Under a clear blue sky, I watched them dive and tumble like little jesters opening the way for a royal carriage. By the time I went to the cabin to take out my camera they were gone.

On the thirteenth morning I got up very early and commenced packing. Someone yelled into the cabins, 'Come and look at the Sydney Harbour Bridge!' I followed the others and ran up to the upper deck. A gigantic curved steel structure passed overhead and dwarfed our ship. It was awesome! Not long after that our ship came to berth and Uncle Tat was there to welcome me, but there was no sign of Ah Sing.

'Is Ah Sing here?' I asked.

Uncle Tat betrayed an uneasy smile. 'Let's talk about it after we get home,' he said.

Thus I landed on this distant piece of land where, so it now seems, I was destined to spend the rest of my life. It was 28 April 1961 – an Upside-Down Year indeed.

The Water Buffalo

Thao Nguyen

He was not crowned or otherwise adorned. He did not look so different, though his horns curved a little more than the rest. His back was solid and strong. Even though many flies came to rest on him, he did not flick his tail to shoo them away like the others did. He was willing to share his body. 'A product and companion of nature,' he would say. His stance was noble. He was the king.

32

As they gathered around him in silent acknowledgment, he looked at each one of them. He thought of his dreams for them and he imagined the future. They all nodded in agreement.

The water buffalo grazes in herds of about fifty animals. Both wild and domesticated buffaloes have a keen sense of smell.

The sky was fading and the slight breeze in the air was momentarily trapped in the tall bamboo. The herd had dissipated and he was on his own. An occasional tinker could be heard from a bell that hung around the neck of a distant cow. But the king smelled unease. His bones told him of something impending.

The darkness came and he waited. It was an unusually black night. The stars did not emerge and the slight moon was hiding. Still, the wind innocently played hide-and-seek with the bamboo.

Then, as deafening as the thunderous roar of an immense storm, screams echoed so hideous that they carved themselves onto the field. The noises came quickly, one after another, producing a monstrous earthquake of terror. The king knew it. He smelled it coming. He cocked his head to the left and listened for the next anguish. He paused. Then with graceful swiftness he sped towards the echo. Just behind the bamboo cluster, he slowed to a halt. He lowered his head and listened to the silence. After the horrific cries, the silence emerged like a lost, curious child. Then with all his might, the king groaned to the starless sky, a sound so mournful the moon came out from its hiding and sobbed. As he walked slowly among the dead herd, he knew the time had come.

He had no reason to stay and fight. What was left of his strength was buried. He was no longer a king, but an ordinary buffalo, an animal soon to be domesticated to graze and work. Leaving his heart behind, he walked towards the South.

The Indian water buffalo is used in Asian rice fields, but has been taken to many other parts of the world, including the East Indies, the Philippines, Egypt, Hungary, Spain and other countries. Its bone structure and the distribution of weight across its legs make it well suited to agricultural labour.

When the king arrived in the South, he was astonished. There was so much abundance! So much fertility in the soil! Its green was so bright and wholesome he began to weep for his herd. It was busy and exciting. There was movement everywhere. No one noticed his arrival. He took up work at a local farm and, as the days and nights passed, contentment began to seep through his skin. He worked and rested and worked and rested and was fed and worked and rested. The cries of that horrific night began to fade from his ears.

After one long day, as the sky began to fade and he began to rest, he noticed that the stars did not emerge and the moon was hiding behind a cloud. It was an unusually black night and the spirits of his herd came to visit, each one gently rolling over his eyelids. The cries came back and haunted his ears and he groaned a mournful sigh to the starless night, wishing for the heart that he had left behind.

Then, suddenly, the ground began to move and the trees began to shake and divide. The moon split up into twenty pieces and the ground tore beneath him. He was frightened and tried to hold on to anything, but even the air was being torn and ravaged. Suddenly he felt a sense of lightness, something he had never experienced before, a lightness so beautiful he felt he was going to drift away. Then with horror and amazement, he saw the horns on his head begin to fall out as if some giant hand was plucking them from his skull. His dark blackish-blue skin began to fade and his feet were dividing into five short stalks.

Then his snout began to flatten like a mound of clay melting in the sun. His ears began retreating into his head. Afraid he would no longer be able to hear, he twitched them vigorously in a futile effort to stop them receding. He felt as if someone was stretching out his body on a canvas and he could not bear it any longer. But his eyes did not change. He squeezed them shut while rubbing them, hoping it would all disappear. Then with all his might, he yelled out a raging roar. As the rivers rippled with the sound and then became calm again, a freakish stillness overcame him. The land had stopped tearing.

Despite the buffalo's ability to adapt to its environment, physiologically it is less able to adapt to extremes of heat and cold than various breeds of cattle.

Slowly, he peeled away his hands and un-squinted his eyes. What had become of him? Who was he?

He looked around and saw concrete paths, shops, a coke machine gleaming from a shop window and a bus pulling up to the kerb. He was confused and dazed. But these surroundings felt strangely familiar.

He slowly learned to walk. It took many weeks. After he had mastered walking on two feet, he ventured to learn to talk. This was much harder than he ever could have imagined. What was this language that these people were using and why could they not understand him? Every now and then, he would let out a groan to the sky above, but this was always quickly met with, 'Why don't you speak English?'

Buffalo hide is thick and tough and makes good leather. The water buffalo is hard working and powerfully ploughs deep into the mud, making rice farming possible in many places.

As a stranger in a new land, he began to fade into the background. He became a working man and thought, 'At least I am safe here,' but he knew where he had left his heart. He tried hard to forget.

He had children and they graduated from medicine, pharmacy and computer science. They were all driven by his desire for them to walk faster and talk smarter than he could. And they succumbed to the pressure, never knowing why they always did better in maths than their colleagues who spoke English at home. Maybe it was the extra tutoring.

Though the water buffalo is strong and versatile, its greatest loss is among its calves. Newborn buffalo calves can fall victim in large numbers to diseases and poor nutrition. The most dangerous and susceptible period for the calf is the first two months of its life.

His only daughter, sick of treating girls with chlamydia at the hospital, gave up her career and returned to college to become a painter. This destroyed her father. They had an angry fight. She said shameful things like, 'You're worthless.' He said, 'You're a selfish, ungrateful daughter. I wish you were never born.' The schism lasted for years.

Then one day, the daughter found herself lying on an expensive couch, drinking expensive red wine, reading *Norwegian Wood* by Haruki Murakami. She glanced out the window of her apartment at the hundreds of people scurrying along, and she noticed an old man. He was trying to catch the bus, but was still learning how to walk and how to talk. She returned to her novel, but the feeling of loneliness would not leave her. Maybe that man was from the same land as her father. Then she realised she did not even know where that land was.

She had exhibited her paintings widely and won numerous awards. But from that day on, her work changed and the critics were harsh. 'Too sentimental,' they said. 'The artist is in a professionally dark phase, she has lost her edge and traded it for the human condition. It is rather unfortunate.'

She existed on a plane far away, staying still while the world moved faster and faster around her. She never did belong, here, there or anywhere. She was a stranger in a familiar land. She was fatherless.

One day she returned home. It had been years. Her father was sitting on his favourite chair – a milk crate in the garage. She grabbed another milk crate and sat beside him. They looked at each other and sat in silence until the sky faded.

'I know you have suffered, but I want to know where it came from. I want to know where your heart is. I want to find it because it has never been here, and I have never been complete,' she said.

He replied, 'It is in another lifetime, my daughter. It is impossible to reach. It is gone.'

The water buffalo when wild is very fierce, and it is said that it is a match for a large lion. But generally, the water buffalo is a docile creature, as seen in many postcards from South-East Asia, carrying children on their backs.

She took out a large blank canvas and her paints and told him, 'Father, I want you to paint your life.'

He took the brushes and began with efficiency. He painted a landscape with hues the daughter had never seen before. Then he painted himself, the second-hand Levi's jeans, the T-shirt. Hours passed and the sun rose. The daughter woke up and found her father asleep near the canvas, the paints strewn across the linoleum floor. She inspected the picture. It was beautifully peculiar with these vibrant colours and foreign feelings. Amongst it all, there was an image of a man without a face.

Time passed, but the daughter was still trapped in a world she could neither explore nor explain. She was caught in a dimension between reality and a dream world; a world that belonged to her father. She became consumed by the search for his lost heart, to understand it and to bring it home.

More than five per cent of the world's milk comes from water buffaloes. It is high in fat and solids, which gives it a rich flavour. In many countries, it is much more highly valued than cow's milk, resulting in high levels of calf mortality, as milk is taken from the parent to be sold.

Years later, she received a note, brief and empty. Callously typed in Times New Roman, 12-point font: 'Father is dying. St Albert Hospital. Intensive Care. Room 12 Bed 6.'

She arrived. His body had shrunk and he looked like a creature from a fantasy novel. He glanced up at her and asked her to bring him the canvas, the one he had painted for her all those years ago. She did not understand but left immediately. She searched the garage violently. There it stood, in bubble wrap, under a wise layer of black dust. She took it to him, along with some paints. He asked her to leave and to come back in two days. For two days she sat outside the door; the old man locked himself in tightly, refusing food and aid.

His frail hands shakily picked up the paints and began to mix them with precision and grace. As the clock ticked slowly, doctors and nurses scurried along holding bedpans and needles.

The water buffalo, though strong, works quite slowly, and walks along at about three kilometers per hour. It feeds on pastures and farm waste such as crop stubble and sugarcane. The average working life of a buffalo is about eleven years, but some can work to age twenty.

It was time. She opened the door to see her father a transformed being, yellowed and shrivelled. She was filled with bewilderment: not sadness – just confusion. As he drew her near, he whispered, 'This is my last and only gift to you; carry it with pride and keep it warm beside your heart.' And with this, his body collapsed, with a gentle sense of deflation.

She sat for a few moments watching this now empty body, a carcass. The air felt crisp. The old air-conditioner hummed nonchalantly. Remembering the painting, she held it up to the light. The world stopped and her head began to buzz. The ground began to fade. Looking at the painting, she finally saw the endless pain in his eyes, the hundreds of stories buried in the abyss. She saw a lifetime of heroism and pockets of private hopes. She saw time and humanity, war and life. The face of the painted buffalo stared at her with so much sorrow and nobility, she felt her heart dissolving.

She looked back at the body on the hospital bed and didn't know what to do. She ran outside as fast as she could, but there was no one on the streets. It was 4 a.m. and the air was chilly. There was a homeless man sleeping among some green rubbish bags. She ran towards him and rambled some incomprehensible sentences about a buffalo and a great man passing. The homeless man shrugged her off and went back to sleep.

Finally, she was on the border of the dream world, but it was too late. She would never know and she would be caught forever in this place between dream and reality. As she collapsed on the ground, she gave a mournful groan to the still-dark sky.

She slowly returned to the empty halls of the hospital and made her way back to the room where the body lay. Sitting on a grey plastic chair across from the bed she watched. As the sun came up and forced itself through the sterile venetian blinds, it cast itself on the painting, highlighting the hues she had never seen before, those foreign but brilliant colors. Somewhere between this reality and her father's dream world was where she now existed, a place of truth.

She picked up the bedpan, walked out the door and closed it gently behind her.

The Ganges and Its Tributaries

Christopher Cyrill

My mother said that empty houses were protected by the spirit of Visakha, who would guard the house until the family of his choice had inspected it. He would then leave a sign to convince them that they had found their home. My mother said that she had bought our house because the spirit of Visakha had arranged nails in the shape of three crucifixes on the windowsill of what eventually became my bedroom. My great-grandmother kept three crucifixes on every windowsill of her home in Howrah. My mother remembered having to kiss each crucifix before going to bed when she stayed with my great-grandmother during the festival of Divali.

My mother said that everyone in India lived in their rightful homes because they understood the signs of Visakha.

*

When we first moved into our house in Dandenong it smelt of the wet newspapers that had been laid out in front of the doors of all the houses. Later, when we peeled away the newspaper pages, fragments remained stuck to the doorsteps, and thresholds to rooms, as if all the doors of our home were epigraphed. When we walked on the timber floorboards small puffs of dust coated our shoes. The backyard was full of tiny hills over which I led my army of clothes-peg soldiers, and elephants that my father had carved out of sandalwood for me. My father used an iron mallet to flatten out the hills and I remember feeling the ground shake every time he brought the mallet down.

For four weekends workmen brought truckloads of soil and

39

sand. My father raked the soil and sand into the backyard and sprinkled lawn seed over it.

When the grass began to grow, my father cut out a three-metre square of dirt from one corner of the backyard. He placed a fibreglass mould into the square. He covered the mould with sheets of plastic and weighed it down with pebbles that more workmen brought in trucks on the weekends. It seems now as if there were always mountains of materials on the nature strip of our Dandenong home. My father stapled the plastic to the fibreglass mould, and filled the mould with water.

When the pond was ready, my father spent three days and nights building his model of India. He pencilled a map of India onto a piece of chipboard, and then went over the outline with a texta. He went over the texta outline with a razorblade and then, with a knife, he cut away the excess chipboard. He was left with the rough borders of India, with room enough at the northern point for the Himalayas.

My father pasted paper maps of India onto the chipboard and wrapped it tightly in plastic. He carved mountains out of sandalwood to represent the Himalayas. He painted the mountains a darker brown and glued them to the line that divided India from Tibet.

My father ignored all terrain outside the borders of India, except for the Himalayas. I believe he omitted the neighbouring countries solely to banish Pakistan from the map of the world in his mind.

My father used blue thread to represent such rivers as the Tapti and Penner, but for the Ganges he used shoelaces, dyed blue and stitched together. The shoelaces were as thick as the shoelaces of desert boots, and when he glued them to the map the Ganges and all its tributaries looked out of proportion to the rest of the map, as if they had been designed to a different scale. The shoelaces covered the point where Calcutta was supposed to be, so my father had to move the toothpick marker a centimetre from its proper place.

Around each toothpick marker my father glued a folded piece of paper. Each piece of paper was printed with a small flag of India. My father marked only the places on the map that interested him: his birthplace of Lucknow; Calcutta, where my mother was born; Bombay, where the great Sunil Gavaskar would bat on the streets with a plank of wood. He ignored Bhopal, Akola and Jaipur. He used swatches of brown silk to represent the Thar Desert and he carved the Eastern and Western Ghats, the Cardamom Hills and the Nilgiri Hills out of the remainder of the sandalwood.

My father mounted the model on a large slab of cork and left it to dry on the living-room table. When the model was dry, and the toothpicks secure, he placed it in the pond. He let the model drift in the water without securing it. It looked as if India had pulled itself away from Asia, ripping the Himalayas with it, and was powering itself through the Indian Ocean in whatever direction it chose. The Ganges would no longer flow into the Bay of Bengal but into all the oceans of the world.

It occurred to me one day as I watched the model float around the pond that India had roughly the same outline as Australia. When the model turned in the water so that Nagercoil pointed directly east, I could transplant the Great Australian Bight onto the Gulf of Cambay and transplant Arnhem Land onto Calcutta.

After my father had finished the model he returned to work on the garden. He placed a stone birdbath in the middle of our front lawn. On the edge of the shallow birdbath, the shape of which reminded me of a chalice, he cemented a sculpture of Brahma. In his four hands Brahma held a book, which I now know to be the Vedas, a sceptre, a string of pearls and a cup. Water was sculpted falling from the cup into the birdbath. If it rained for long enough, the cup would fill and water would drip off the stone into the bath.

My father grew palm trees along the side fence, planted strawberries in a stone flowerpot shaped like an elephant, and nailed a bronze sun wheel above the front door.

*

My mother packed the cupboards with our plates and cups, washed each of our tin dishes three times, and hung a mask of a god, whose name I have forgotten, in the cupboard where she stored our masalas, onions and chillies. The mask was green with two

41

locks of thread on either side of the forehead, holes for the eyes and mouth, and a horsehair goatee. It had paper incisors, which tickled my bottom lip whenever I tried it on, and a glass dot was glued to its forehead.

My mother glued three crucifixes to the windowsill of every room and placed statues of Mary and Joseph on my bedside table. I kissed the stone feet of the statues every night before going to bed. My father had planted a rosebush outside my window, and on nights when the thorns scratched against the glass, or the wind swung the iron gates of our house against each other, or when possums ran over our roof, I would turn the faces of Mary and Joseph directly toward me.

This is an edited extract from *The Ganges and Its Tributaries* (McPhee-Gribble, 1993).

The Beat of a Different Drum

Simon Tong

Geelong. February, 1982.

Only one person was in the cool, shadowed tuckshop when I tottered in, starving for a reprieve from the badgering and the flinty heat. I took my time to write down my lunch order on the brown paper bag, making sure it was legible before handing it to the middle-aged woman behind the counter.

She looked at my order, chuckled, then crossed out the second 'p' in 'meat pipe.'

My ears burned. *She must think I'm an illiterate idiot.*

'Sorry,' I said, sotto voce. She probably didn't even hear me. I kept my gaze on the scarred countertop and my fists in the pockets of the school trousers I had put on for the first time that morning.

'No worries, luv. It'll be waiting for you at lunchtime.'

Why would an Australian woman three times my age, someone I had never met before, call me her love?

Searching the ground for something to kick hard, I gulped in a deep breath, gritted my teeth and scurried back out to face the waiting hordes of rowdy teenagers.

*

I wasn't an angry child in Hong Kong.

I loved badminton, went to a public primary school and spent too much of my pocket money playing Space Invaders in unlicensed premises. My favourite outing was going to the public library in the Central district. I would run ahead, shove open the heavy glass door and plunge into the bouquet of old books. I peeked at the foxing on the coarse yellowed papers and wondered if the brown spots would coalesce into a discernable pictogram, a secret message slowly released by the book.

Like many people who missed out on a good education, my mum compensated by reading eclectically. She managed to shoehorn a few bookshelves into our small apartment. Books were stacked two, three layers deep and they made the apartment seem bigger.

I loved the pictures of dinosaurs and animals in the science books my uncle sent me from Taiwan, but I liked the pleasure of words even more. The rhythm of a mellifluous poem was honey on my tongue, the shape of a well-balanced *duilian* made me grin and grin. I won the school's essay competition every year; teachers marvelled at my vocabulary, rich and sophisticated for my age. I fantasised about growing up to be a writer.

Just before I finished primary school, I became obsessed with Jin Yong's martial arts novels. I devoured *The Legend of the Condor Heroes* in one week, *Laughing in the Wind* the next. The protagonists were gallant, principled scholar-swordsmen, equally adept at calligraphy, music and poetry. I was enthralled with the *I Ching*, too. It presented a method for divination, but as I was happy with things as they were, I had no need for its prognostic powers. I was far more intrigued by the principles by which it purported the universe was governed.

Some primary schools used English for teaching, but mine used Cantonese. I was an attentive and conscientious student. Hong Kong's quirky colonial education system awarded my good

43

results by assigning me to a Christian high school run by the Lasallian Brothers. Every subject, except Chinese, would be taught entirely in English. Despite more than six years of classroom English, I couldn't even understand the first question my teacher asked me on the first day of high school: 'Are you a Catholic?'

Crossing the classroom threshold was like stumbling through a portal into a foreign country. I was robbed of speech, hearing and literacy. Each lesson was like a foreign movie without subtitles. I took hours to read one chapter in a textbook; I had to look up a word in the dictionary every few minutes. I didn't make a peep in class, always dreading the glance from a teacher that might precede a question. My parents, who had barely finished primary school, couldn't help. My marks deteriorated quickly. If it wasn't for Margaret Thatcher's intervention, dropping out at fourteen would have been my lot.

In 1982, Thatcher formally started negotiating with Deng Xiaoping to transfer the sovereignty of Hong Kong to China. The Cultural Revolution and all the subsequent madness were still fresh in people's minds. My mother decided it was prudent for us to join the new wave of diaspora and we fled to Australia.

*

The whole plane of passengers from Hong Kong had crammed into the small Sydney airport transit lounge, airless as an underground fallout shelter, to wait for our connecting flight to Melbourne. The sluggish ceiling fans did nothing to alleviate the stifling heat.

I had noticed a middle-aged man and an old woman when we were still in the air. He reeked of sweat and unwashed hair; his well-worn vinyl shoes were scuffed from toe to heel. The woman, wearing traditional baggy trousers and loose blouse, her silver hair swept into a severe bun, slumped in a chair with her eyes closed.

When I saw the man saunter towards me in the lounge, I wrinkled my nose and looked away.

'Excuse me, little brother, could you do me a favour, please?'

I stared at him.

'Could you please buy a bottle of orange juice for my mother?

She is very thirsty, but I can't speak English. Here is some money. Very sorry for the bother.' The pleading in his voice embarrassed me. There was a look in his eyes that I couldn't read.

'Of course he would. And get this uncle some food, too,' my mother replied.

He thanked me profusely, but didn't look me in the eyes when I handed him the juice and biscuits.

*

I knew the exact moment when my mother realised we hadn't collected our luggage.

Turning away from the transit lounge's warm window, I was about to ask her if she wanted another drink. She was frowning, and had a far away look in her eyes. Then they widened, and she gasped, 'Our luggage!'

'What about it?'

'It's still on the plane! What are we going to do?' She stamped her foot, hammered the air with her clenched fists. I had never seen her panic before.

'No, it's not, Mum. They are transferring everything to the new plane for us. The pilot told us over the loudspeakers before we landed.'

'But he spoke English! Are you sure you understood what he said?'

'Ah. I did ... I think.'

She didn't relax until she could lay her hands on our luggage again in Melbourne.

*

The sum total of what I knew about Australia came to three things: it had an opera house, kangaroos and Australians spoke the dreaded English.

My aunt said I was the first Asian student at the Christian Brothers' school she had enrolled me in. I greeted that piece of news with indifference. I told myself I would be fine if I just sat quietly in a corner in class like I did in Hong Kong. Perhaps, at fourteen, I was too naive to be afraid. I was gripped by curiosity and glee.

My first day at school in Australia was stinking hot, the only kind of weather this desiccated country seemed to have. I squinted against the refulgent sun, the enormous expanse of bleached sky and the exposed open space. I was on a different planet. Even the thick air, superheated, utterly bereft of moisture (but so clean!), felt alien on my skin.

The principal took me to the classroom and sat me down at a desk by the door. The kids silently stared at me. The teacher, Brother O'Brien, was the second oldest person I had ever met. He was younger than my great-grandfather, who was in his nineties then, but not by much. He dressed like a priest in a black shirt and white collar, hunched behind a desk on a dais raised above us. His gaze behind his thick black-rimmed glasses swept through the whole class without his head moving an inch. His croaky voice had a strange cadence; I managed to understand a whole sentence a few times. No one said anything to me during the whole morning.

At the first recess, I followed the others out of the classroom. A surge of kids immediately swept me up and pushed-dragged me to a bench in the shade. More kids scampered over from all directions to join the ruckus. The crowd loomed over me, blocking out the sun, but the rising heat from the asphalt still turned the soles of my shoes into marshmallows.

I was the new animal at the zoo, fenced in by concentric throngs of teenage boys. Apart from the Lasallian Brothers in my Hong Kong high school, I had never met a white person before. The boys' faces fascinated and unsettled me. One orange-haired kid's face and arms seemed to be covered with hideous skin lesions, until I realised they were only freckles. Another boy's eyebrows wriggled like a single furry caterpillar as he squinted and pushed the corners of his eyes upward with his fingers, bowing and yawping monkey noises at the same time. Another's head was covered with little coiled springs of implausibly curly hair.

Their questions pelted down on me.

'Are you from Japan?'

'Are you from China?'

'Do you speak English?'

'Do you play footy?'

'Did you come here by boat?'
Then they became a torrent.
'How long have you been here?'
'Are you a virgin?'
'Konichiwa!'
'Toyota!'
'Do you eat dogs?'
They were all hooting, making faces. There was nowhere to shelter. They were standing too close, yammering too loud. I had no voice to scream, no strength to shove. *Leave me alone! I don't understand!*

Emboldened by my silence, or sensing easy prey, the circles of kids swirled, tightened.
'Do you wipe your arse?'
'Do you have a boyfriend?'
'Do you eat raw fish?'
'YUCK!'
'Ching-chong Chinaman!'
'Do you know kung-fu? Karate?'
'How do you cook a dog?'
'Come stand here in the sun, it's cooler!'
The questions hurtled at me, a stinging barrage of blows. I dodged, weaved and parried. With grunts, with gestures and monosyllabic answers. I tried to snatch the words as they whizzed past. My inchoate replies were snuffed out by more questions, spat at me with increasing menace. I turned my face away, cowered, tried to hide from the heckling. Something warm in my chest coagulated, clotting my lungs. I shivered in the silver heat even as rivulets of sweat ran down my back. *Leave me alone …*

Finally a teacher broke up the crowd and told me to go to the tuckshop to order my lunch. I elbowed my way through the pack and bolted.

*

The mere thought of going to school would throw me into a sweat.

Robbed of speech again, but this time both inside and outside the classroom, I was stripped of my dignity and personality as well. I didn't have the words to object, to defend myself, to argue, to cajole or control. My ethnicity made me conspicuous, but my reticence made me invisible.

People using simple words to talk to me annoyed me, their condescension made me dizzy with fury. They treated me like a child, assumed I was stupid – and I lacked the language skills to prove them wrong, to demand to be taken seriously. A fourteen-year-old boy doesn't want to be a stuttering baby making gurgling sounds. He wants to be a suave Don Juan who can amble nonchalantly over to the emerald-eyed girl, make her laugh with his wise cracks and buy her a Sunny Boy to share.

I was always angry, feeling a compulsion to withdraw and reach out at the same time. I had no one to talk to about these feelings. I couldn't tell my mother; it would only upset her. Were my feelings less real if I couldn't articulate them? Were they festering into something pernicious? If I couldn't express myself, then who was my self?

What to do when I thought I had pronounced a word perfectly and no one could understand me? I found using irregular verbs particularly difficult, although I had memorised their inflections years ago. Verbs are not conjugated in Chinese; the temporal flow of events is entirely indicated by adjuncts like 'last week' and 'tomorrow.' I wasn't used to matching a verb's tense with the action's place in time. What to do when I thought I had nailed a tense and people were still confused and I was confused about why they were confused?

I buried my nose in my beloved martial arts novels to escape. Even at their most abject, the swordsmen never sulked in gloom. Even when they were nailed to a slimy wall at the bottom of a black pit half-filled with fetid water in a far-flung hell hole, subsisting on cockroaches and rage, they were always plotting their revenge. I could do without the cockroaches, but I had plenty of rage.

*

Stewart was in my science class; we both liked Asimov's robot stories. I envied his swimmer's physique; he thought it was cool that I could read Chinese.

48

'Did you see Nigel sucking Brother Smith yesterday?' I asked Stewart.

'WHAT did you say? Nigel did WHAT?'

'Sucking Brother Smith. Because he wanted Smithy to pick him for the football team.'

Stewart stared at me.

'Do you mean sucking him or sucking up to him?'

'Ah. I don't know. What do I mean? What's the difference?'

Stewart looked away, shaking his head. 'Bloody hell ...'

'By the way, what is a wanker?'

'Oh god.'

Stewart was very patient with me.

*

I discovered that soap operas were excellent learning aids: their plots universal and repetitive, the histrionic acting transpicuous; I could concentrate on the colloquial dialogues. I watched the cast of *Sons and Daughters* squabble and *The Young Doctors* flirt with the nubile nurses. I sat in front of the TV and repeated the dialogue line by line. I copied the rhythm, the idioms and the tone. I discovered that to learn to speak is to learn to listen.

I couldn't formulate sentences quickly enough to converse at normal speed, so I took to planning for a conversation like for a game of chess; the first 'hello' was the opening gambit. I anticipated all the possible responses from my opponent and devised my replies accordingly. Preparing such a script gave me the semblance of a spontaneous speaker in common situations like asking for directions or ordering fast food. But I was still utterly useless when talking to girls, who always came up with startling lines that reduced me to a stammering idiot. When I did finally think of a witty response, it was usually hours after they had left.

No English teacher in Hong Kong had ever mentioned the prosodic characteristics of the language. It has its own distinctive pitch, melody, tempo and tones. Even meaningful noises, like a gasp of surprise, a moan for pleasure or pain, a grunt for admiration or contempt, are all different in English and Chinese.

Curiously, dozing in a busy shopping mall helped me to tune in to this. In the never-never land between wakefulness and sleep, vowels and consonants receded while the musical quality of English became prominent; its intonations tintinnabulated like glass bells, its distinct rhythm became a drumbeat I could clap to.

My relationship with English became a lot friendlier once I started to learn not just its grammar and vocabulary, but also to listen to its music.

Battlers

Pigs from Home

Hop Dac

Pigs in real life, I'm told, are meant to be charming, but no pig has ever endeared itself to me. George Clooney may have mourned the death of his companion of fifteen years, a Vietnamese potbellied pig called Max, but the only name I've ever given to an incarnation of the porcine genus was 'breakfast.' Of all the animals one can keep, pigs are by far the worst smelling. Pig shit is the most repulsive smelling of all shits. No pig has ever been a friend of mine.

*

I was brought up in the belief that any good Vietnamese family was a self-sustaining one. We kept animals for meat and maintained an abundant herb and vegetable garden. My mother's herbs were sought after; her friends would come over and take away armfuls of the aromatic plants for their own kitchens. Throughout my childhood in Geraldton, Western Australia, a basket of herbs was a permanent fixture on the dining table. Each plant had a health benefit. For example, my mother ate a pennywort leaf a day: 'Good for arthritis,' she'd say. She has a flair for natural medicine, which is handy, as she comes from a long line of hypochondriacs. We always kept poultry, including chickens, ducks, geese and bush pigeons (the pigeons were killed by holding their legs while whacking their heads against the cast-iron stove) – all for the table. Sometimes we had other animals. For a while there were goats and because we didn't ever trim them, their hooves would grow long and curl around upon themselves like elves' shoes. But this story isn't about herbal medicine or any of the animals mentioned so far, although they play a part; it involves that miraculous, repugnant beast: The Pig.

Our nameless pigs lived with the chickens, ducks and geese in their corrugated-iron houses in the animal enclosure. We kept no more than four at any one time, and they were greedy, bullying animals that pushed the poultry away from the troughs until they had eaten their fill. Each day after school, it was the job of my brother Tam and I to feed the animals, a thankless task that was handed down to each brother as the older ones left home. We had a wheelbarrow that we'd load up with half-rotten tomatoes and we'd have to take a run-up to get it up the slope to the animal enclosure nestled in amongst the Banksia trees. We'd negotiate carefully through the minefield of droppings to the centre of the yard and up-end the contents of the wheelbarrow into a mound. Then we'd pour the slops bucket from the kitchen into the trough. The ducks would come waggling up, yakking away, and gleefully bury their heads in the rotten matter like they were blowing raspberries on the bellies of babies. The chickens pecked amidst the kitchen scraps, flinging up bits of lettuce, noodle and eggshell. The pigs would lumber over, grunting noisily, and shoulder their way into prime position. I have never trusted pigs: something about them always made me nervous, and I would hurry out of the enclosure while the feeding frenzy took place.

Now, on one occasion when I went out to feed the animals, I saw something truly extraordinary. It was a Saturday and I was feeding them around lunchtime. We mustn't have given them enough food the night before because the birds came running up hungrily as soon as they saw me approaching with the wheelbarrow. The ducks, always the noisiest of the bunch, were off their heads with excitement. In the corner of my eye I saw a large sow coming across the yard, but she wasn't after the pile of tomatoes. She crept up behind a duck that was oblivious to anything other than gorging itself and before the duck knew what was happening, the pig had bitten its arse off. The duck stood up straight, looking around wildly like it had heard an explosion. It started to waddle off, its guts trailing behind it. I didn't know what was going to happen next. I'd always thought pigs were vegetarians, but this confirmed my suspicions. A pig is like the ocean: don't ever turn your back on it. Perhaps she didn't like the taste of the duck: the sow was already neck-deep in tomatoes.

I went inside to wash my hands and told my grandmother about the incident.

Her eyes lit up. 'Where's the duck now?' she asked.

'Still walking around, I guess,' I said.

My grandmother's hypochondria meant that the only reason she'd leave the house was to sun herself by standing in the driveway and turning herself slowly like a rotisserie chicken. She'd complain about her phlegm rising, which to Vietnamese people is symptomatic of oncoming sickness, but hers was always rising. She had a plastic bag hanging from a bedknob; she'd hawk up and spit the phlegm into it between decades of the rosary. Upon hearing this news of the duck, my grandmother grabbed a pot from the kitchen and bolted out the door, up towards the animal enclosure. I went outside and saw her banging what was left of the poor creature on the ground, finishing it off once and for all. Then she de-feathered it and made congee out of it.

'Do you want some?' she asked.

'No thanks, Grandma.'

Right there was the divide between the old world and the new.

*

The pigs my parents kept were for slaughtering. They used to do it themselves. On special occasions, like New Year or the Tet festival, Dad would get his mates around and have a day of pig killing, gutting and shaving. Mum and her friends would be in the garden, picking herbs and leafy greens. After which, the women would spend the rest of the day turning the pig into numerous dishes as the men sat around drinking beer with ice in their stein glasses. Usually the slaughtering was done in the morning. One time, though, it happened in the dark of night.

I would have been about thirteen or fourteen. It was a quiet weeknight; I was doing my homework when several vehicles turned into our driveway. It must have been around 10 p.m. Some of my parents' friends had an interstate visitor; they were having a party and needed a whole pig right away. My father shouted from the courtyard for Tam and me to come out and help. Our job was to hold the torches. It was eerie, walking through the Banksia trees to the animal enclosure at night-time. It was windy, and loose sheets of corrugated iron flapped about, making unpleasant metallic screeching noises. We led the party with our beams of light, and found the pig we were going to slaughter sleeping innocently below the roosting chickens in their coop. We gathered around it, about six men and Tam and I. Some of the men had bailing twine. Then all of a sudden my dad gave the signal and they all jumped on it. The pig woke up in fright.

'Keep the torch on the pig!' Dad shouted at me.

A couple of the men held its hind legs, some others held its front legs, my dad jumped on top of it to keep it from struggling. One of his mates, a man we kids called Cookie, plunged a carving knife deep into the pig's throat.

It let out a scream that I will never forget.

Blood gushed over Cookie's hand; it spurted over his arm. The pig struggled and kicked as the men held on to it tightly. My brother and I stood there transfixed. After a few moments the screaming grew fainter as the pig laboured for breath and died. I thought about our neighbours, the girls who caught the school bus with us, and wondered if they'd heard the commotion.

Then the men bailed it up and carried the pig to the shed, where they strung it up, gutted it and shaved it, and Dad's mates took it away to their party.

*

The last pig we had was killed by a snake. It was the middle of summer and the pig turned grey and putrefied. Dad found its stinking carcass in the chicken coop, next to the drums in which we kept wheat for the chickens and pigeons. Dad dug a pit and he, Tam and I, with our T-shirts tied around our faces, carried the animal out of the enclosure. While the poultry gawked at us solemnly, we dropped the pig unceremoniously into the hole.

My parents don't keep pigs any more. They don't need to. They have a friend now named Reg, a pig farmer out in Northern Gully, who practically throws pork at them whenever he visits.

*

While a pig is being strung up, Mum will put some salt into an ice-cream container. She'll then fill it with blood as it drains out of the pig and the salt will stop the blood from congealing too quickly. She'll take the container into the kitchen and add onion, pepper and water. About five minutes later, depending on the salt content, it congeals. Once that has set, she carefully lifts cubes of the fragile jelly out of the container and cooks it in boiling water until it hardens. She adds slices of the hardened blood to noodle soups or congee.

Now I live on the other side of the country, in Footscray, where alongside the traditional beef noodle soup, *pho*, there is a spicy noodle soup called *bun bo hue* that is also very popular. I have it with pig's blood and it reminds me of home.

Spiderbait

Annette Shun Wah

You don't have to go back to medieval times to find the worst jobs in history. Not if you grow up on a poultry farm run by Chinese parents with a cleanliness obsession.

I was eight years old when my father bought his little piece of Australian bush – seven acres in the Pine Rivers District, the first shire north of Brisbane. These days it's filled with shopping centres and project homes, but in the late sixties it was mostly empty stretches of bush punctuated with fibro shacks, rusted-out tractors, car wrecks and the occasional farm. While the properties around us tended to be sparse and run down, the road that linked them was wide and impressive, probably built by American soldiers during the war, my father proudly surmised. He'd been an ardent fan of all things American since the Second World War, when he'd served as an interpreter with US Marines in China. The Yanks not only rescued the Chinese from invading Japanese forces, but also gave my dad a job and respectability.

Our road had the mighty name of Samsonvale Road. A long smooth strip of bitumen, it lured the area's speed freaks, seventeen-year-old boys newly licensed to drive, a few Fourexes under their belts and heavy right feet. I don't know how you lose control on such a straight road, but people did – often right where a solid tree trunk or telegraph pole has no business being.

In this neck of the woods my father decided to build his poultry farm. Sick of slaughtering chooks for a living in his previous business, he thought he'd have a go at raising them. True to form, he tried to do much of it himself – which is to say the whole family had to pitch in. Why would you pay good money for something you could handle yourself? Those *gweilos* would only try to rip you off, so better to save yourself the angst.

He did make an exception for the man with a bobcat to clear and level the building site, although I have cloudy memories of family members wielding pickaxes at tree stumps. Even my stepmother, a 148-centimetre-short former seamstress from Hong Kong, was pretty handy with a pickaxe. I think it belied her true origins in some Chinese rural village.

Once our land was levelled the real work began. What my father had in mind was BIG. I can't tell you how big, because to an eight-year-old just about everything is big. Stage One was an enclosed shed that would become the main area for cleaning and packing eggs and would house the chicks through the early stages of life. When it was complete, we received our first batch of fluffy yellow day-old chicks, the cutest things I'd ever seen. Even Dad couldn't restrain a smile as we carefully lifted them – handfuls at a time – out of the cardboard delivery boxes, into the special heated cages we'd assembled days before. As the chicks grew, they'd be moved to bigger and bigger enclosures (Stage Two), until finally, they'd be ready for the laying cages – the Final Stage.

That first batch of fragile chicks set the construction schedule. As they lost their down, sprouted feathers and grew, so did the laying shed. Eventually it would accommodate over 3000 cluckers. The wooden pegs and bits of string that plotted out its foundations seemed to go for miles. It wasn't just one expanse of concrete, but long parallel rows, with a concrete strip at each end. I had an instant lesson in construction. For weeks, my father, brothers Tom and Doug, and occasionally our two Hong Kong cousins Clarence and Clifford – who'd come to Australia to study, not to toil as builders' labourers for free – set about feeding shovelfuls of sand and cement into a cantankerous petrol-powered concrete mixer. One section at a time the concrete was poured, smoothed with trowels, levelled with lengths of wood pushed back and forth between two people, then trowelled again. Sturdy metal girders were set in place to hold up the corrugated-iron roof. No doubt my father would have attempted to cast these himself if he'd had a smelter on hand. But he satisfied his DIY bent by nailing in the hundreds of wooden slats that enclosed the shed on three sides.

The concrete rows would become walkways and in the gaps between we assembled the cages, elevated on stands above the bare earth. That's where the chook poo would drop and mound up over years and years, until it nearly reached the cages. Then big trucks would come in to clear the lot. The whole neighbourhood would know about it for days. Good thing then that there weren't many neighbours, and we didn't talk to any of them long enough for them to complain. Anyway, the man who owned the local pig farm smelt almost as bad all on his own.

The wooden slatted walls were good for ventilation, but they also multiplied the possibilities for the freeloaders who sheltered in the shed. Between each slat, between the slats and the girders, between the girders and the roof, grew clouds of cobwebs. They'd look particularly messy when lots of insects had been snaffled, and while you may think the spiders were doing us a service, my mother had another way of looking at things. *Ai-ya! Woo-joo!* Filthy, filthy, filthy. So every few months, she'd recruit me for spider patrol.

It wasn't enough to sweep the cobwebs away with a broom. We swept everything else in the joint – the paths, the cages and the food troughs. But when it came to the spiders Mum was looking for a more satisfying solution. It took a few experiments, but finally she succeeded. Armed with a gas-jet burner, a box of matches and a stepladder, she'd turn those webs to cinders. Quickly, efficiently, cleansingly, the gas flame would disappear those silken threads like magic. The spider's prey, shrouded in silk, would sizzle and dissolve into fine ash. The only problem was the pesky spiders. They'd make a quick sidestep, squirt out a lifeline and descend to safety, ready to re-colonise at the first opportunity.

That's where I came in. My job was to stand below my mother as she perched on her stepladder and squash the spiders as they dropped. Don't worry, I didn't wear my usual rubber thongs for this job. I'd slide my feet into sturdy rubber boots and make like Fred Astaire. The problem was, the spiders would land on my head or fall inside my shirt, or down the back of my pants. My mother would roll her eyes at my shrieks of horror as I jumped up and down, trying to dislodge whatever was crawling up my bum.

The next time we faced this job, I dressed for the occasion in one of my father's cast-off long-sleeved shirts buttoned right up, long pants tucked into the wellies, and a wide-brimmed straw hat. Plop, plop plop. Big black and brown spiders, with stomachs bloated like ball bearings, bounced off the hat onto the floor, ready for my tap dance. We just had to hope there weren't any with the telltale red markings on their backs. There were hundreds, thousands of the critters abseiling down like US commandos. How's that for a swell job?

The shed had doors every few metres, which opened outwards to let in the breeze, and guess whose duty it was to open and close these according to climatic conditions. It wasn't too tough a task except when summer storms broke in the middle of the night. Of course the doors had been left open to give the poor fowls some respite in the custard-thick humidity of the day, but the last thing you wanted was the delicate things to get wet and catch cold. They do catch cold, as well as flu. We'd find ourselves feeding slivers of garlic to sick chooks – or perhaps that was that for hiccups. My parents would probably have had me blowing the hens' noses if they'd thought of it … and if hens had blowable noses. So in the interests of sanity, and dry fowls, I'd have to race up to the laying shed in the pitch dark to close the doors, clutching a clapped-out cheap umbrella in one hand and a big torch in the other, with our dog Mickey (as in Mouse) my only security.

The umbrella was pretty well useless in conditions that had the rain coming in sideways, but it balanced out the torch, which spotlighted the very strange sight of the gravel road ahead of me seeming to come alive. The thing was heaving, bits were bouncing up and down – too solid for raindrops and too big for gravel. The rain was making my feet slide in my rubber thongs, and I slowed down to avoid stepping on the dark shapes that landed with soft splats around me. The joint was jumpin' all right – with cane toads! The dog's four skinny paws were having no trouble sidestepping them, although one or two of the ugly critters slammed into the side of him as they leapt. I found myself tiptoeing the rest of the way, trying not to imagine the sensation of stepping on one, bare foot sliding out of my thong onto the rough skin, the squelch of it exploding under my weight, spraying black sticky goo everywhere, warts up my legs for all eternity. YUCK!

But there are worse jobs. Who'd want to be a battery hen in the height of a Queensland summer? Two years in a row, severe heatwaves hit right on Baby Jesus' birthday. My father was always careful to answer 'Church of England' whenever an official form enquired after our religion, but the only time I remember seeing him in an actual church was when I was baptised at the age of six. I had no idea what was going on, or why the man in a frock was allowed to lift me up, tuck me under one arm like a roll of newspaper, and threaten to dunk me like an Anzac biscuit in a hand basin. I tried to squirm out of his vice-like grip before he splashed my pretty best dress. Why on earth were my parents tolerating this behaviour in a complete stranger?

That one occasion didn't qualify us as churchgoers, but there was one day on the Christian calendar we observed: Christmas. Perhaps it made up for the Chinese festivals we no longer celebrated. Estranged from family thanks to a long-running feud that dated back to the Second World War, and being the only Asian family in the entire district, it was pointless carrying on a ritual no one else understood. Our parents had enough trouble making us *speak* Chinese, let alone believe in Chinese ghosts and ancestor worship. If we ever went along with it, it was only to get the money in little red packets they were supposed to give us at the beginning of each new year, but money was so scarce even a few cents couldn't be spared. So my parents gave up the old traditions and all we had was Christmas. It was the only day of the year when we were allowed to beg off the daily duties of collecting, cleaning, weighing and packing eggs. But on these two Christmases, when temperatures soared above century Fahrenheit, the eggs were the least of our worries.

The chooks were dying. They'd grown tough enough to be manhandled from cage to cage, shoved two abreast into tiny wire prisons, growing callouses where feathers and skin had rubbed off, but they couldn't cope with the formidable heat.

I could barely move myself. The humidity sapped my strength and made my head pound as if someone was hitting my skull with a mallet. But there was no respite on this day. My brothers, stripped down to stubbies and old sandshoes, were up on the tin roof hosing the shed with precious tank-water in an effort to cool things down. My job was to revive the hens that were fading. I saved a few, but many were too far gone. I'd dribble cool water over their heads, try to make them drink, or let them roam free on the ground for the only time in their short lives. But they'd stumble about pathetically in the dust, wings splayed, gasping for life, too weak even to dream of escape. That's when I had the grisly task of wringing their necks to put them out of their misery, and carrying them to where my parents had set up a make-shift abattoir.

Even a heatwave couldn't stop them. They'd managed to set up the old copper boiler, filled it with water, stoked a fire underneath and had the thing steaming away like a Turkish bathhouse. My limp little casualties were dunked in the water to make the de-feathering easier. I'd help a bit, cleaning off some feathers, sticking my small hands into the still-warm cavities to pull out the gizzards. But mostly it was my task to walk the rows of cages like a paramedic, trying to save as many hens as I could. Often I got there way too late. Rigor mortis set in, and all I could do was pile up the carcasses away from the full glare of the sun.

Clarence, my cousin, dropped in at one point with a mate from Hong Kong, hoping to give him a taste of my mother's usual Chinese-Australian Christmas feast – roast turkey or chicken swollen with stuffing made from stale bread and fresh mint, served with rice and a soy-sauce gravy. The whole hot, heavy deal would be washed down with an ice-cold Fourex or a once-a-year shandy for me and Mum. Not this time. Clarence and his friend, chubby faces frozen in shock, glumly watched my parents expertly plucking and gutting, not missing a beat even when they wished each other a Merry Christmas. 'There'll be no Christmas lunch this year. Got to save as many of the chooks as possible – get them dressed and into the deep freeze as quickly as we can. There isn't a minute to spare. Can't let them go to waste.'

Clarence and friend mutely nodded their understanding and waved a greeting up to my brothers, who were still hosing down the roof, glistening from the occasional watering-down they gave each other to keep themselves amused. Quietly, discreetly, Clarence and his companion slipped away. He may have missed out on Christmas dinner, but I reckon Clarence received a gift. If he hadn't brought his friend with him, he'd have been roped in to do some plucking and gutting too.

Anyway, social niceties over, it was back to trudging up and down the rows of chooks, looking for the ailing ones. I remembered stories about the Black Plague. 'Bring out your dead!' I yelled. The chooks weren't listening. As usual they were clucking away, 3000 of them making quite a racket. I used to practise being a rock star when we collected eggs. I could do Janis Joplin at the top of my voice and no one heard but the chooks. Sometimes I'd swear they were singing along with me. Every now and then something would spook one of them, and like magic the whole lot would go quiet. Three thousand bird-brains communicating as one – not a peep. I could do Janis Ian at that stage and you'd hear it. Spookily they would collude in silence for about a minute, then one would screech loudly, 'bu-GAIR, bu-GAIR,' then another would chime in, then a third, then a fourth. Soon the whole bloody lot would be making an even bigger din than before, to scare off the imagined threat, I suppose. You could bring an entire rock band in for rehearsal at this point and it would be drowned out.

Anyway, the chooks were too busy staying alive this day to be spooked by anything, and my pile of stiff feathered carcasses grew, one by one, to about chest-height. When the sun finally dropped, and things cooled marginally, my brothers climbed back down to earth, and my parents finally tired of the boiling copper and the stench of wet plucked feathers. Actually, I think they only stopped because they couldn't cram any more into the freezer, the fridge or the Esky.

We finally let ourselves sit for a while before my mother and I had to stoke the combustion stove to cook dinner. My brothers and I guzzled cold soft-drinks. My mother sipped warm water. My father, shirt limp with sweat, grimly walked up to survey the pile of dead chooks. For a moment, I thought I was going to get into terrible trouble for letting so many die. Instead, he did what he always does at important moments. He started to count.

We lost about ten percent of our stock. We couldn't afford it, but that's farm life for you. Tomorrow or the next day we'd get out the pickaxe and chisel out a deep hole in the red clay for the grisly job of burying them.

No one would get into trouble. It was Christmas.

Take Me Away, Please

Lily Chan

It was four o'clock. I sighed. Every day, six days a week, I dreaded this moment, and hoped the hands on the clock would miraculously spin forward a couple of hours. For 4 p.m. signified that it was time to start work.

Every quintessential Australian town had a local Chinese take-away shop, and my parents were the proud owners of one such establishment in Mareeba, a largely agricultural township in Far North Queensland. Rather than adopting a traditional and fortuitous sounding name such as Golden Dragon Restaurant or Happy Fortune Inn, my father preferred a simpler approach. Peter Chan's Chinese Take-Away resided on the quieter end of the town's main street, nestled between a video store and a chiropractor's practice. This was where I grew up, and where my family lived and worked from 1983 until my parents' retirement in the late 1990s.

The shop officially opened at 4.30 p.m., but we needed to prepare half an hour beforehand. I changed out of my blue school dress and roused Mum and Dad from their daily twenty-minute siesta. Getting to work wasn't an issue, but getting away was, as our small living quarters were attached to the shop. The quarters consisted of two rooms separated by a sliding wooden door. One room served as a combined family living area and was also where my parents slept. The other room, a small storage-area-turned-bedroom, I shared with my sister. The shop's restroom also served as our family bathroom, and was located outside the main premises.

Mum and Dad started organising the kitchen, taking out a vast array of ingredients from the cold room, all of which they had meticulously chopped, sliced and marinated only hours earlier. Dad lit the gas rings under each of the woks, including the big wok containing the vegetable oil reserved for deep frying.

My sister and I were responsible for the front of house. Our chores consisted of switching on the lights and turning the 'open' sign that was hung on the front sliding door. As the elder child, I had the added responsibility of managing the cash float. Instead of a cash register, we used several plastic take-away containers to separate the various notes and coins. This was how I was able to develop my arithmetic skills early on. I learned quickly, for non-reconciliation of cash to the total orders at the evening's end would earn a stern word from Mum.

After opening up shop, I took my usual place behind the counter and scrounged in my school bag for the day's homework. One of the few benefits of working after school every day was that I became very diligent at homework. It gave me something to do to pass the time. That, and the fact that I wanted to get out of this town very badly.

If not doing homework, I could either talk with my sister or watch television. More often than not, my sister preferred to play outside when she wasn't on duty, so I usually resorted to switching between the two free-to-air channels to see what was most palatable. I became a big fan of shows like *Get Smart* and *The Goodies*, and the theme song to *Come and Get It*, Peter Russell-Clarke's five-minute cooking show, became forever ingrained in my memory.

Having finished my algebra questions, I again looked at my watch. It was now 5.30 p.m. Any moment now, the bodybuilder from across the road would ring up and place his usual Tuesday order: a steak omelette and four steamed dim sims. Bodybuilder

Man was the classic 'same time, same dish' kind of customer. We had a lot of those, which was good because they were our bread and butter. If one didn't turn up when he or she was supposed to, then the person was either on holidays or had passed on from this earth. To call them reliable was an understatement.

The most popular dishes included special fried rice, chicken with almonds, and sweet and sour pork. Those who were indecisive could order the shandy special, which was basically a combination of the three dishes in one meal. Our more adventurous clientele would choose from the specials board, which included exotic-sounding dishes such as Mongolian lamb and Singapore noodles.

Mum and Dad were already busy in the kitchen, standing over the five smoking woks. A customer from Cooktown had called the previous evening to place a large order of twenty dishes. Every three months, this customer would make the 200-kilometre journey to do her shopping and, of course, pick up her supply of Chinese food. I could hear the faint sizzling of the wok in the background as Dad tossed the ingredients around with his steel spade-like cooking implements. Mum was writing the name of each dish on plastic container lids with a thick blue felt pen so the customer could identify them easily.

I bet they were looking forward to finishing up tonight. They had invited the town's only other Chinese family over to dinner. The Laus were, in fact, our competitors; they owned the Hong Kong Restaurant down the road. However, they were also our friends, simply because in this small, prejudiced town, all we had was each other.

We got together every now and then, especially to celebrate events on the Chinese calendar. However, the reason for tonight's gathering was that Mum had cooked her special salted pork and century-egg congee. This was complemented by several plates of *you zha gwei*, Chinese savoury dough-sticks, which we had ordered from a Brisbane bakery the previous week and which had only arrived by freight today.

Our families shared many things, including Chinese magazines, newspapers and videos, as well as gifts of various delicacies from overseas visitors. But the adults' favourite thing to exchange was gossip, particularly concerning other Chinese in the Table-lands and Cairns region. This provided endless hours of specula-tion, analysis and discussion, which they would enjoy while sipping Chinese tea and munching on Sao biscuits.

The phone rang. Ah, Bodybuilder Man, on time as usual. I jumped up, pushed through the swinging doors into the kitchen and picked up the receiver.

'Peter Chan's Chinese Take-Away. Can I help you?'

ABC Supermarket
Kevin Lai • Matt Huynh

My parents owned a store in Cabra. It was located exactly where Tomatec Tutoring is today.

Back then (1990-1996) that entire complex (including where Bing Lee is) was filled with small shops.

Ours was probably the biggest asian grocery store in Cabra.

Before we owned the store, it was a Franklins. The layout wasn't like a typical asian store with tight aisles.

We had six long, wide aisles, large enough to accomodate a fleet of trolleys. Besides mum and dad, there were five employees.

Sometime around '94 - '95 business went down. Not only for us, but all the shops in the centre. The free parking lot underneath the centre became privatised and only accessible to people looking for long-term, reserved spots. Looking back, that's what I imagine caused business to go down. One by one, shops either closed or moved away.

The ABC Supermarket was the last store to remain.

By then, I was old enough to stay home alone so I wasn't exposed to the decline of my parent's business.

One scene I'll always remember though: I was at home and my parents called for me from work to bring them lunch.

When I arrived, the store was completely devoid of customers and employees.

It was just mum and dad.

They told me, we love you though at the time I didn't understand why because they never said that before.

I just thought it was very weird.

But I got it soon enough.

Coming home from school one afternoon, I remember seeing just a few boxes of unopened stock in our garage, but I knew exactly what it meant.

In '96 the store closed and my parents declared bankruptcy.

At one point, we were down to our last $20.

To this day I feel uncomfortable being around that area.

I prefer not to walk by or use the parking lot. I've only been in Bing Lee once or twice and felt very uneasy in there. Even the furniture store next to it seems really dark.

Too many unnecessary connotations.

In the past ten years, my mum has walked through Cabra twice.

But there's two things I've learnt from all that.

To appreciate more important things and that eventually things will get better.

Mates

Wei-Lei and Me

Aditi Gouvernel

Barry West was a rude little boy with a pug nose. He had the red stained face of Australian summers.

'Don't touch me!' he screamed.

All the kids were playing tag and I was 'it.' I was running through the playground, my pony-tail slapping my back as my feet hit the ground. My heartbeat pulsed in my head. I grazed Barry's left shoulder with the palm of my hand. He stopped, turned around and faced me.

Anger stretched across his face and he screamed, 'I'll have to wash this shirt now – you wipe your butt with your hands.'

'No I don't,' I screamed back, startled and confused.

'Yes you do … You're Indian and I've got your Indian shit on me.' He ripped off his shirt and threw it on the ground. The other kids gathered around us, watching and listening.

*

I was six. It was the early eighties and my parents had moved our family from the aristocratic world of Delhi, a city filled with palaces, temples, gardens and tombs. They moved me from my playground under the tower of the Qutab Minar to Canberra. The only thing the two places had in common was they were both national capitals. Our new suburb, Melba, spread its backside up Mount Rogers, a lofty title for what was really a hill. Each night my father and I would climb the hill and watch the sunset turn Lake Ginninderra a bright pink. 'This is our chance,' he would say, as Belconnen became a small cluster of lights. 'This is a place we can make ours.'

Delhi, with its eons of history, was not a place that could be 'added to.' Australia, on the other hand, large, spacious and full of gaps, would be a place where we could create a new identity.

We became Australian in 1982. I recall very little of this ceremony, which took place in a small room in the cinder-block building of the Department of Immigration. My parents held up their palms while a man read an oath from a piece of paper. People clapped, some whistled and small flags were waved. The citizenship papers given to my parents were locked in a bank vault with my mother's jewellery.

My parents met Australia when they started work and I met Australia in the school playground.

*

The playground consisted of a large expanse of grass, at the centre of which stood a dark wooden structure rising out of a pit of tanbark. Some days it would be a fort, and we would defend ourselves from an imaginary attack. Other days it would be a ship, and we would be pirates and sailors. The days our child fantasy minds were tired it would just be the playground and we would hang from the monkey bars, or jump off the platforms. It was fun until the day Barry told the world I wiped my butt with my hands.

That lunchtime as I climbed the fort, Barry screamed, 'She's infected. Don't touch the fort! You'll get her germs.' I watched as the kids around me jumped off it like a crew abandoning a sinking ship.

Over the next couple of days the kids stopped talking to me, as though my words, like my body, carried an infection their immune systems couldn't fight. On the rare occasions they did pay attention to me they would combine their hatred in a human circle around me.

'She even looks like shit,' said Amy Pulawski.

'That's so gross,' added Cris Kovacic.

'No I don't,' I screamed again and again at them. Once I was forced to pull my top up and bare my chest to prove I had nipples when Barry had the idea Indian girls 'have no tits.'

On these days, I would go home with tears in my eyes and wonder why we couldn't move back to Delhi. I would beg my mother not to send me back to school. 'You have to face the world,' she would say. If this was the world, I wanted nothing to do with it. I pretended to have various illnesses – flu, malaria. Once I claimed I had gout. My mother ignored all my attempts to miss school. Each day she would send me out the door with a brown paper bag and a piece of fruit and each day I hoped things would change. They did, the day Wei-Li arrived.

*

It was a cold autumn day. I ran into the classroom and warmed my hands against the metal gas heater bordering the walls. My teacher walked in, a halo of curly red hair, her arm attached to a honey-coloured boy with a smile of excitement on his face.

She wrote his name on the blackboard, 'WEI-LI,' in white chalk. The boy stood in front of the class and in a sing-song voice introduced himself.

'My name is Wee Lee.' He smiled.

Titters ran through the classroom. It took the class exactly thirty seconds to shorten his name to Wee. By morning recess he was called Piss. He lost his smile at lunchtime when, to my relief, he became the object of their attention. The kids mauled Wei-Li the way a cat would maul a toy. They pawed and prodded him and the circles that used to form around me formed around him. He was hit, spanked and kicked. He was spat on and forced to pull down his pants and show his penis when Barry had the idea Chinese boys 'have no dicks.'

Wei-Li's shoulders started to stoop and after a week he would walk outside and avoid talking to anyone.

*

I watched everything from an aluminium bench. It was far enough away from the kids to avoid their attention but close enough to watch their activities.

Today the bench was freezing. I was folding my legs underneath myself in a sort of lotus position when Wei-Li walked into the playground. I saw Barry walk straight towards him, his arm held behind him and his hand in a fist. As Wei-Li faced the playground, Barry made a full arc with his arm and punched Wei-Li in the head. Wei-Li fell to the ground. Barry jumped on Wei-Li, his butt on his chest and both his hands pulling at Wei-Li's school tie. Wei-Li's face turned red and a strange sound escaped his mouth.

'Think you can tell on me?' Barry threatened.

Wei-Li shook his head.

Anger rose inside me. I wanted to help him. When the abuse had been directed at me, I had always wanted one of the other kids to hit Barry. I wanted someone to make it all stop, and for the first time I realised the 'someone' could be me.

To the left of the bench was a rock the size of my foot. I picked it up and walked up behind Barry, the rock firmly in my hands. I could see Wei-Li's tongue poking out between his lips. I threw my arms over my head and brought the rock down as hard as I could. It made a loud crack when it connected with Barry's head. He fell forward, lying on top of Wei-Li, who had regained his breath and was wiggling out from under him. When Barry started moving, Wei-Li and I ran in opposite directions. I could hear Barry screaming, 'You're both dead.'

The afternoon passed like a death sentence. Barry stared menacingly at me from his desk. As soon as the bell rang I leapt out of my seat and ran out of the class. I started running up Le Gallienne Street and as I was about to reach the first cross street, I saw Wei-Li standing there. He grabbed my hand. 'C'mon,' he said. I followed him up the narrow side-street and onto a foot-path. On one side was a row of houses and on the other side a nature reserve. 'Lets go this way. It's longer – but we'll be alone,' he said.

*

In Tamil, my father's native tongue, there is a word, *jalrah*, that means shadow. From that day on, Wei-Li became my jalrah.

That Saturday, Wei-Li stood on my doorstep and rang the bell twice. My mother was cooking and the house smelt of mixed spices. Cumin, chilli powder and garam masala floated through the air like a scented rainbow. My mother opened the door and called out my name with a smile on her face. I saw Wei-Li standing there. A second later, as he entered my house, I saw everything Indian come to the foreground as if lit by a spotlight: the wooden statue of Ganesh, the fabric birds hanging on a string, my father lounging around in a dhoti. Everything Wei-Li saw could be used as evidence for my difference. But Wei-Li didn't notice anything, or if he did he never mentioned it.

From that day on we spent every possible second together. We would ride our bikes or secretly rifle through our mothers' purses, pilfering loose change that we would then pool and buy a Mars Bar. All sugared up, we would re-enact our favourite TV show, *Monkey Magic*. Wei-Li would be Monkey and I would be Tripitaka. We would find large sticks and pretend they were swords and staffs and fight imaginary foes who looked like Barry.

*

Hiding from Barry had become an art. At lunchtimes, Wei-Li and I would sit in the library, or jump on the Olympic-size trampoline in the gym. If there was no adult supervision we would be sent to the playground no matter how much we pleaded. On those days we would sit on our aluminium bench and share our lunches. Wei-Li would eat my samosas and I would eat his sandwiches, filled with pork balls and grated carrot. When we were together, we felt safe.

But one day, there would be no lunchtime. We were going on an excursion to Parliament House. The day was divided into two sections. In the morning, half of the class would play cricket on the lawns while the other half took a guided tour. When the first tour was finished the groups would swap. I was excited until I realised the teachers were filing us alphabetically onto the bus. My last name was Vishwanathan and I was told to sit directly in front of Barry West. For the first time since the incident with the rock, I was alone. The bus ride lasted thirty minutes. Thirty minutes of Barry kicking the back of my seat. I didn't say anything. I just stared straight ahead.

The bus stopped and the kids pointed at the white building with its small steps. I couldn't enjoy it; I was angry. It was a gut-wrenching anger that was growing each second in its volatility. Barry left his seat and walked towards mine. When he reached mine, he leant close to me and spat straight in my face. He walked off laughing, leaving me to wipe my face with my sleeve. Tears gathered in my eyes, but this time I felt I could do something – the rock had taught me that.

I walked off the bus, and as the bus driver opened the cargo hold, I waited. As the bus driver brought out the sports bags, I cal-culated. Wei- Li walked up to me. 'What's going on?'

'Nothing,' I said, my arms folded and a look of determination on my face. I waited until the bags were opened and the teachers had started organising the activities. When I was confident the teachers were distracted, I walked over to a sports bag and grabbed one of the bright yellow cricket bats. I ran over to Barry and bashed it against the back of his neck. He fell and again I held up the cricket bat; this time I bashed it against his face. I couldn't hit him anymore because the teachers had grabbed the bat and were pulling me off him.

Barry was as fine as he could be with a bloody nose, tissues and tears. While the other kids walked through the House of Repre-sentatives and the Senate, I sat on a seat, guarded by a teacher who phoned my parents.

My mother arrived, apologetic and angry. She bustled me into our red Subaru and said repeatedly, 'What's gotten into you? You can't behave like this.' I was silent until she said, 'You must apolo-gise to that boy.'

'Never,' I said.

My parents had a meeting with the school principal and Barry's parents. I wasn't punished and neither was Barry. The next day I discovered why.

*

It was Friday and our teacher stood in front of the class and said, 'Barry has an announcement. Come up here and tell the class your news.'

Barry walked to the front of the class and stood there for a sec-ond.

'I'm moving to Jakarta. I'm leaving next week,' he said.

That lunchtime Wei-Li asked, 'Do you think it's because of the cricket bat?'

'Nah,' I said, shaking my head.

Wei-Li and I counted the days, crossing them off an imagi-nary calendar in our minds. Barry's departure was marked with cupcakes and wide smiles.

On our first day of freedom, Wei-Li and I went home. We

walked up Le Gallienne Street, now claiming it for ourselves. Wei-Li's grandmother opened the door to two beaming kids.

'Why you so happy?' she asked suspiciously.

'Barry's moving to Jakarta,' Wei-Li said.

She smiled and hugged her grandson.

*

Things changed rapidly after that. We grew up and as our faces changed, so did Canberra. An Indian restaurant, *Jehangir*, opened on Swinger Hill. Canberra's Chinatown became so busy you couldn't find parking. When I was sixteen I went to a private high school on the other side of town where people described me as 'pretty.'

Wei-Li and I gained a group of friends who we would meet at the chess-pit in the centre of the city. We would sip lattes under the gas heaters at Gus's Café and dream about a better life after uni. At night we would sit on scrappy vinyl-covered chairs in a bar called The Phoenix and, after a couple of beers, rant about how we hated homogeneity and longed for difference. We had become what we thought we could never be: Australian.

Hot and Spicy

Oliver Phommavanh

My tongue is on fire. My nose is clogged up with chilli. I can't breathe.

'Do you think it's too hot, Albert?' Mum asks.

I run over to the tap and try to suck it dry. It's no use. My taste buds are shot.

My parents run a tiny Thai restaurant called Yip's. We live at the back of the restaurant and we have our dinner just before the restaurant opens in the evening. It's an innocent dinner until Mum drills me with questions. I am their guinea pig. Tonight's experiment is red curry. Dad tastes the curry with his spoon. 'Not bad for a mild curry.'

My ears prick up. 'Mild? I can melt polar ice caps with my breath.' My dad has a metal tongue. He makes his own famous chilli paste. He chooses the hottest chilli from the garden and chops them up, mixing in some curry powder. Dad smiles and messes up my hair. 'Your brother's not complaining.'

Kitchai is happily eating his rice and curry. He's only in Year 2. His taste buds aren't fully developed yet. I'm in Year 6 and I can already tell the difference between red and blue M&Ms. 'That's because he's got so much rice,' I say. I grab my spoon and pour red curry all over his mountain of rice. It looks like an erupted volcano. He turns into an erupted volcano: 'Mummmmmm.'

I quickly sit back down and finish off my curry. I have a glass of water in one hand. People always say how lucky I am to have parents who are cooks. But I'm sick of Thai food. I'm tired of having the same stuff all the time. The canteen is the best thing about school. It's got meat pies, sausage rolls and chicken burgers. It's another reason to love lunchtime. At eating time, my teacher Mr Winfree walks around and makes sure we're eating healthy food. He comes across Rajiv, who's eating his fourth Turkish wrap.

'What's inside the wrap?' Mr Winfree asks.

'Um … curry paste,' Rajiv says.

Mr Winfree narrows his eyes. 'Smells like Nutella to me. I want to see something healthy tomorrow.'

Mr Winfree walks away and Rajiv smirks. 'I'll have it with jam, then.' Rajiv loves food. He could eat my parents out of house and restaurant.

In the afternoon, Mr Winfree hands out a bright yellow note. 'There's going to be a Year 5/6 feast to celebrate our multicultural unit. Bring something tasty.'

I thump my desk. 'We have to bring our own food?'

'Just a dish from your own cultural background.'

I groan. 'That's so booorrrrriiinnnggg, sir.'

The bell rings. I shove the note in my bag and walk off. Mr Winfree stands in my way. 'Albert, I need to have a word to you.'

Great. Another boring lecture about how school events are not boring. I try to save a few minutes. 'Sir, it's just that I always bring the same crap to these celebrations.'

Mr Winfree gives me a blank look. 'Well, the teachers don't think its crap. That's why we'd like to order some extra dishes for a school luncheon.'

'You want more Thai food?'

'Well, you're the only Thai kid in Year 5/6 who happens to know a good Thai restaurant,' Mr Winfree says. 'How about you bring in a menu tomorrow? I reckon your parents will love the publicity.'

I can't believe it. The whole school is craving Thai food. Before I know it, the canteen will be selling fish cakes and pad Thai. It'll be my worst nightmare. I want to ignore Mr Winfree's request. But if the teachers don't crush me into coconut cream, my parents will. Mum and Dad dance around the kitchen like they've won lotto. Mum hands me a stack of menus with cards and magnets.

I groan. 'Aw, Mum, why don't I just wear a giant "Eat at Yip's" sign?'

Mum looks bemused. 'Would that be okay with you?'

'This is better than any newspaper ad,' Dad says. 'If the teachers love us, business will increase.'

'We need to make sure our food is excellent,' Mum says. 'Whatever they order, we need to try out for dinner.'

The next day, I give Mr Winfree the menus and he comes back with the teachers' list of dishes in the afternoon. They're typical Thai specialities. Thai fried rice, pad see mow noodles, beef salad and red curry. I see a small note down the bottom. *All mild dishes.* Mr Winfree points to the warning. 'We don't want anything too spicy. It'll freak the teachers out.'

I walk outside with an idea stirring around in my head. I'm going to make sure the school becomes a Thai-food-free zone.

*

Tonight, Mum cooks the pad see mow noodles. I make sure she knows I'm enjoying the food. 'It's great, Mum, but it could use a little more chilli.'

Mum looks at me weirdly. 'Are you sure? Your teachers want mild food.'

Dad comes to my rescue. 'Albert's right. A little more chilli won't hurt.' He slaps me on the back. 'It'll put hairs on your chest.'

I don't think the female teachers want hair on their chests. But I'm glad he takes my side. The next night, Mum sprinkles a little more curry powder on the noodles. The spices hit the roof of my mouth. My eyes are watering, but I quickly push the food down my throat. I try to remain still. 'Not bad, Mum, but it's still pretty plain.'

Kitchai takes a whiff and backs away. 'Looks pretty hot to me.'

I turn to Kitchai, forcing the words through my shrewd lips. 'Believe me, Aussies love chilli, they put it on all their dishes, even in their meat pies.'

Kitchai has never had a pie in his life. He takes my word for it, and he helps himself to a bowl of rice and some tame satay chicken. Over the next few days, Mum adds a little more spice and curry powder. I try to stay cool, even though it feels like I've been grilled on the BBQ. When the teachers eat this food, they will never ask my parents for Thai food again. Every half an hour before dinner, I make myself spice-proof. I scoff bubblegum and gummi bears in my mouth. I smack my lips with a lollypop. I hide a little sherbet beneath my tongue.

I feel sick walking over to the table but I sit there and eat the food in silence. I can actually see bits of chilli on my spoon. I shrug my shoulders and brace myself. It's pure torture. The heat is intense. The sherbet evaporates. I can't taste gummi bears any-more. I can't taste anything. I take a sip of water, breathing heav-ily through my nose. I stick my spoon in my mouth to cool my tongue.

Mum walks over and smiles. 'Are you sure your teachers will be able to handle it?'

I want to dunk my head into a bathtub of ice cubes. 'It's fine, Mum.'

She cracks up. 'You're kidding me.'

Dad comes from the kitchen with a jar. 'We knew you were up to something. So I added some of my famous chopped chilli paste.'

I don't know what is more embarrassing: my parents playing a prank on me, or chilli snot trickling down to my lips. I quickly grab a napkin and rush to the bathroom. I come back, chewing my towel. Mum hands me a plate of an ordinary beef salad. 'We need to cook Aussie Thai for your teachers.'

I almost choke on my fork. 'Aussie Thai? Is that like putting satay on a steak?'

Mum shakes her head. 'We cook differently for people who don't have Thai often. Even if your teachers didn't request mild food, we would still take it easy on the chilli.'

Dad comes in and gives me another glass of water. 'I always laugh at the Thai-style sausages and chicken sticks in the supermarket. There's hardly any flavour on them.'

I shovel down my food. It's not hot but I'm still fuming.

*

I can hear stomachs rumbling all around me. I don't think anyone has had breakfast. We're all waiting for the multicultural feast. Rajiv licks his lips at the food on display. 'Where's your food, Albert?'

'Mum's going to deliver it at recess, so it'll be nice and fresh,' I say, echoing Mum's voice in my head.

Mr Winfree leaves the classroom open at recess. Mum comes in with two huge bags. We take the foil trays out onto the table. She dumps a load of plastic sporks next to them. 'These are for your classmates.'

I roll my eyes like giant marbles. 'Mum, why did you bring sporks for?'

'Well, can they use chopsticks?' she asks.

I shake my head. Mum shuffles outside. I wait until she is out of sight before I grab my bag. I take out the jar of Dad's special chilli paste and a wooden spoon. I carefully lift the foil lids of the trays. I smear paste on the spoon and mix it into the food. Mum and Dad aren't going to stop me this time. I'm up to the red curry when Jennie walks in with a bowl. 'What are you up to?'

I quickly put the jar in my bag. 'Mum just wanted me to keep mixing the stuff,' I say, making circles in the curry.

Jennie puts her bowl down. Her sweet and sour pork is neon pink. My mum's Chinese friends cook sweet and sour pork but it doesn't look like it would glow in the dark. 'The pork looks so bright,' I finally say.

Jennie grins. 'Yeah, my mum made it Aussie style.' I smile back.

Mr Winfree walks in and claps his hands. 'That smells delicious. Mr Murphy is going to be the world's luckiest principal.'

'Yeah, if he survives the deadly Thai food,' I mutter under my breath.

Jennie picks up a lid on the floor. 'Is this yours?'

Oh no! I open my bag. The paste is on all my books and pencil case.

Mr Winfree doesn't suspect a thing. 'Let's start bringing our food down to the hall,'

Rajiv helps me carry my mum's stuff. 'I can't wait to try your curry.'

'You can, once the teachers are finished with it,' I say.

'There's not going to be much left over.'

'Trust me, you'll have plenty.'

The celebration begins with a speech from Mr Murphy and Mrs Schwartz, 5/6S's teacher. The talk only makes us even hungrier. Finally Mrs Schwartz announces: 'Okay, Years 5 and 6, it's time for our feast. Get a plastic plate from your teachers.'

Mr Winfree flicks the plates out like frisbees. Rajiv looks at his plate in dismay. 'Can I have another one? I can barely even fit one spring roll.'

Mr Winfree taps him with the plate. 'There needs to be enough food for everybody.'

'Tell that to the teachers, sir,' Rajiv says, pointing to the teachers, who are digging in to my mum's food. My eyes are glued to their table. This is going to be awesome. I wish I'd brought my camera. Mr Murphy approaches me with a plate of my mum's red curry.

'I have a surprise for you, Albert.' He leads me outside. My nose springs to life. I can smell something burning. It smells wonderful. It's a BBQ. Jim, the general assistant, is cooking sausages and a few steaks.

Mr Murphy hands me a large plastic plate. 'Because your family has been such a big help, you're going to get some Aussie tucker.'

Jim plants a sizzling, juicy steak on my plate. 'This is kangaroo meat. Be careful, it's a little tough.'

Mr Murphy grabs a bowl of hot chips and tosses some next to my steak. 'Help yourself to the tomato sauce inside.'

I stare at the steak and chips. I am in heaven. 'Thanks, this is going to be so yummy.'

Mr Murphy grins. 'I'm sure we can say the same thing about your mum's food.'

I almost drop the plate. Suddenly the steak weighs a ton. I walk back into the hall. My shoulders are slouched. My eyes are glued to the steak. Kids are drawn to its smoky scent, they scream like seagulls. I ignore them and sit next to Rajiv. 'What country is that from?' he asks.

'Australia,' I say.

'Australian food? That's a bit weird for a multicultural festival.'

Mr Murphy yells out, 'Albert, come here for a photo.' He is armed with a camera. 'I want a picture of you eating some Thai food for the newsletter.' He gives me a spoon and leads me over to the teachers' table. 'Just one bite and you can get back to your steak.'

I take a spoonful of the curry. My nostrils want to run away. I look at Mr Murphy's eager face. He's so proud of me. I don't think a tiny taste will hurt. The spoon enters my mouth. The chilli lashes my tongue. I quickly swallow the curry. Big mistake. The heat rises up my throat and blasts out of my mouth, ears and nose.

Mr Murphy doesn't take the photo. He's too busy chasing Mrs Schwartz. She's humming around the hall, using her hands to fan her mouth. Mr Winfree goes for his can of coke. I want to tell him soft drink actually makes things worse. I don't need to tell him. 'Ahhh, it burns, it burns!' he yells. Mr Winfree goes for his bottle of water and he almost swallows it whole. 'I need more,' he croaks. He runs out of the hall. Mr Murphy and I quickly follow him out. Mr Winfree is on his knees, bending over the small bubblers. The water trickles into his mouth.

I tug Mr Murphy's shirt. 'Now that's a photo for the newsletter.'

Mr Murphy heads back into the hall and gets his plate of curry.

'Wow, this is really good,' he says. I can't believe it. I thought his head would explode. The other teachers are pale but they slowly go back to their tables.

Mrs Schwartz takes another mouthful of beef salad. 'Yum, this is pretty tasty.'

Mr Winfree clutches his water bottle like a baby, but he gives me a thumbs up.

Maybe the teachers are being nice or the chilli has numbed their brains. I walk back to my plate. Most of the chips are gone. Rajiv is grinning, with potato bits between his teeth. 'They were getting cold,' he says.

'It doesn't matter,' I say. I cut out a piece of kangaroo meat and chew on it. It's no use. All I can taste is guilt. It tastes a lot like chilli.

*

Everyone in 5/6W is nursing a giant belly after lunch.

'I never want to see any food again,' Jennie says.

Mr Winfree nods. 'I don't think I can eat until next week.'

Rajiv proudly plays with a toothpick. 'I can't believe there was no dessert.'

At the end of the day, we all trudge outside with our empty trays and bowls. I carry my schoolbag like a soiled nappy. The stench of chilli is unbearable. Mum is talking to Mr Murphy and Mrs Schwartz. I wonder how many hours of detention I'll get.

'Well done Mrs Yip, you and your husband are magnificent cooks,' he says. 'Every dish was delicious.'

Mum smiles. 'I'm happy you liked the food.'

'We'll definitely be asking for more in the future,' Mr Murphy says.

'Next time,' Mum says, 'maybe you can try something spicy.'

Lessons from My School Years

Ray Wing-Lun

My sister held my hand and led me through the gate.

'Just sit over there on the benches by the monkey bars. Wait for Sister Mary to call all the kindy kids. And do what you're told.'

I had waited years for this day to find out what people did at school, and to find something to do other than kick stones, play in the sand pile and shine the apples in my parents' fruit shop.

*

Sydney's North Shore in the 1950s was not, for me, leafy streets and solid brick houses. It was our fruit shop in Lindfield, where my family lived and worked. My world was the stretch of shops along the highway, a back lane where mechanics drove cars backwards and forwards, the railway line behind the back lane and the library and park at the end of the lane.

Our fruit shop was always shiny and clean with fancy displays of fruit. Its doors opened wide across the whole shopfront, welcoming customers to come in. And they came in. They were friendly and chatted with my mum and my dad. They asked about what was fresh and gave advice on clothes and gadgets and schools and on ways of doing all kinds of things in the local community.

My dad had come to Australia when he was seventeen with no English and no business experience. Now, he was a successful businessman who drew customers in. He had a wide smile. He was keen to ask what people wanted and what they knew about this and that. He always made sure that he had a chat and that they were happy. He was friends with all the local shop-owners and enjoyed the dinners and parties held by the local Chamber of Commerce.

Dad loved everything modern. He had a huge refrigerated cool-room built for the shop; it was the talk of all the shop-owners around. Mum got an automatic washing machine to replace the old wringer and Dad had a camera, tape recorder, movie camera and movie projector. He also worked hard. He loaded and unloaded the trucks with crates of fruit and vegetables. He was not tall, but he was strong. At night, in the little office under the stairs, he would do the accounts. You would hear the rapid clicking of the Chinese abacus as he checked all the figures. The neat and perfect columns tracked every item down to the last penny. Afterwards he would practise his calligraphy in both Chinese and English. Skinny and shy with a scratchy scrawl, I always wanted to be strong and to write as beautifully as my dad. I wanted to be the warm big-hearted man my dad was.

My mum was beautiful. Whether in her simple work frocks or silky cheongsams, she drew constant admiration from shop-keepers and customers, and most of all from me. She was a little more careful in what she said and did than my dad. She had to be, because of Dad's big eyes and big plans. She taught us to respect our elders and look after our family. She watched the pennies. She made our clothes. She gave us advice about working hard, being careful with our money and getting on with the *gweilos*.

Aware that she had no education and how much there was to learn about this new country, she read magazines, listened to the radio and chatted with the customers to make sure she knew what to say at the right time, and what to advise us to do when visiting friends or going to school. We learnt table manners and the formalities of polite conversation. Our politeness and deferential demeanor singled us out as those shy Chinese kids from the fruit shop.

The shop was busy enough for all kinds of relatives and friends to come to work there. This helped Dad to fulfill his family duties by bringing relatives out from China. It brought an audience of Chinese relatives and workers to listen to my dad's stories and to share in the secrets of business success in Australia. It brought the only Chinese people in Lindfield to Lindfield.

I didn't play much with the few local kids from the other shops. I mostly tagged along with my older sisters and brother when they had friends over. Sometimes, I would go to the markets with my dad early in the morning, or accompany him on his home deliveries. We would go as far as Pymble, a good five or six miles away. I was amazed by the green trees and gardens, the houses that looked like the ones on TV. I wondered how people got to live in those homes.

As the fruit shop prospered, my dad began to plan for weekends. At first we only had Sunday afternoons, but eventually we took the whole of Sunday off. We would go on picnics with relatives and workers from the shop, and sometimes with the families of the local policeman or other shop-owners. We would visit distant relatives somewhere on the other side of Sydney. Their shops were very different from our open, airy, sunlit fruit shop. They were dark and narrow with the strong smell of salted fish, dried prawns and other Chinese foodstuffs. Unlike all the workers in our shop, these relatives spoke Chinese to us. I felt uncomfortable. They were the only other Chinese people we knew. They were very different from the people whose shining houses we visited on home deliveries.

Most of the time, I did my jobs and played my games and kept out of the way. Customers smiled, chatted and patted me on the head. My siblings came home from school with stories to tell and ribbons and stamps that showed they had done well. There didn't seem to be room for me to ask questions, for me to do things that counted. I watched and I listened.

*

I was going to school now. It was my turn to do things that mattered. I wouldn't have to just watch and listen any more.

Boys and girls were running around shouting and screaming. I couldn't understand anything. My mother had warned me, 'We have to watch out for *gweilos*. They can be nice sometimes but they won't always treat you the same.' I stuck to watching and listening, trying to work out if I should be scared or afraid. I stuck to my guns and said nothing.

One day, I was sitting by the low brick fence counting the cars and trucks on the highway. Tony was one of the biggest boys in the class. He came up with three or four kids behind him, chanting 'Ching chong! Ching chong! Don't even know how to talk! Don't even know how to fight!' I didn't know what to say but I did know what to do. I had had many fights with my older brother. I used my arms to cover my stomach and my face. He punched and punched until he got tired. I think I counted seventeen. I got a few red marks and bruises. I punched him once in the stomach. He cried and Mick ran to dob me in to Mother Fabian. Whatever else might happen, I now knew that I could look after myself.

I became involved in everything after that. Tony invited me over to play at his house. I had rock fights and cracker fights with my brother's mates in our back lane. I learned to grit my teeth as rocks hit my garbage-can lid and tuppeny bungers rang in my ears or sizzled in my hand as I waited for the wick to run low before throwing it.

Even though we were in the back lane behind the shop, my parents didn't seem to know what we were doing. They only found out when we broke the windscreen of a car or when my brother got run over by one of the mechanics in the back lane. We felt the rough timber of packing-case planks then.

Mum and Dad were busy: they were starting a restaurant next to our fruit shop. Dad was up before we were awake and didn't finish work until late at night. All our Chinese workers were learning English and getting ready to join the ranks of the many Chinese grocers and restaurant-owners across Sydney.

My second cousin came from China to live with us. Her dad was a captain of a Chinese freighter. She took me to the library, bought me milkshakes and read to me. Her name was Carmel. I loved her. She ran away with one of the workers in the fruit shop instead of marrying one of the educated people Dad had picked out for her. Dad said she hadn't done the right thing and told us not to talk to her again.

So much was happening. I was learning a lot. I am not sure whether anyone could have said what I was learning. I didn't know.

*

When I was nine I went to 'big school,' run by the Christian Brothers. It was a couple of stations away, in Chatswood. Chatswood was like a slow country town; there was no sign of the bustling centre it would become.

On my first day, my straw boater was trampled and I got the strap because I didn't know whether my second name was 'George' or 'Wing' or 'Lun.' A lot of other boys didn't know their second names, either. We all got two each. The sixty-five or seventy boys in the class lived in dread from that day on. We were in Strap-Happy Jack's class. Almost every day, the whole class would be lined up at least once to get the strap. We got the strap for making mistakes in our homework, or in mental arithmetic, or in spelling bees. We got it if our ticks were too big, for standing in the wrong place, sitting next to the wrong boy, moving too fast or walking too slow, being part of a rowdy group of boys … There were lots of ways to get the strap, and not too many ways to avoid it.

I can still feel the tingling fear in the boys as they waited for the strap. The sight of them writhing on the ground shocked me and stays with me as a picture of what evil we can do to each other, what pain we can bear, and what horrors we can hide. This memory haunts me. It paints the dark side of human nature better than any history book has been able to do for me.

We didn't just sit there and take it. We placed bets on who would get the most straps each week. We rubbed gum leaves on our hands to numb them and dared each other not to flinch or cry. I remember getting fifty-seven one week and I still didn't win. Sometimes there is no winning.

My brother always came first in class and got lots of attention and praise at home. Despite nearly always being the last to get an answer wrong in spelling bees and mental arithmetic quizzes, I only came ninth in my class, and for some reason was pushed back to thirteenth. I had to wait quite a few years before I could stand up on speech night to get a prize.

The swimming carnival approached. I couldn't swim. My sisters and brother asked my dad if I could have swimming lessons at the local public school, but Dad was too busy. My sisters wrote a note asking for me to be excused from the carnival. Strap-Happy Jack read it out in class. He said, 'We all know these Chinese people don't contribute to anything. They are worthless and shouldn't be part of this school. They should all be sent back on a slow boat to China.'

For Strap-Happy Jack, this might not have meant much. After all, there weren't many Chinese people to worry about. The only other Chinese people I remember seeing in Chatswood were my brother, our two second cousins who went to our school, and another boy who went to the public high school.

School, my great opportunity to find out about the world and to do things that mattered, had become a very bad dream that I could not understand or escape. I could not do anything to make it better. I was nine. If I was a quiet boy before, I now became a ghost. I walked the playground in the middle of a thousand boys, invisible and absolutely alone.

*

A couple of years rolled on and life stirred. Shintaro the Samurai arrived on Australian TV screens and inspired new activity. The playground was alive with star knives and ninjas. I breathed in the noble traditions of the black-haired heroes and villains. I began to feel some value in my Asian culture. I was a samurai in a foreign culture. I was still a quiet boy, but I began to feel alive again. I became an observer, a thinker and a judge of the world around me.

As I went through high school, some teachers and students began to find something of value or interest in me. One teacher mentioned that my performance in tests indicated good opportunities for the future. I was selected to appear on television in a school-team quiz show. My teachers let me do whatever level of mathematics, science or English that I chose, despite my total lack of application. I became friends with all the leading boys of the school and became active in school activities. The other boys were curious about this quiet boy, and perhaps even worried about me. They treated me very well.

But in my final years of school, confusion began to boil.

I was at the top of the school social tree, enjoying all the benefits of a competitive system that looked after those who made the school look good. I was uncomfortable.

My mother, like every Chinese mother then, always wanted a doctor in the family. I wanted to shine for her. I knew I hadn't done the work to get the marks. I didn't like the sight of blood. I knew how much it was all for show – to show that she had done a good job. I wanted recognition, too. I thought that just once, recognition would be good.

Teachers focused on blue-eyed boys who did well in sport or school, or they harassed the boys who were already headed for the scrap heap. The new school counsellor, much loved by the boys, said only one thing to me: 'Five foot seven, hey? Not short enough to have an inferiority complex. Go on and get on with it!'

But I couldn't focus or study. I couldn't take advantage of the one thing the school did provide: discipline. As one of my friends has said, 'The school was all about discipline. Without the focus on results and punishment, I wouldn't have been able to do so well in the HSC.' But for me, punishment came whether I studied or not. I did well or badly whether I studied or not. I could see that the strap didn't help those who struggled to do their work. I would work extra hours in Dad's restaurant rather than study for an exam the next day. I didn't have discipline. I was stuck. I couldn't do what a good Chinese boy should do.

I needed to do something to shut out the guilt. I needed to shut out the questions about wasted opportunities, a wasted life, questions about what was a good thing to do. My brain, my heart, were pounding. If I couldn't help myself, I could do something about this competitive system that didn't look after those who most needed it.

So in 1971, in my final year of high school, I decided to set up a workshop program. The best students would present papers on the biggest topics in each subject (something similar seems to happen online now at my sons' school). I put it to the deputy principal and, almost voiceless, presented it to the class. I recruited a team of helpers, booked workshop times, collected money, stencilled and printed the presentation papers, and sat back exhausted with a month to go to the final exams.

I am not sure whether what I did was unique or remembered by anyone. But it gave me a sense of purpose. It taught me how to work with people. It taught me to be passionate. It taught me how satisfying it is to care about what happens to other people.

*

I don't think I ever spoke to my mum about what really happened at school. Once I must have mentioned that I didn't like what we did there. She said I had to learn what the teachers wanted; when

I grew up I could do what I wanted. I was a frustrated boy of nine, and replied, 'If I spend all my time learning what they want, I won't have time to learn to think and do things for myself.' I don't think I spoke to anyone again about what I thought about school until it was all over.

I never got used to doing only what I was supposed to do. Sometimes, I wondered if I was a bit slow on the uptake. But I just thought differently; I had different ideas about what was important. I just had to find the right opportunity to use the kind of thinking that I had.

I learned a lot in those school years. I learned enough to set me up for a lifetime of learning.

Exotic Rissole

Tanveer Ahmed

I loved everything about my best friend, Daryl. I called him Lynchy, performing the Australian practice of elongating someone's name with an 'o' or 'y'. I admired his crew cut and was riveted by his rat's tail, which he sported with great confidence. I wished I had a rat's tail, but my parents were horrified, believing it would be my first step towards juvenile justice.

My dad still cut my hair once a month, a ritual we undertook while I sat on a stool in the bathroom. Each time he reminded me how he had cut his relatives' hair while he was growing up in a small Bangladeshi village. He almost collapsed in his armchair when my mother came home once and confessed to a $100 haircut. He was adamant, it seemed, that I would never pay for a haircut again.

Lynchy advised me gently that my father's forays into hairdressing had to stop. We were almost twelve years old and were beginning to take an interest in girls. My chances of meeting a girl were zip while my father was channelling 1970s rural Bangladeshi fashion through me, Lynchy said.

Lynchy would visit my house every day after school and we

would ride our BMX bikes to the local creek. There we would play marbles, skim rocks across the water or play French cricket with a plastic bat. I had never visited Lynchy's house. He always made an excuse about his annoying older sister or explained that his parents didn't like having guests. I didn't push it. I thought my parents were annoying too and I was embarrassed that my house always smelt like curry.

But he seemed to love hanging out at my house. He would sit with my mother and talk about school. He helped her to make snacks, dipping doughy mixtures into Indian spices and passing them to her. He spoke of how all his family ate were rissoles, steak and baked potatoes. I looked at him with envy, wishing my mother could cook such things. She treated him like her long-lost Aussie son, hand feeding him and stroking him across his blond flat-top.

'You are a very nice boy, Darr-el,' she would say while patting him on the head. 'Not like my son, who never eats his vegetable curry.'

I never felt jealous. I knew my mother was just being nice, because she lamented how poorly Daryl performed in his studies. She would encourage us to do homework together, but the chances of that happening were slim. I can't say I was ever disappointed. It was embarrassing to be good at studies and I tried to hide my scholastic abilities as much as possible. I even failed a couple of exams on purpose. The teachers freaked and thought about sending me to counselling. That was enough motivation to make me top the class again.

But in the afternoons, once Lynchy had chowed down on his samosas, it was time to ride to the creek.

That was all our suburb really had. Toongabbie it was called, home to the highest concentration of drug addicts, single mothers and ex-cons in all of Sydney. I'm not sure there were census figures to prove it, but everybody seemed sure about it. I would later attend a posh private school in the city and be known as Tanny from Toony. It even flooded when the creek overflowed. Some people thought we lived there because the poverty and flooding resembled Bangladesh.

During one of the very last days of primary school, Lynchy asked me to come over. I was shocked. It felt like some kind of goodbye before we headed off to high school. For all our talk of maintaining our friendship, I thought his invite was some kind of admission that this would be futile.

'We'll still see each other, man,' I said, genuinely believing it. 'I'll still live in Toony.'

Lynchy reassured me that the invitation had nothing to do with this. It was his mother's idea as a kind of repayment for all the food my mother had fed him. I nodded with approval. I longed to taste the mouth-watering promise of his family's rissole, the delicate balance of mince, breadcrumbs and egg. I had asked at the local milkbar, but they said they didn't cook rissoles anymore. At last, my dream was to come true.

I didn't even bother going home, but walked straight to Lynchy's weatherboard house near the train station. There was a front patio where his father used to sit and read car magazines, but it had been empty for months. I had often walked past and seen his mother watering the garden, which consisted of a handful of azaleas in a zigzag. She would smile, but she always looked like she had bigger worries in her life.

Lynchy's elder sister Stacey never paid much attention to me, aside from once telling me that I was too short for any girls to like me. I had become a loyal cadre of Lynchy's Stacey Complaints Commission: 'Eww, Stacey's face is a zit factory,' or 'Stacey is meeting her boyfriend at the parole office.'

That afternoon Stacey was at work. Only Lynchy's mother was home. Lynchy's father no longer lived there. Daryl had told me recently and I was confused and asked dumb questions. He had told me about his parents' divorce a few months ago, while we sat by the creek and gave each other horse bites, slapping each other on the leg. It might have been a rare tender moment between two boys entering manhood, except I had no idea what divorce was. He said his parents fought a lot and his mum thought it was better they lived apart. I didn't get it because as far as I could see, my parents had nothing in common and barely had any relationship to speak of. My father just worked in the garden and told me to go and study while my mother did the housework and made my little sister and me eat all the time. My parents fought a lot too, but they seemed to have no problems staying together.

But I worked out that it wasn't a topic to dwell upon. At Lynchy's house, we sat at a breakfast table and were served green cordial. His mother asked me to call her Bridget. She had weathered, reptilian skin like many older Australians who had spent too much time in the sun. Her droopy eyes and furrowed forehead gave her a melancholy air. She patted me on the head like my mother did to Lynchy. I liked it. She told me I must have been really smart and wished me well at my new school. My parents never told me I was smart. I was thrilled.

I had been to very few houses where non-Bangladeshis lived. My other friends were also from overseas from countries like Turkey and the Philippines. Aussies were definitely different, I thought to myself. Lynchy's house had pets and smelt a bit like the dog, a big German shepherd that intermittently sniffed my shoes. They had an air conditioner and a soda-stream machine. I was amazed. My parents would never buy such a wonderful thing. Bridget sensed my awe and offered me a fizzy orange drink from the machine. She dropped two ice cubes into a glass before I was allowed to taste a piece of liquid heaven.

She spoke of her garden and how hard it was to keep her azaleas alive in the heat. I was riveted. Daryl sat beside me quietly, looking as embarrassed as I felt when he was friendly with my mother. He rubbed his fingers through his hair and gloated about being checked for head lice at school but coming out clean. Bridget patted him on his head before asking me questions.

'Have you been back to Bangladesh, Tanny?' she asked. Daryl had told her of my origins, after lengthy lessons at my place showing him where the country was on the map and how it had been formed after repeated wars with India and Pakistan.

I told her yes, and described how I'd had diarrhoea all the time, but still enjoyed village life more than the crowded, dirty cities. Bridget laughed and said she wished she had travelled more. I looked at her cropped hair with interest. My mother always kept her hair long.

'Daryl's father never had any interest in the world beyond, only his tools.'

Lynchy bowed his head and a frown appeared. I felt embarrassed and sad for him as the jovial mood turned sour for an instant. Bridget patted him across his crew cut again and motioned to some food on a plate.

'I put some rissoles in sandwiches for you two. Dig in.'

Lynchy motioned towards me, a smile replacing his momentary sadness. He grabbed two and handed me one. We bit into them while sipping our soda-stream soft drinks. A rush came over me as I tasted the spice-free rissole bursting across my taste buds. It was worth the wait.

I saw Daryl a few more times that year, but we became more distant as our worlds grew apart. At the end of the year, his mother decided to sell their house and move to the North Coast. I never saw him again.

After gentle urging on my part, my mother taught herself how to cook rissoles, although she would mix pieces of chilli and turmeric paste into them.

The Folks

Perfect Chinese Children

Vanessa Woods

If there was ever anyone I wanted to stab in the heart with a chopstick, it was my cousin David.

'What happened to the four per cent?' my mother says, looking at my maths exam.

'I got ninety-six. What else do you want?'

'Don't talk back,' my mother snaps. 'Ninety-six isn't 100. If you want to do well you have to try harder. David just got 99.9 on his HSC.'

I dig my nails into my chair and wait for the punchline.

'He asked me to ring up the school board and contest the score. Ha! Imagine that. The lady on the phone laughed.'

My mother shakes her head in wonder, as though David is the god of a new religion she's following.

'It really was 100,' she says confidentially. 'They had to scale it down for the school.'

Usually Chinese parents don't have bragging rights over other people's children, but my mother tutored David through high school, so his HSC score is her crowning victory.

My maths exam, with the scrawled red '96' that I was so proud of, begins to look ratty. Untidy figures rush across the page as if they're about to make a run for it. David's handwriting is famous for looking like it came out of a typewriter.

'He's going to medical school,' she sighs. 'He's going to be a heart surgeon, just like Victor Chang.'

The reason my mother harps on about David so much is probably that her own two children don't warrant much praising over the mahjong table. My sister Bronnie has been expelled from piano lessons twice, and me, well, I am trouble on all fronts. I'm the child who talks back and gives viperous looks to her elders. In all my life I've only learnt two Cantonese phrases: *Kung Hei Fat Choi*, Happy New Year (saying this at the right time earned you *lycee*, red envelopes stuffed with cash), and *gno sat neyko say yun tow*, a phrase I hear often from my Aunty Yee

Mah that roughly translates to 'I will chop off your dead man's head.'

'Jasmine just bought her mother a $600,000 apartment in Hong Kong,' mother says wistfully before going for the touch-down. '*In cash*.'

Jasmine is David's perfect sibling. She is a stockbroker in New York, married to an investment banker. The photographer at her Sydney wedding cost $12,000.

'Jasmine only got 80 per cent on her HSC.' My mother looks hopeful, as though retards like me might have a chance after all. Then she shakes herself out of it. 'But no one paid any attention to her until she started making money.'

My mother looks around our tiny two-bedroom apartment. The kitchen is fine if you're a troll and enjoy dim, cramped spaces. The carpet is grey and curling around the edges. The furnishings are the type you pick up by the side of the road. There are occasional glimpses of the life we had before. A Ming vase. A black lacquered screen with flourishes of gold. But the priceless antiques give the apartment the ambience of a refugee camp, as though we managed to save a few precious things before catastrophe threw us into squalor.

When I visit my cousins in their two-storey palaces, their kitchens as big as our apartment and their lucky trees with life-sized peaches of jade in the foyer, my secret pleasure is to creep upstairs and press my face into the pale, plush carpet.

*

We are poor because my mother's financial history has been over-shadowed by unlucky four – *sie*, which sounds uncomfortably close to *sei*, death. She was the fourth child born in the fourth decade of the century. Her father gave all his money to Chiang Kai-shek, the Chinese leader of the Nationalist Party who lost China to the Communists in 1949. My mother's brothers and sister were also left destitute, but they all married suitable Chinese spouses who helped them earn back the family fortune.

My mother, with her silken black hair and face like a doll, could have done better than anyone. But instead, she married my father, a *gweilo*, a ghost person, a white man. In our world, interracial marriages are unheard of. We don't know any other Chinese who married Australians.

'Barbarians,' Yee Mah would say. 'Chinese were using chopsticks while *gweilos* were eating with their hands.'

My father was a charming but troubled Vietnam vet, prone to occasional psychotic episodes and heavy drinking. When he brought my mother home to meet his family, my grandfather's first words to her were, 'Jesus Christ – a chongalewy-chow Sheila!'

My mother did everything required of a dutiful Chinese wife. She spent three hours baking *dun tahts*, the pastry as flaky around the warm egg custard as those served for the Kangxi Emperor at the Manchu imperial feast. She did the ritualistic two-day preparation for Peking duck and gave herself RSI from rolling perfectly circular Mandarin pancakes. She served orgasmic banquets to my father's friends and unwittingly to his mistresses.

It wasn't a surprise to anyone except my mother when my father divorced her and left her for a white barbarian when I was five and my sister was two.

My mother almost slit her wrists in shame. We didn't know anyone who was divorced. Chinese spouses had affairs, slept in separate rooms and barely spoke to each other, but no one divorced. It was a matter of saving face.

Her own life in shreds and two dollars in her pocket, we became her only hope. We would be brilliant at school, earn accolades and awards until the day when we were educated, rich and could lavish her with the money and attention she deserved.

Unfortunately, it isn't quite working out that way. As a result of the impure blood of my father, my sister and I don't even look Chinese. We both have Chinese hair, dead straight and completely resistant to the crimping tools crucial to the '80s, but my sister's hair is blonde and mine is the colour of burnt toast.

As time goes by, it becomes clear to her that we are going the way of *Australian* children. The ones who don't work as hard, are loud and uncouth and, worst of all, talk back to their parents and hold chopsticks near the pointed ends, like peasants.

Until the divorce, we had barely seen my Chinese relatives. Suddenly, from our big, comfortable house in Turramurra, we were living in a troll cave in Kingsford near Vietnamese boat people. Instead of a mother who stayed home all day cooking delicious and exotic meals, I had a mother who worked as a secretary for fourteen hours a day. And every day after school, my sister and I get dumped with my Aunty Yee Mah and my three cousins.

It is well known among all my new relatives under the age of sixteen that you do not fuck with Yee Mah. Yee Mah isn't fat but there is a heaviness to her. The back of her hand feels like a ton of bricks. She once broke a bed just by sitting on it. Besides the famous 'I will chop off your dead man's head,' she sometimes pulls out a box of matches, holds one out close to our mouths and hisses, 'If you are lying to me I will burn out your tongue.' In a way that convinces you she absolutely is not joking.

Her daughter Erica is seventeen and the high-achieving darling. Robert is number one son and therefore immune to any criticism or punishment. However, her other son, Patrick, my sister Bronnie and I, we are all under ten and therefore under her complete jurisdiction.

So every day after school, Bronnie, Patrick and I get up to mischief and then try to stop Yee Mah finding out. On the weekends there are more cousins, aunties and uncles to visit, most of whom aren't even related to us. The hope is that some of their Chineseness will rub off on us and Bronnie and I will become bright, smart vessels and alleviate some of my mother's disgrace.

Bronnie and I never quite blend in, but our new playmates are always too polite to mention it until one day, Erica storms out of the playground.

'Australians are retarded,' she says churlishly. Erica is seven years older than me and I worship her. She is everything a good girl should be: smart, respectful, and her boyfriends buy her large stuffed animals that I secretly covet.

There's a rhyme going around the playground. The kids pull up the corners of their eyes, then pull them down, chanting: 'Chinese, Japanese, hope your kids turn Pickanese.' On 'Pickanese,' they lift one eye up and one eye down, giving the clear impression of mental retardation. Like all bad jokes that come into fashion, this one is going around like wildfire, and Erica has apparently been socked with it 150 times during lunch.

As we wait outside school for Yee Mah, I catch Erica giving me a sideways look, as though she is seeing me for the first time, realising that I look more like one of *them* than like her.

'Yeah,' I quickly say. 'Australians are dog shit. Their babies will all eat dog shit and die.'

I have to be liberal with the faeces because the week before, my cousin Victor was bashed at the 7Eleven in Maroubra. A local gang was targeting Asians, and a couple of them beat up Victor and stole his bike. I saw him staggering down the road, bleeding from his nose with scrapes along his arms. The cheekbone beneath his eye was swollen and red, like a ripe fruit about to burst.

There is also a rumour going around that Asian-haters have been stabbing Asians with syringes full of AIDS blood in the cinemas on George Street. As a result, we don't go to the cinema for at least a year.

Yee Mah's car pulls up and we all climb in. Erica doesn't speak to me for the rest of the day. Without knowing why, I am ashamed.

*

Every Saturday, about twenty of our 'inner circle' go to yum cha. The children are fed *cha siu bao* pork buns to fill us up so we don't eat any of the expensive stuff, while the grown-ups brag about themselves by bragging about their children.

'Patrick just passed his Grade Seven piano exam,' says Yee Mah. 'And Erica is top of her class. Again.'

Aunty Helen talks about Jasmine's new office in the World Trade Centre and David's internship.

And my poor mother sits with nothing to say. No awards we have won. No praise from our teachers. No marks high enough for medical or law school. It is the ultimate aspiration for any Chinese mother to have a child who is a lawyer or a doctor. The best-case scenario would be a lawyer who defends doctors in court.

'You would make such a good barrister,' my mother sometimes tells me. 'You and that slippery tongue of yours.'

Such two-faced compliments are the staple of my existence. '*Ho liang*,' my relatives say. 'How pretty.' But I always sense another implication: at least I am pretty, because there isn't much else going for me.

Even worse, Bronnie wants to be an actress and I want to be a writer. My mother can't think of anything less likely to lead to one of us buying her an apartment.

'You'll end up penniless in an attic,' she tells my sister. As for me, she clips out cuttings from the newspaper to prove that most writers end up dead of starvation in the gutter.

*

To twist the chopstick even deeper, I am developing an aversion to school. In class, I am miserable, churlish and awkward. I don't have any friends, and a boy called Owen throws rocks at me after class. There is another charming game going around the playground in which you pinch someone and say, 'Tip, you've got the germs.'

I am always the original source of the germs.

Finally, to escape being the human turd, I lock myself in the school toilets for three hours. When a teacher comes to find me, I tell her I've been vomiting. Half an hour later my mother pulls up outside school and drives me back to our apartment. She cooks me chicken soup with noodles and wraps the bed sheets around me so tight I feel like I am in an envelope, about to be posted somewhere exotic. I love the garlic and chilli smell of her hands. She takes my temperature and smoothes my forehead and continually asks if I am all right.

I suffer another week through the germ game until I lock myself in the toilet again. This time, Yee Mah picks me up from school.

'What's wrong with you?' she demands.

'I threw up in the toilet.'

'You don't smell like vomit,' she says suspiciously.

'It was only a little bit.'

She looks at me slyly from the corner of her eye.

'Do you know why your mother is poor?'

I shake my head.

'Because of you. She has to pay your school feels, very expensive. You see how tired she is? You must pay her back with good marks. Otherwise you will make her shamed.'

The emotional terrorism continues until we get to her house. There is no chicken soup or tucking into bed. I have to sit on the couch with Bobo, her mother-in-law, for six hours, watching day-time television until my sister and Patrick come home.

*

'Mum,' I tug on my mother's arm during Saturday yum cha as she chews on a prawn dumpling, part of yet another meal she can't pay for. She looks down at me absentmindedly. 'Mum!'

'Yes, sweetheart?'

'Can you buy me that fish?'

'What?'

There are over fifty bream stuffed in the tank of the yum cha restaurant. They are squashed so tight together they can hardly move. In the middle there is a beautiful golden one, with scales that shimmer in the light of the crystal chandeliers. I want my mother to buy it so I can take it to Bondi Beach in a plastic bag and set it free in the ocean.

'Don't be stupid,' my mother says. 'They are for eating.'

The eating habits of my sister and I are yet another source of embarrassment. We are very wasteful. We don't eat chicken's feet. We don't suck the jelly out of fish eyeballs and we refuse to eat the creamy filling inside prawn heads.

'Just that one. *Pleeeeeeease.*'

'No.'

'Why?'

'We can't afford it,' she hisses.

I let go of her hand and catch up with my sister and Patrick, who are playing in the elevators. We like to go into the elevators and push all the buttons. Go all the way up. Go all the way down. Occasionally, we get out on a floor we aren't supposed to be on and run up and down the corridors.

It doesn't bother me that we are poor. I've found a way to com-bat it – I steal from other children. When I get kicked out of class for misbehaving, which is often, I rifle through the school bags of all the other kids and steal their lunch money, as well as anything else I like.

When I finally get caught, I'm terrified Yee Mah will burn off my tongue like she's always threatening. Instead, my mother sits me down at the dining-room table. She is very quiet. She puts her hand on my hand and says, 'What do other children have that you don't?'

If I were smarter, I would hear her heart breaking.

'Erasers with Snow White on them,' I say without hesitating.

'All right,' says my mother. 'Go to your room.'

As I leave, I see her bow her head, as if she's carrying a great burden. It's shame. And she's not ashamed of me, she's ashamed of herself. For failing to teach me the difference between right and wrong. For failing to make me feel like I am warm and safe and don't need to steal from other kids to make up for everything I don't have.

The next day, the Snow White erasers are on the dining-room table. I don't even want them.

*

When I finally ring my mother to tell her my HSC score, she sounds delighted.

'You got 88.8? Very lucky number. You will be rich for sure.'

There is an odd note in her voice, one of momentary regret. That this isn't the moment when I exceed all her expectations.

'Very rich,' she says again, as if to comfort herself with an ancient Confucian wisdom: *Just think how it could have been worse.*

As for me, I've given up hoping she will tell me she is proud. I no longer begrudge my friends their mothers who overflow with constant affirmation and nurturing encouragement. When she criticises me with all the sensitivity of a Japanese scientist harpooning a whale, and I feel the slow-burning resentment building to rage, I bite my slippery tongue.

Instead, I fossick through my memory for one of my earliest recollections.

My mother is in the kitchen. Steam rises from the wok and oil spatters over her hands. There is a delicious smell of soy sauce, garlic and chicken. She tips the contents of the wok into a dish, then spoons out chicken wings onto beds of rice. Chicken wings are the cheapest part of a chicken. She has bought all her salary can afford.

On my sister's plate there are two. On mine there are two. On hers, there is only one.

And in her sacrifice, I see love.

The Asian Disease

Simone Lazaroo

It's getting closer, I know it is.

I can feel it at my back, a cold, static darkness that makes the hairs along my spine stand on end. I'm almost certain it's my father's death, drawing nearer. His family has a saying: *You haven't grown up until you've faced your parents' death.* And I haven't, not yet. I'm still trying to make sense of his disease.

I'm not sure if his disease is Asian or Australian in origin. It makes his body and speech shake, or sometimes freeze for minutes at a time. Over the years, the medications have lost their effectiveness in combating these symptoms.

'I'm ... not ... sure ... how mmmuch ... lllonger ... I can ... go ... on,' my father says each time I visit him in the nursing home in Perth's new blond-brick outer suburbs. I hear the long slow tremor of death in his voice, see it moving through his body. 'Sssorry ... the ... bbrroadcast's ... a bit... sslurred today,' he apologises. 'Like ... the BBC in ... Sssingapore when ... I was a child.'

One day soon, I warn myself, this disease will freeze him forever.

It already demands all his willpower and concentration to swallow. He refuses the liquefied food the nurses offer him. As it times his days, the gold Swiss wrist-watch given to him by Singapore's government fifty years ago for his services to the island's post-war plumbing is smeared with rejected puree and soup.

'Tasteless ... mmush,' he complains to me. 'I ... will ... vvomit ... or die ffaster ... if... they mmmake me ... eat ... that again. Sssspeech ... mmmovement ... now even... my ffood ... is ssslurred.'

How much longer will my father be able to endure such loss

of control? Despite so much slurring, his watch still keeps perfect time.

'Do you have anything tastier?' I ask the matron.

'We don't cater for foreign appetites here,' she tells me. 'And there's duty of care, Miss Nazario. Your father's disease might make him choke on solid food, and that would be distressing for the other residents.'

But I take the risk and buy him take-away curry, kuey teow and ginger tea, so that he might taste memories of his mother and Singapore. Anything to delay the final freeze. I feed him in his room, to avoid distressing the other residents.

'Thank ... you,' he says. Two slow tears run down his face. 'Aunty ... Mercedes ... visited me ... today.'

I don't have the heart to remind him that his sister Mercedes died five years ago in Singapore, and never made it across the Indian Ocean to visit him. His memory, too, has been slurred by the disease. Only a few episodes from his more distant past are clear.

*

Covering his thinness and uncertainty with his recently deceased father's suit jacket and his almost-BBC English pronunciation, twenty-year-old Eurasian civil servant Emanuel Nazario stood in the dirt amongst the chickens and goats and briefed the residents of several Singaporean kampongs about a new pipeline planned to service them. It was the late 1950s, and the government had recently unfurled blueprints for an intricate system of plumbing and housing. Emanuel held the crisp plans high in the air so the goats couldn't eat them, and assured the kampong dwellers that the new pipelines would deliver them unprecedented convenience and release them from centuries of filth, disease and bad spirits.

Emanuel's parents had recently died, their bodies prematurely aged by starvation during the war almost fifteen years earlier. His own body was still skinny from his malnourished childhood. He did push-ups three times a day in front of his poster of Charles Atlas, and he fortified himself with Milo and Dutch Maid powdered milk after double helpings of nasi lemak and kuey teow from Singapore's street hawkers. Cold storage had recently come to Singapore, and he bought himself a small serve of their expensive ice-cream once a week as a treat. He tried not to think too often about his mother's piquant gaze and curries. Within a few weeks, he'd be journeying to the university in Perth on a Colombo Plan scholarship to study water supply and sewerage disposal, and he was worried that insufficient nourishment and unchecked grief would diminish his ability to apply modern Western plumbing methods to Singapore's future.

*

Wearing pleat-fronted chino trousers and a large, spotlessly white shirt to disguise his slenderness, Emanuel Nazario met Maureen Jones on his first morning at the student boarding house in Perth. It was 1959, and the boarding house hallway smelled of boiled cabbage and milk, with not even the faintest whiff of spice. Maureen's room was just across the hall from Emanuel's. Despite this proximity, it seemed at first that they were latitudes apart, at least on the surface.

Think of it, the sinewy golden-brownness of the civil engineering student from the teeming South-East Asian island city; the voluptuous paleness of the young education and English literature student from a small Western Australian wheat-belt town. But imagine too their loneliness so many miles away from home; their youthful fascination with one another's skin and history. The only spice for miles around, it seemed.

*

'Jolly Asians bring nothing but disease. Your life will be a disaster if you marry one of them,' her mother with the frosted hair and gaze warned the lovelorn Maureen when she returned to her little wheat-belt town for the summer vacation.

*

Emanuel returned to Singapore qualified as a water-supply and waste-disposal engineer. There, he was handed a spade, a pair of rubber boots, a plan of the proposed sewage-disposal system for a cramped kampong near the CBD, and a white cotton handkerchief to tie over his nose and mouth as he dug.

His new job called for single-minded heroism. The soil around the kampong was clayey, and people still emptied their waste into open drains on the street. He had no maps to help him locate these outpourings of human bodies. He ducked a bucketful here, an ammoniac-smelling puddle there. One morning he surfaced from a newly dug tunnel into a tiny room full of ten Chinese labourers sleeping the day shift on straw mats. The closest man woke afraid and hit the young engineer, causing his palm to slip against the spade handle.

'The government sent me,' Emanuel said to the rudely woken labourer, 'I'm laying pipes against disease.' But neither of them spoke one another's language. Emanuel retreated through the tunnel he'd just dug. The cut on his dirt-stained palm was shaped like the white crescent on Malaya's recently unfurled flag, symbolising a new moon and nation, but the crescent on his hand was the blood red of mortality. Had a disease already entered his body? Afraid of contracting tetanus, cholera, hepatitis and diseases beyond diagnosis, he doused the crescent in Jeye's Disinfectant and went to the government clinic for every available inoculation, but a longing for permanent escape from disease entered his bloodstream with each needle jab. That night he dreamed of Perth, where Maureen Jones and an efficient sewage-disposal system were already in place, and tropical diseases were almost unheard of. He wrote a letter to Maureen the next day, lightly smeared with blood from his wound.

When Maureen flew to Singapore to visit him two months later, he proposed to her. He did this under a gnarled old angsana tree at the new reservoir, one of the sites in her tour of the infrastructure he was helping to build. He didn't tell Maureen that the tree was more often used for suicides than proposals.

*

'*Ah-yah!* Why not a nice Eurasian girl?' Emanuel's oldest sister Mercedes muttered when he announced his engagement.

'You never know what could happen if you marry one of *them*,' Maureen's mother warned her through the white noise of the long-distance phone call to Western Australia.

Despite the consternation of their families, Maureen and

Emanuel married within a few weeks at his old school chapel, under the sorrowful gazes of a mildewed plaster Christ and the two Nazario sisters. When Maureen ran her fingers gently over his immunisation scars that night, Emanuel understood how wounds could be transformed into rewards.

*

When we three children were born in Kadang Kerbau, the Pregnant Cow maternity hospital, in the years leading up to Singapore's independence, Emanuel was sure to have us immunised for everything going. Our buttocks were dimpled not only by our mother's milk, but by immunisation scars that puckered our tender skin into tiny rosettes.

After his youngest child was born, he was presented with the gold Swiss watch. *To Emanuel Nazario from the Government of Singapore, for helping to lay the groundwork against disease*, the inscription on the back read.

*

Emanuel Nazario knew that the most serious diseases were best avoided by putting as much distance as possible between us and the tropics. He hoped to migrate with his young family to Australia, but he had dark skin and the White Australia Policy was still in force. We three Singaporean-born children had 'come out various shades in the wash,' as my father's expatriate English boss put it. The Australian embassy officers in Singapore were perplexed when the white mother, brown father and three colour-gradated children presented themselves at the desk to apply for migration.

'We don't get many families like yours applying,' the Australian man in the striped blue, red and white tie said. 'We're not sure how you'll measure up against policy.' Years later in Perth, my maternal grandfather, a public servant, would tell me that the White Australia Policy had screened us out, and that we were only permitted to migrate to Australia after he'd pulled some strings. This grandfather died before I found out what the strings were attached to.

*

It was 1965 when the strings released us to fly to Perth. Down at the local supermarket in the State Housing Commission suburb where we first lived, the walls were a cool, sparkling white. There were pink sausages, white bread, milk and more flavours of ice-cream than Dad had ever seen. There were a few Aboriginal people, conspicuous against all that paleness and fluorescent light, but no Asian faces or food. Milo and Jeye's Disinfectant were available, though. Dad stockpiled them, as if fortifying himself against new diseases.

My father took his job at the Water Board seriously. On the weekends, we went on picnics to the new dams and pipelines he'd helped design. He checked water levels and dam walls while we picnicked on sausages wrapped in white bread and smothered in tomato sauce. Deprived of meat and dairy foods during his war-time childhood, my father finished up every sausage, every scoop of ice-cream, every pat of butter, as if his life depended on it.

*

The evening my father picked up his gleaming new white 1968 Valiant Safari station wagon, he drove it down to the local post-box to send Christmas cards to his sisters back in Singapore. Withdrawing his hand from the slot, he was salivating slightly as he thought wistfully of the achar pickles and curried devil they'd be preparing for Christmas lunch over there, when he was blinded by two beams of light and slammed face-first against the super-market wall by two hard hands at his back. He felt his glasses cut into his left cheek. He closed his eyes against the glare of the car headlights upon the bare white wall as the saliva dribbled from the corner of his mouth.

'Keep yer hands up!' the two policemen shouted together in their harsh Australian accents when my father moved to wipe his saliva away. He did as he was told, saliva running from the corner of his mouth, palms flat against the white supermarket wall, unsure of his crime.

'You're the boong who robbed the deli,' the first policeman said, frisking him. My father had been in Australia just long enough to be familiar with this insulting term for Aboriginals.

'I am not Aboriginal,' he murmured.

'Nah, you're a boong.'

'I am Eurasian,' he said.

'Never heard of it.'

'I am an Australian citizen, too,' my father concluded.

'You're a dribbling blackie,' the second policeman sneered.

When he arrived home, the only thing my father could remember about the policemen's appearance was their plump ham-coloured faces, a kind of boiled greyish pink. A cut like a question mark bled on his left cheek. Only when he cleaned himself up in the bathroom did he start crying, just a little. He was crying, he said, for Aboriginal people, and anyone else in Australia with dark skin.

'Unwhiteness is a notifiable crime in Perth,' he warned us. 'They only let me go because of the new car and my BBC accent.'

He sat down and shovelled two platefuls of sausages and potatoes into his mouth.

'One day, Asians will be rewarded for what they bring to this country,' my mother said. In the silence, I could hear his reward from the Singaporean government counting down on his wrist.

'It's getting closer, Dad, I know it is,' I agreed.

But he just kept eating, as if he were fortifying himself against future disaster. That night I dreamed of running with my father from the Australian police, shielding him from their gaze, placing my inadequate paleness between him and them.

*

'Let's play nurses,' the girl over the road said behind the chook-pen. 'I'm the nurse, you're the patient. You have to drop your knickers.'

'You're different,' she concluded. 'Darker, and what are those things? They look like something's bitten you on the bum.'

'They're from needles I had when I was a baby so I didn't get the disease.'

'Which disease?'

'I forget its name.'

'Dad says you're Asian.'

'Is that a disease?'

Up until then, I'd almost succeeded in forgetting where I came from.

*

Around the time the White Australia Policy was officially abolished by Gough Whitlam in the 1970s, we met newer immigrants with faces a bit like ours, mowing lawns and learning how to barbecue sausages in streets near ours.

'We come to Australia, we must learn to be Australian,' I heard a group of recent immigrants from Singapore agree at one of these barbecues.

But they weren't as adrift from their pasts as we'd been when we'd arrived in Perth in 1965. By the early seventies, Asian grocers and restaurants began appearing in shopping centres. At last! Nasi lemak and salted plums! Ginger tea and kuey teow! Although we were still sometimes insulted in the streets of our suburb, even spat upon, young Australian men and old ladies stopped my sister and me in the shopping centre and told us that we were beautiful. My schoolteacher, captain of a Western Australian Football League team, declared me prefect with a rosette-shaped badge, and a man in a suit at the bus stop declared mine the face of the future in the same week that our local Chinese restaurant won a Gold Plate Award. At last! Rewarded for being Asian! Twelve years old, on the brink of trainer bras from China, official multiculturalism and adolescent vanity, I thought we'd never look back.

*

Towards the end of my adolescence, my father divorced my wheat-belt mother and remarried, the only one in generations of his family to do so.

'It's an Australian illness,' his younger sister Mary told me when she visited us during a package tour of Australia some time between his divorce and his second wedding.

*

'The disease is probably not genetic in your father's case,' the doctor at the nursing home tells me. 'We suspect he suffers from the type caused by childhood malnutrition.'

'The war,' I say. 'When he was a boy, his father was imprisoned and the rest of the family were sent by the Japanese to fend for themselves in the Malayan jungle.'

But this is an Asian history, not an Australian one, and the doctor is already moving on to the next patient.

*

The slurring disease has doubled my father's foreignness for people who don't know him well. Suffering from advanced symptoms, he sometimes struggles to make himself understood to hospital and nursing-home staff.

'Can he understand English?' two relief nurses ask me after glancing at his dark skin and failing to comprehend his speech.

'He's spoken English since he was an infant,' I tell them. 'The British and the BBC were big in Singapore and Malaya when he was a child.'

'But he sounds so ... foreign,' one of them replied.

'It's the disease, not a foreign language. You have to listen carefully.'

'But he *looks* foreign, too. You're his daughter? But you're so ... pale.'

'My mother ...' I begin. But the story is too long.

*

If Dad's lucky, a Malay nurse, Jamilah, is rostered to look after him at the nursing home. Like my father, she is slender and looks younger than she is. She's sixty years old, but she looks about forty.

'It's the Asian blood in us,' she says.

Jamilah migrated to Australia a few years after the White Australia Policy had been lifted, but she understands the bruise of being dark-skinned in Australia.

'When we first came, we were the first Asians in my street. Next to all the white fences and people, I felt blacker than I'd ever felt. And none of the Australian neighbours dropped in to eat with us, even when we invited them.'

'I've ... been ... up ... against ... the great ... w-w-white wall ... too,' my dad nods, slowly but adamantly.

'But after all these years, we know we're great, don't we, Manny?' Jess says, breaking the nursing-home rules and giving him a home-made curry puff.

'We'll … rule … the world … one … day,' my father concurs in his trembling drawl.

But I know that he also sometimes hallucinates that he's being arrested by police for not having a passport, or that he's being locked up to freeze to death in cold storage, or being taken to court because he is stateless. In these delusions, he's never sure whether he's in Singapore or Australia.

'The hallucinations are another symptom of the advanced stages of the disease,' the doctor says, but I make other interpretations.

Sometimes, my father tells me, he is nursed by a large Australian woman with permed hair and gaze who refuses to speak to him, except to mutter that his slurred speech and occasional incontinence are symptoms of his Asian-ness. She withholds smiles and his cups of ginger tea, and pushes bland mush into his mouth, cursing as he chokes on it. I haven't met this nurse yet, the nursing-home staff deny that she exists when I question them about her, and I have to conclude that she is at least partly a product of my father's hallucinations. He tells me she's ham-faced, and that she speaks in a frosty wheat-belt accent. I wonder if hers is the face of the policemen in 1968, or if she speaks in my maternal grandmother's disapproving voice.

As he tells me this story about the nurse, Dad dribbles slightly and looks almost unbearably forlorn and lost. One thing's for sure: my father's up against the white wall again. For him, this Australian who wishes him ill is still real, a nightmare from our first years in Perth that never quite disappeared.

'Please … bring me … some Jeyes' Disinfectant … next time,' he begs me. 'The … disease is … everywhere.'

*

On my most recent visit, my father was almost unable to speak or walk at all. The medications he takes to control the disease have almost no effect.

'He may have a few days left, he may have a few months,' the doctor told me in the corridor outside my father's room.

When I waved my father goodbye last time, he held out both his hands towards me. I could hear the ticking of his watch. I could see the crescent-shaped scar on his palm, the inoculation marks on his upper arm, the question mark on his cheek; I could see the tremor in his fingers, the symptom of his disease.

Emanuel Joseph Nazario. His trembling outstretched hands might have been giving me his blessing. They might have been begging me to take him with me. They might have been bidding me farewell for the last time.

*

At home afterwards, I soak in the bath a long time, as if the water from the hills reservoir my father helped design in his first years in Perth might wash away any lingering bad spirits.

I see my father's fine outstretched Eurasian hands blessing, begging, farewelling me; trembling with all the diseases he's endured – Asian, Australian, and everything in between.

When I dry myself, I notice the inoculation marks I received in infancy on my left buttock. Like Dad's marks but smaller, they're shaped like medals or like sores, depending on how you look at them. They are still with us nearly fifty years later, after living through the final years of the White Australia Policy, several years of assimilation, a couple of decades of multiculturalism.

Is it my pulse I can hear, or my father's battered old wrist-watch counting down again?

If I ever meet the large Australian ham-faced nurse with the frosted voice and hair, I will point to his scars and ask her the question: 'A punishment, or a reward?'

It's getting closer, I know it is.

Crackers

Rudi Soman

It was after we moved to the new house that the cracks grew into fissures and then a mighty black crevasse.

One night Acha set three cheese-baited mousetraps on the floor at the back of the walk-in pantry. Later that night Amma opened the pantry door and quietly laid down a saucer containing a couple of broken Ritz crackers.

'We should give him a chance,' she said to me in a low voice, taking a tea towel and wiping a coffee mug.

The next morning the crackers were gone. Only a crumb remained. Amma removed the saucer and rinsed it under hot water in the sink. In the pantry the little wooden traps were still tightly coiled. They looked ominous despite the cheerful cubes of Coon.

'This is a crafty mouse,' Acha said when inspecting the traps after his morning prayers. 'Still, we will see how long he can resist the temptation.' He disappeared into the corridor to get ready for work.

That night Acha baited the traps with fresh Coon. After he went to bed I heard Amma moving around in the kitchen. I went in to take a look. This time she was breaking a Sao biscuit into tiny pieces.

'He's not hurting anyone,' she said as she placed the saucer in the pantry.

'What about the poo? It could be unhygienic.'

'He doesn't poo here.'

'He or she must poo somewhere.'

'Can you see any poo?'

Amma was right. There was no sign of mouse poo. But we had all seen the mouse at one time or another in the last two weeks.

The next morning I was first up, closely followed by Amma. Once again the traps were untouched while Amma's nibbles were, we presumed, completely devoured.

That afternoon when I arrived home from football practice I

threw my school bag down and hurried to the kitchen. I was looking forward to a snack of heavily buttered white bread sprinkled with granulated garlic and then toasted under the griller. In the kitchen, Acha, in his suit trousers and a white singlet, was backing out of the pantry with the Dustbuster. He revered his Dustbuster in the way that other suburban fathers loved their power drills. This explained the absence of mouse shit in the pantry. Acha turned to face me. He held the device with the nozzle pointing up, as a soldier would handle a combat rifle amongst civilians.

'As cunning as an outhouse rat,' he said. I had recently noticed the *Dictionary of Australian Colloquialisms* on Acha's desk in the study-cum-prayer-room. I imagined him methodically consulting the index under 'M' for mouse and then 'R' for rat. I had heard this expression before the arrival of the dictionary. I suspected Acha had sanitised the phrase by replacing *shithouse* with *outhouse*, and not just for my benefit. He was a pious man after all.

'This time he has been nibbling the edges but not taking the whole cheese. Not exerting enough pressure to set off the trap,' he said.

'Maybe the Coon isn't tasty enough,' I mumbled. 'Maybe try Cracker Barrel.'

'Don't say stupid things.' He pronounced stupid as if it was spelt with two Os and a T at the end. 'Coon is very tasty.'

Acha opened the back of the Dustbuster and emptied its contents into the kitchen bin. The specks of dung made soft, almost inaudible tapping sounds as they hit the puffy sides of the bin liner. It sounded as if he had let fall half-a-dozen grains of basmati rice.

'*Cheh!*' he spat out in disgust. He went back to the study-cum-prayer-room, where I heard him hang his Dustbuster on the special wall fixture between the altar and his desk.

*

That night Acha decided to modify his tactics.

'The aroma of celery is very strong. Together with Coon it is bound to attract a mouse,' he announced.

Using toothpicks he pierced together cubes of cheese with cross-sectional slices of celery. With great concentration he fastened the new improved baits to the traps and set them. Each device now looked like a menacing bionic canapé.

Acha summarised the plan. 'The toothpick will hold the food-stuffs firmly together with the trap so that when the bait is inter-fered with, the trap *must* spring. The rodent now has only a Buckley's chance of survival and none other.' Looking solemn, he retired to his study-cum-prayer-room. I heard the sound of matches being lit. Soon the smell of incense wafted down the hall together with muffled intonations of the Gayatri mantra.

Later, before going to bed, I went back to the kitchen to get a glass of water. I found Amma with a jar of peanut paste in her hands. The open packet of Sao crackers was on the counter.

'I asked my Year 12 class today which foods a mouse would like. Many of the children said their parents would use bacon to catch a mouse. Some said peanut paste. We do not have any bacon so I will use peanut paste. *Crunchy.* He will find it a delicious diversion. The celery and cheese cannot compete. Don't tell Acha.'

This was quite logical for my mother, compared with her past behaviour with animals and food. Nearly twelve months earlier, on our first day at the house on Ormsby Street, I had acquired a new pet. While sullenly exploring the backyard, mentally cursing my father, there in front of me on the garden path had been a tor-toise. Its shell was dull green and the size of a cereal bowl. It car-ried some illegible paint markings, like old, faded graffiti. The tortoise's neck was fully extended in five or six centimetres of friendly greeting. It was winking at me, slowly and steadily.

I winked back. I bent down and softly touched its leathery head but it did not shrink away.

I named him Bronchi. In biology we had just studied the human respiratory system. The name given to the air tubes lead-ing from the trachea to the lungs had reminded me of a dinosaur but it seemed ideal for a tortoise too. Over the following weeks I would find Bronchi in various corners and niches of the large sloping yard. He soon became my pet and a redeeming feature of the new house.

I wasn't sure if Bronchi was a long-time resident of 3 Ormsby Street. I couldn't believe that the previous occupants would have left such a cute pet behind. I assumed he subsisted on the fat of the land – maybe a diet of leaves, bugs, grasshoppers and whatever else it was that tortoises ate. I soon discovered that Amma had taken a liking to Bronchi too. One day I arrived home from school to find, on the same section of concrete path where I had first encountered him, a brown plastic two-litre ice-cream container. It was laden with leftover Keralan chicken curry and rice. The steep-sided receptacle also contained a small amount of sambar complemented by a crushed pappadam. Even with his neck fully extended and standing upright Bronchi would have needed a small crane to get anywhere near the curries and the stale, broken accompaniment.

I asked Amma about it when she got home from school.

'What?' she said. 'He will eat it when he is hungry.'

'Yes, but how, Amma, how? How is a tortoise supposed to get into an ice-cream container?'

'Don't worry. He will eat if he is hungry,' she said, squinting through her glasses at a pile of test papers. 'Look at this nonsense. *Au* is the symbol for gold. There is no such element as *Australium!*' She continued crossing and ticking. Then without looking up she added, 'He is already a good-looking tortoise. How could somebody paint on his shell like that?'

*

A few days later Amma had called me outside to show me the ice-cream container. 'See?' she said, pointing down the verandah towards the path. 'Half eaten. Poor thing was starving.'

Indeed, it looked as if some of the food had been consumed. A drumstick lay on the path, some savage looking gashes exposing grey bone. There were a few salient depressions in the thick bed of rice and curry.

'Amma, that was probably the neighbour's dog, or a stray cat. Could have even been a possum.'

'I told you he would eat if he was hungry.' She went back into the house. 'Tonight I can give him yesterday's chapattis and some vada.'

A few months later Bronchi disappeared. Not having seen my tortoise for a week I searched every inch of the yard, in vain. I also searched the garage though I knew that not even a curry and rice diet would have enabled a tortoise to open a roller door. I tried the yard again and discovered a small gap under the back fence. I came to the unwelcome conclusion that Bronchi had moved on. I remember how sadly I trudged to the back door, carefully stepping over the ice-cream container. That day it was half-filled with dhosa, coconut chutney and two intact Arnott's Yo-Yos. Presumably, Amma had deemed Bronchi's appetite hearty enough to warrant dessert. I looked for signs of tortoise-sized teeth marks in the savoury pancakes but the dhosas looked as pristine as when Amma had flipped them off the ghee-oiled griddle two nights before.

So, in light of her menu for Bronchi a year ago, it seemed remarkable that today Amma had undertaken research into the most effective way to attract, or rather distract, a mouse. She was spreading the lumpy peanut paste thickly and evenly, right to the corners of the cracker. This was a quality that I admired even if I had tossed ninety percent of my school lunches over fences or into bins. My mother *was* thorough.

'If we can divert the mouse for long enough with these nice foods then your father will eventually become interested in some other project. Then everything will return to normal.' Using the butter knife she carefully broke the cracker into pieces and placed the saucer in its spot near the traps on the pantry floor.

I wasn't so sure that Acha would forget about the mouse. And what if there were two mice, and they were of opposite sex, and compatible, and they decided to breed? What then? We would live in a house overrun with vermin. I was ashamed enough of my parents and this ugly house in this depressing suburb, without having to cope with that.

That night I lay in bed listening intently for any sound coming from the kitchen. As much as I sympathised with Amma's cause I hoped for the sound of a snapping mousetrap so that this episode might quickly come to an end.

No snapping came and I soon fell asleep.

*

I woke to the sound of shouting. It was coming from the kitchen. I looked around my room. The blinds were framed with light. The shouting stopped but I could hear Amma and Acha talking.

Not looking forward to the gory scene that might await in the pantry I threw off the blankets and stumbled out of my room.

Amma and Acha were at either end of the kitchen in their dressing gowns.

'Why do you do this? So unfriendly sometimes! Always showing a sad face whenever I ask anyone to come here!' said Acha. He was muttering to himself as he poured boiled milk into the small metal jug that he used for morning offerings at the altar. 'Soon nobody will want to come here at all!'

'What do you expect? I have no time to cook dinner parties with end of term so near. All my marking. All the cleaning and washing. Why don't you ask me before you invite people for dinner?' Amma replied to herself, dropping a couple of Weetbix into a bowl.

I walked over to the sink to get some water. Acha turned towards me.

'Why do you sleep wearing sports clothes? You are jogging at night? Why don't you wear a pyjama?'

At that moment, low down in my peripheral vision, I saw a small scurrying form. I jumped.

It was the mouse. It now stood frozen against the skirting, a metre from the open pantry door, clutching in its mouth a large corner of a SAO cracker still scrupulously covered with peanut paste. It was healthy looking, plump – almost muscular. I wondered just how long Amma had been leaving snacks on a saucer in the pantry.

Acha was the first to move. He lunged towards the mouse as if to stomp on it with a slipper-shod foot. Instead he reached over and slammed shut the pantry door. The mouse abandoned the Sao and bolted between Acha's feet. In an instant it had darted behind the stove. Acha grabbed a broom and with the handle began to poke violently behind the cooker. It sounded like he was banging pots and pans. I thought that at any moment the gas pipe would be ruptured, causing a major emergency.

After a minute the barrage of prodding seemed to work. The mouse shot out and raced along the skirting back towards the pantry. Startled, I jumped again and grabbed the first thing I saw, a plastic colander, from the dish rack by the sink. Acha attempted to swat the mouse with his broom handle, flailing a trail of cobwebs and sooty dust. The mouse changed course in the only way it could – towards me. I let out a yap and involuntarily flung the colander down in front of me in the direction of the advancing rodent.

My aim was precise to a degree, my timing exact to the milli-second. The colander landed horizontally and base-up, completely enclosing the little creature. The utensil and its captive skidded half a metre before coming to rest in the centre of the linoleum floor.

There was a moment of silence and then the colander started to gently jiggle this way and that as the mouse attempted to escape.

'He's all right,' I said. I was astounded. 'I think he ... or she ... is all right.'

'The end result is that it was a very good shot,' said Acha. 'But why were you so frightened by a little mouse? In any case, now we have to get rid of it. At least this way we can eradicate him in a more hygienic way.'

I wasn't sure how he intended to despatch it. Would he gas it in the stove or perhaps quickly break its neck? Whatever he had in mind, I had no intention of witnessing it. I started to leave the kitchen.

'NO!' said Amma, who had been silent throughout the marvel of the capture. 'We will collect him and let him go outside. We will not kill him. Poor thing.'

Standing there with her bowl of Weetbix and glaring into Acha's eyes, she looked as resolute as I had ever seen her in my life.

It appeared Acha thought so too. After a small hesitation he said, 'You do what you want. Just get rid of it, that's all. I must go light the lamp.' He picked up the tray containing the milk jug and some fruit and went into the study-cum-prayer-room, closing the door behind him.

'Can you take a placement from the dining room and bring it here?' asked Amma.

'Placemat, Amma, placemat,' I said.

I went and got her one of the cork-backed placemats that carried a picture of Ayers Rock. She knelt down and gently prised it under the edge of the colander and then slid it across, providing a floor for the cage. She carefully lifted it and placed it on the counter. We had a look inside. The mouse was dashing around in panic, twitching and blinking in terror and confusion. There were already several droppings in the blue sky over Ayers Rock.

'Don't worry,' Amma said. 'It's best if you go live outside now. But what will prevent you from sneaking back and returning to our pantry?'

'I might know a good place to release a mouse,' I said.

It was cold in the backyard. We stood by the gap under the fence where Bronchi had apparently made his exit from our lives. Amma held the placemat-cage on the palm of one hand like a small, rotund waiter about to serve a delicacy in a fancy restaurant.

'Wait a minute,' I said. I stooped down and quickly tucked my tracksuit pants into my socks. 'Just in case. Okay, you can let him, or her, go now.'

Amma bent down.

'Be a good mouse,' she said. 'We hope you have a better life next door, or wherever you may choose to settle.'

She squatted and gently placed the colander against the gap and slid out the placemat. From where I stood I could not see the mouse through the tiny openings of the colander.

'He is gone. He ran straight through the opening,' said Amma, rising.

'I'll fill it up.' I crouched down and dug into the moist ground with my hands. The dirt was rich and dark and there were a few small earthworms, which I was careful not to crush. I soon filled the little depression under the fence and firmly patted down the earth. There was no longer a gap.

'Okay, that's that,' I said and stood up.

I looked at Amma's face. Her lips were flat against each other, and she was looking back at the house, four parts mournful and one part morose, it seemed. With arms crossed she held the empty colander, the placemat and herself. For a few seconds she said nothing.

'Okay, that's that,' she finally repeated and began slowly walking back towards the concrete path and the verandah steps.

Conversations with My Parents

Oanh Thi Tran

Conversations with my parents are not especially long.

Before I left Brisbane, my father fell sick again. I ditched appointments and farewell lunches with friends to sit in hospital with him, listening to him regaling me with stories of his childhood.

Many years ago when Ba fell very sick the first time, and we had not been talking for ages because of what he saw as my wayward behaviour (I moved out of home before I was married – gasp!), I sat in hospital with him until the wee hours, when the nurses would regretfully kick me out. Some of his hospital time coincided with my exams, so I took my books into his hospital room and sat beside him, studying my exciting law texts while he slept. Once, he shook me awake – I had slumped over my textbooks, resting on his tea tray – and told me to go home.

His first illness was the turning-point in our relationship. I liked being in the hospital with him because it was one of the few ways I could express that I was a dutiful daughter, even though my values were not his. We did not talk much, initially. Then I began to ask questions about his life in Vietnam, questions I'd never really asked before. He would talk and talk at me, but only when we were in the hospital room together. I would go home and scribble frantic notes.

During his most recent bout of hospital time, I sat listening to him tell me about how much he liked school when he was younger.

He paused and said, 'When you are in England, you must telephone your Um and me every three weeks. Promise?'

I was bemused by the precision of the instruction, and said, 'Yes, okay. Every three weeks.'

*

I have not quite kept the every-three-weeks rule: I am a bit absent-minded and time slips away from me. My first conversation with my parents was very brief.

Me: Hello, Um. It's me, Oanh. (Actually what I say is: 'It's your child.' I don't always say my name, which seems silly given how many children my parents have, but they always know it's me. I wonder what my siblings say to identify themselves?)

Um: Is that you, child? (aside) Old Man! Your daughter is on the phone!

Me: Yes.

Ba: Oanh?

Me: (Not knowing who I am speaking to anymore.) Yes. Are you well?

Ba: What time is it there?

Me: (I tell them the time.) What about you? What time is it there?

Ba: (He tells me the time. I don't tell them that I have worked it out.) Are you cold? Is it cold there?

Me: Yes. It's cold. Are you well?

Ba: Where are you calling from? A phone box?

Me: Yes. We are still staying in a hotel.

Ba: Well, this phone call must be costing you a lot of money. Are you well?

Me: Yes. Don't worry about it. It is not costing very much at all. And you? Are you well?

Ba: Yes. I am well. Your Um is also well. Is there anything else? Are you okay? Your partner, is he okay?

Me: Yes.

Um: I am well. Are you cold?

Me: No. Not really. It is cold here.

Ba: Well, goodbye then. Call again.

The phone dies before I even say goodbye. I stand shocked in the phone box, staring at the receiver in my hand.

My next three conversations with my parents follow exactly this pattern. I find it somewhat funny. I never get the opportunity to tell my parents I miss them (in Vietnamese, the word for miss is the same as the word for remember) or that I love them. I am not even sure exactly what words I should use to tell my parents I love them in Vietnamese. I have never told them. This worries me, because I am so far away now. I feel I should tell them, but I don't know how.

*

I had the following conversation with one of my nieces. She is starting to talk in complete sentences:

Me: Hi! How are you?

Niece: Good. I ate pasta today, so I get to have some special (dessert).

Me: Hey, lucky you! Do you miss me?

Niece: No. Oh. Mummy is telling me to say yes. Should I say yes?

Me: (laughing) No. You don't have to miss me. What did you do today?

Niece: Well, I was playing with my cousin until Mummy told me to come talk to you.

Me: Oh. Well, why don't you go play with your cousin again?

Niece: Okay. Bye!

My family does not waste time on sentiment.

*

My mother is currently grilling me about how I obtain Vietnamese groceries. She lists what the family has been eating, and how she remembers me at every meal, particularly when she cooks my favourite dishes. 'We had crab the other day,' she says. 'We all missed you.' Then she says, 'This weekend, I am cooking banh xeo. You like to eat banh xeo so much. We will remember you.'

*

I had the longest telephone conversation with my parents ever this morning: about ten minutes. The ritual is completed first: time, weather, health. I half expect my father to harangue my mother to hang up but I get in first and tell them that we have a telephone deal where it only costs me about six Australian cents per minute of chatter with them. I then plough on and tell them that I hope my sister is showing them my photos, which I have posted to a website. My mother says no.

Then she remembers something: 'Your sister says you have been walking a lot.'

I have to agree to this. I do walk a lot. My mother tells me not to. I try to tell her that I am walking for fun, but then I just let

132

her lecture me and I make listening noises. She then tells me about her weekend, how great Bunnings hardware store is. I listen.

Then she says, 'Is that all? Do you want to say anything else?'

Here's my chance! I think about which words to use, how to tell her I love her without sounding too formal or ponderous.

'No? Okay, call again. Bye.'

And she has hung up, and I have missed my opportunity.

In another three weeks, I shall try again.

The Year of the Rooster

Bon-Wai Chou

My father grew up in the country. When he discovered he had terminal cancer his one wish was to return from Australia to his home village in China. It was a futile wish because the cancer had destroyed the bone at the base of his spine; he could not bend and when he sat he suffered intense pain, so flying was out of the question.

As compensation, he bought three silky chickens to remind him of his childhood. The silkies were fluffy, beautiful young things. They occupied my father. He smiled at them, petted them, carried them in his arms like newborn babes. When he put them on the grass they followed him trustingly like gentle innocents, tended with magic.

But it was not long before two of the silkies picked up a bacterial infection and they died within days of each other. They were replaced. My father gave the new chickens his full attention. They grew in strength. One of them even started laying eggs, delivering one each day under the hydrangea.

One morning my mother accompanied my father to his chemotherapy appointment. When they returned home the silkies had disappeared. A trail of feathers suggested the predator was a fox or a large cat. Then we found a cigarette butt near the chicken pen.

Dunhill brand. None of us smoked. My father was in a state of shock. Why would anyone want to steal a chicken? We bought more chickens as a mark of defiance.

A year passed. Visitors came from all over the world to see my father. They came to reminisce and to reconnect but inevitably the subject turned to his health. They told him he must rest and recuperate. They gave him Chinese herbal medicine. They advised him on new types of pain management.

My father was losing weight rapidly, losing his vitality. He dozed in front of the television, his legs stretched out like logs, his feet bloated with fluid. He struggled to get out of his chair and then he would rely heavily on his walking stick. He walked short distances with enormous effort. The cancer in his lungs was depriving him of oxygen. Depriving him of interest. He gave up on things that used to matter. He grew his hair out and looked like Einstein. One day he looked at his fingernails, gnarled and blackened by the radiation treatment, and he said to me:

'They're getting better, aren't they?'

'Yes,' I said. 'The bad parts are growing out.'

We were all stretching hope. My father knew it was only a matter of time. He knew the enemy well because he was a pathologist.

Omens of sacrifice were warning us from every direction. I saw the signs in the mug that slipped from his hand one day, shattering as an exclamation mark. His favourite mug of thirty years, smashed, just like that. Then his much-prized Omega watch, which he had worn since he was a young medical student, stopped dead one afternoon, just as the hands came together on the half-hour. My mother tried to get it fixed in Hong Kong. The jeweller told her it was a superb watch, but they didn't make parts for them any more.

It was all proving prophetic. I saw the signs in the front garden when the pump for the fishpond stopped working. The water thickened overnight like soup. Dead goldfish floated to the surface.

We had one of the worst storms ever. Lightning had struck the oldest tree in my parents' garden, splitting it right down the middle, like an axe had fallen through it. *Murder*, I shouted in my head, as I looked at the ravaged trunk.

Then a chicken went missing again. My mother admitted liability.

'I forgot to lock the pen,' she said as we watched the two remaining silkies, traumatised by their ordeal, hop cautiously about the lawn. 'It's terrible how forgetful I'm becoming.'

'When were they taken?'

'I heard a loud squawking at four in the morning.'

I stifled a gasp. That dreadful Chinese symbol of death, the number four ...

Drugged by morphine, my father was now nauseous virtually every hour of the day. He ate little and vomited up everything, even water. He was as thin as a skeleton and his clothes hung baggily over his shrivelled limbs.

One afternoon he beckoned me lightly and I went up to him.

'What do you think of this?' he asked and pulled out a pad containing two fine sketches.

'My dream kitchen,' he explained proudly. 'This is the bird's-eye view. And this is how it would look from the living room.'

My heart raced with a mixture of admiration and emotion. My father was a wonderful cook but in all the years of raising his three children he had not seen the need to spoil himself with a kitchen he deserved, preferring to make do with what he had.

'What's this door?' I asked.

'The door to the cellar.'

I smiled in spite of myself. With our spirits considerably brightened, we decided to go downstairs and measure up the space for the proposed renovations. We took with us tape, pencil, paper and calculator and spent a good while with the measurements. My father marvelled at the closeness of his mental calculations. When he got back upstairs to his favourite chair, he was breathing hard but his face was exuberant. His dream was going to be realised after all. He could never have predicted it would turn out like this. He sat up all night refining his sketches.

A week later, he was taken to hospital.

'A mild dose of pneumonia,' said the doctor, when he had finished the examination and settled himself next to my mother. The sombre note reverberated in the room for a while before he leaned in and spoke again.

'The cancer has spread to the liver. I'm sorry. Terribly sorry.'

Some little time later it was Christmas. A warm, still day. The birds chirped in the trees and my father took a seat at the edge of the patio to look out at the garden he so loved. It was when he was picking quietly at his plate of food and all around him the voices were eddying and the glasses were clinking that his true nature came back to me. Hating to hurt others, he had spent his whole life holding back information.

He was brought up by his mother and his grandmother. He hardly knew his father, who was away in the army. One of his sisters was married out as a child and another sister had died in childbirth. He had two younger brothers and a cousin who lived with them but her true identity was concealed for twenty years. She was my father's half-sister.

At the onset of the civil war in China, people in my father's village began vanishing. Fearful rumours were circulating but the villagers sealed their mouths, as a rash word or a hasty act could be followed by annihilation. Troubled by the sinister developments, my father's mother secretly arranged papers for an escape. But only one person would be able to leave. As the eldest son, my father was chosen. He was then thirteen years old. He never laid eyes on his mother again. She was killed in the Cultural Revolution, shot in the back of the head with a single bullet. Days before, her second son was beaten to death by the Red Guards. She was caught when she tried to help him. They made an example of her by strapping her to a board and parading her through the streets for all to see with a dunce's cap slapped on her head. When she could walk no more, they forced her to kneel on broken glass before shooting her.

My father wrestled alone with the weight and the depth of his suffering. He knew that no matter how far he travelled or how high he soared, the tragedy of his people was embedded in him. He tried to do what he could for his surviving younger brother when he was released from a re-education camp. But by then they had been cut off from each other for more than ten years. I don't know what they talked about then but they corresponded regularly for the next thirty years. Perhaps they only wrote about the things that could easily be discussed, while living separately, each to himself.

As Chinese New Year approached, I had an irrational wish to alter what must be. I went about sprucing up the garden and putting up auspicious signs to welcome in the Year of the Rooster. I gathered up all the symbolic ingredients for the big family meal. Moss hair for good fortune, red dates for progeny, gingko nuts for long life.

I placed a quaint porcelain rooster figurine near where my father sat one afternoon.

'It will give you luck,' I explained.

He smiled at my antics. 'You little fool,' his eyes said.

But he played along and listened to my explanations of the hidden commentaries of the zodiac. When I had finished, he insisted on getting his hair cut to welcome in the new year.

'That would be too much for you.'

'Rubbish!' he snapped, and sweated and gasped for air as he put one foot in front of the other.

It was no use my protesting. He simply had to go there. The whole exercise of getting out of the house to the hairdresser's took a great deal out of him. When he came back, moisture was glistening all over his brows but his eyes were gleaming. He had retained his dignity.

Then came the slurred speech a few days later. My father said the strangest things, as if he was losing his reason. He alternated between being very talkative and being gloomy. One day he started watching cartoons. At first I thought I was imagining things. But no, he was reverting to his early childhood. My brother, with his medical knowledge, suspected a stroke.

'Daddy, you have to go to hospital,' he said very gently. But my father's face remained blank, unsurprised.

We remained standing around him, full of suspense. I could see it was on his mind as his eyes stayed glued to the television set. After a pause, we heard: 'Can't I go tomorrow?'

*

I put the cutting of a branch of red bougainvillea in a glass of water.

'From the vine you gave me,' I said

'How beautiful ...'

He closed his eyes. I sat by the bed and watched him sleep. His eyelids kept fluttering open, as if they couldn't shut properly, and his eyes rolled in all directions. His pain conveyed itself to me. The beam of light that came through the split in the curtain induced me to brood. I was hardly aware when the nurse came in and hooked an oxygen tube around his ears. She told me he was having trouble eating. Towards the end of breakfast he had mistaken the spoon for a straw.

Death was pulling him away.

Suddenly he woke. His mind was full of wandering. He whispered to me, 'Those two need to be bathed.' He was referring to my sister's children. Then he said he needed someone to help put his things away. He thought of other unfinished business. Day and night were getting crushed together. The next day a fever descended on him. It escalated then mercifully subsided. When he had recovered his lucidity, he couldn't stop crying.

'I'm bedridden. I can't walk, bathe or feed myself ...'

I didn't know what to say but felt defiant. 'You'll get home,' I said. 'We'll make sure you get home.' But I knew my father would never return to his Chinese village.

That afternoon he wanted to get a grip on himself, to make use of his hands again. He asked for his shaver. Propped up against two pillows, he carefully went over his cheeks, his chin and his throat. When I handed him the mirror, he began to sob.

He was in two minds; he didn't see any point in staying, but he didn't want to go just yet. He told me his brother in China had written to him.

'He wants to see me,' he said, 'but I don't think it's necessary.' Then in the same breath he asked me for pen and paper.

I watched him write his last letter. Knotted frown, shaking hand, all strain and obstinance. His Chinese characters, usually so splendid, were now small and scrawled, as if wrung dry.

He was in a great deal of pain. They gave him morphine. He slept. His hands shook and rattled. Suddenly he opened his eyes.

'What are you all doing here?' he said, lowering the air piece around his nose. 'I'm all right.'

He closed his eyes again, mumbling all the time. We sat on either side of the bed, grasping his hands and feeling his body temperature rising. We put on his favourite music as a last little pleasure. His breathing was heavy but steady. The whole night he roared like a lion. The nurse on duty was drawn to look in.

'What a strong heart,' she said, incredulous.

But I saw all the signs. His gums were rotting. Banishing thoughts of decay, I held his hand more tightly. I was hardly aware when the last breaths came – slower, softer, more imperceptible, more delayed.

Then came a pause so long I was unable to bear the weight of the emotion. Suddenly I was terrified. *No. Not now!* But the screams in my head were drowned out by a howl so beseeching I almost lost my footing. He slouched forward. Then all plunged into silence.

Such tears came to me I could not control myself. I cried like any daughter deeply distressed. But it was more than that. It was the cry of despair that I would no longer be whole again. It was grief, pain and emptiness all rolled into one overwhelming entanglement. Bending over my father's face I wanted to tell him how much I loved him and how much I needed to do with my life. But nothing was utterable. Nothing at all.

We were busy for the next five days preparing for the funeral. My mind did not have time to wander. There were hundreds of mourners. People had to stand. I shook hands with everyone. Many faces I had almost forgotten. Everyone looked older. I inhaled the smell of flowers and wondered what I would have given to see my father for a moment. People came up to the front to place a carnation on the coffin while my nephew played a piece on his violin. 'A beautiful service,' I heard again and again, when the mourners began filing out of the chapel.

We had refreshments of dainty sandwiches back at the house. The place was packed. The pair of silkies wandered around the garden. I was asked questions and I answered each carefully. Everyone was sympathetic. Gentleness itself. When they began leaving, I stole into the toilet to be alone.

We had a private cremation a few days later. I drove early to the house to help out with last-minute things. Dressed in black, my mother was silence itself. Her eyes were swollen from crying.

'One of the chickens died,' she said at last, looking up.

'Died! What happened?'

Apparently it had been weakening over the past few days and my mother had been giving it tablets to fight the infection.

'When I checked last night it looked so much stronger ...' She stopped to bite back the tears.

The silky was cremated along with my father.

Are You Different?

Mia Francis

My son didn't come to me in the 'normal' way. I collected him fully clothed, toilet-trained and with a blue and white plastic guitar strung around his neck. The orphanage staff had dressed him in his going away 'trousseau' – a pair of shorts printed with the familiar face of Bart Simpson, a red and white T-shirt, sneakers and a baseball cap. His face was dusted with some type of white cream or powder. Ricky had lived his first three years and three months of life in a Philippine orphanage and he weighed just under eleven kilos. I picked him from the steps of the grey stone building and carried him like a baby – he *was* my baby.

We stayed for a short time in a luxurious hotel in metro Manila while we waiting for the official papers to be signed. The staff, who I suspect were not very well paid for the work they did, were curious about what was happening to Ricky. A young bell-boy asked where I was taking him. When I told him that we were taking him home to Australia I might just as well have told him that we were taking Ricky on a one-way trip to paradise. 'Oh, Ricky ... Australia ... Australia,' the young man crooned longingly.

When we were preparing to leave the country at Manila airport, my husband and I were quite tense. We were on our own now and we had to get Ricky through all the custom officials and red tape without the support of the Filipino social workers. Finally we did, and it was time to make our way to the plane. That was when Ricky began his goodbyes. My husband was carrying Ricky in his arms and to every Filipino man we passed on the long walk to the plane Ricky called out, using a Filipino term of respect for an elder: 'Bye, kuya, goodbye ... Bye, kuya, goodbye ...' It was like a mantra. At three years of age, he knew what was happening to him, perhaps not entirely at a conscious level but certainly at a spiritual level. Ricky was leaving his country for a long time.

What a relief it was finally to be on board the plane and heading home to Australia. While we were waiting for the plane to take off, a turbaned Indian gentleman walked past my seat. He stopped for a second, stared at me, pointed and said, 'You ... you keep your promise!' Flashing me a broad toothy smile, he walked on to the back of the plane and I never saw him again.

*

Did I keep my promise?

Ricky is eighteen now and a very fine young person he has grown to be. I have raised him as my own son, my own flesh and blood, but I have raised him as an Australian. That's not because I didn't want to honour his Asian heritage, but because if I had tried to raise him in his own culture it would have been a falsehood. It would have been an Australian version of Filipino culture, a little like the Australian version of chop suey. (Anybody raised in the seventies would surely remember their mothers and aunties making this exotic modern dish. It contained a lot of cabbage and mince, but the most important ingredient of all was Maggi spring vegetable dried soup mix. Authentic Chinese cuisine?) To know a culture you have to live it, and we didn't live in the Philippines – we lived in suburban Adelaide.

Of course, I did tell him about Filipino ways and traditions, took him to Filipino cultural events, and tried to connect with other adoptive families in Australia. But the older Ricky got, the less 'cool' cultural events became. I remember one particular Filipino Christmas party where I knew quite a few of the women and greeted them by name. Towards the end of the evening Ricky, who was about twelve at the time, gave me a quizzical look and said, 'Mum, how do know all their names? How can you tell them apart? I can't tell one from the other!'

That same evening there was a Filipino family sitting opposite us. One of the older sons had obviously been ordered to attend.

He began the evening looking bored, but by the end of the night he was prostrate, his head in his hands, his tie loosened and his suit jacket spread in desperation across the table. He had obviously seen one bamboo dance too many! He was ready for clubbing, not culture.

*

Unfortunately, the world is full of people eager to judge and express what a terrible thing it is to take a child from their culture and country. But tell me, what culture is there in desperate poverty, hunger, sickness and child labour? Ricky's birth mother made the ultimate sacrifice. She showed the greatest act of love that any mother can show her child. By giving him up for overseas adoption, she knew that he would not die of sickness and hunger and that he would have some kind of chance at life. Once, an acquaintance asked me, 'When you were adopting, did you not think of all the children in Australia who need homes?' What narrow lives some people live.

That is not to say that my husband and I did any great heroic act in bringing Ricky to Australia. No, we did not. We wanted a child of our own – nothing more, nothing less. It was March when we arrived home, a beautiful autumn. I had taken Ricky to the park to play and he came to me crying, holding his head, frightened: '*Untog, untog!* [I bumped my head!]' He had never felt leaves falling on his head before. He was frightened of so many things in those early days: the vacuum cleaner, the dog, the shower, so many things that he had not been exposed to in the orphanage. I remember taking him outside one evening and showing him the moon. I'm sure it was the first time he had ever seen it.

Those early days passed very quickly and for much of that time I would carry Ricky around like a baby. It suited us both that way. My need was as great as his. Before I knew it, it was time for Ricky to go to school. I think that first day was one of the saddest days of my life. I missed him so much. We had only had him for eighteen months and already it was time for him to go out into the world. When Ricky had been at school for about a week he asked me a question I have never forgotten. He was playing outside at the end of the day, riding his bike, when he stopped, looked up at me and said, very quietly, 'Mum … are you different?' I looked down at his shiny black head – he seemed to be looking somewhere far into the distance. I don't remember what I said.

Perhaps further down the track he came to realise that we were both different. We came to live in regional Victoria in a town which at that stage was almost completely mono-cultural. We stood out – fair-haired, light-skinned parents with a dark-skinned Asian child. The school-yard taunts of 'flat-nose,' 'ching-chong Chinaman' and 'dirty black nigger' came and went throughout primary school and I wish I could say that that was where they ended. Ricky never lashed out and usually just said something like 'whatever' and walked away. That was until the wrong person said something, on the wrong day, in the wrong way. A person can be called a 'slit-eye' or a 'Japanese fucker' one too many times. Everyone has a breaking point. So when the year co-ordinator rang to tell me that Ricky had punched a boy and thrown him into a rubbish bin, my first question was, 'Were there any racist taunts involved?'

Ricky was suspended because the boy had to be taken to hospital, but – funny thing – ever since that day he has not had any more problems of that kind. Ricky has lots of good friends at school. They affectionately call each other 'nigger' and 'bro.' His best friend is a gentle blond-haired boy called Daniel whom Ricky and other members of 'the gang' have given the status of 'honorary Asian.'

Now it is nearly time for us to make the return journey to Manila. Ricky wants to find his people; he needs to know his roots. Try as I might, I can't convince Ricky that his family won't be living in a modern house, wearing Nike sneakers, drinking Coke and watching a plasma colour TV. But I will be a fellow searcher with him on his journey for as long he wants me to be.

The fourteen-and-three-quarter years that Ricky has been with us have passed like a blink of an eye. It seems like yesterday that he came crying to me when the autumn leaves fell on his head. Thank-you, Ricky, for all you have given us, for all you have taught us, and above all, thank-you for being our beautiful son.

The Clan

Tourism

Benjamin Law

My family isn't exactly the outdoors type. Despite being raised right on the coastline, Mum detested the beach (all the sand it brought into the house), while Dad actively disapproved of wearing thongs ('It splits the toes'). We never camped. All those things involved in camping – pitching a tent; cooking on open fires; the insects; shitting in the woods; sleeping on rocks; getting murdered and raped in the middle of nowhere – they never appealed to us. 'We were never camping people,' Mum explains now. 'See, Asians – we're scared of dying. White people, they like to "live life to the full" and "die happy."' She pauses, before adding, 'Asians, we're the opposite.'

We preferred theme parks. For parents raising five children, theme parks made so much sense. They were clean. They were safe. There were clear designated activities, and auditory and visual stimuli that transcended barriers of race, language and age. Also: you could buy heaps of useless shit. This seems to be an exercise in which Asians of all nationalities, ages and socio-economic backgrounds naturally excel: buying shit. Venture into my childhood home, and in amongst the epic piles of suburban debris, you'll still find a plush blue whale wearing a Seaworld cap, T-shirts emblazoned with Kenny and Belinda – the now defunct Dreamworld mascots – and a pox of hideous fridge magnets. Oh my god, the fridge magnets.

It was family tradition that once a year, our family of seven (eight, including my Ma-Ma) would cram ourselves into my grandmother's 1990 grey five-seat automatic Honda. *Five seats.* We'd travel like this – faces smashed against the glass; no leg room; the two smallest children illegally wedged between various legs – for a good three hours before we reached the Gold Coast. By the time we got to the theme park, our limbs were numb, our nerve endings destroyed. On the ride home, exhausted and drained like dead batteries, we'd fall asleep in extreme angles, our spines contorted and twisted. We'd wake up, our shirts covered with drool we weren't even sure was ours.

On the day of the trip, we'd wake before sunrise to get there by opening time. Despite having endured three hours of vivid pain, we'd feel an overwhelming sense of awe as the Thunderbolt, Dreamworld's fire-branded rollercoaster, emerged from behind the trees that bordered the highway. It would appear so suddenly, like some strange apparition, or a mirage. Our necks would crane back trying to take in the sheer majesty of it all. For a non-religious family like ours, the experience was borderline spiritual.

Once through the gates, we kids would do our best to distinguish ourselves from the actual Asian tourists. We'd make our Australian accents more pronounced. We ended our sentences with 'eh.' Our trousers were pulled further downwards, away from our navels. We refused to wear bumbags, and spoke English very loudly, with proper grammar and syntax. These hoards of Japanese and Chinese tourists would point to the most innocuous objects and proceed to take photographs like idiots. We could only imagine what they were hollering to each other as they ripped through their film. 'Look, a fire hydrant!' 'Over here, a drinking fountain!' 'Wow, there is a toilet: a public, shared facility and receptacle for my waste. Why not take a photo of it?'

Mum would sabotage all our efforts to set ourselves apart. She wore her hair in a Bozo-esque clown perm, and had a strange insistence on wearing her fluorescent Dreamworld T-shirt if we happened to be at Dreamworld (and her killer-whale Seaworld T-shirt if we were visiting Seaworld).

'Mum, come on,' I'd say as she posed us at the entrance of yet another ride. 'Everyone's going to think we're tourists.'

'We *are* tourists, you idiot,' she'd reply. 'Now smile big!'

It would take her about twenty seconds to finally press the shutter, and another five to release it. We'd groan.

*

When my parents split up, I was twelve years old and had just finished primary school. Trips to theme parks became less frequent. Custody was split. Mum hated driving long distances. Dad threw himself into work. The mood became downbeat and glum. The separation also made our family the subject of gossip amongst the local Chinese community, who were mildly scandalised by all the drama. Elderly Chinese women who smelled like mothballs and grease would corner my siblings and me in the shopping centre, literally pulling us to one side, shaking their heads and tutting their tongues, lecturing us in Cantonese.

'*Wah*, what is going on?' They'd raise their tattooed eyebrows. 'You need to tell your parents they must make an effort to get back together! *Ai-ya*, why would any parents split up like this? You're only children! And no marriage is a walk in the park, is it?'

None of these concerned citizens ever visited my mother during this period. Mum was always a tiny woman, but she began to lose weight quickly. Her low blood pressure got worse. She became prone to intense dizziness that would render her immobile for days on end. She almost fainted at my fourteenth birthday party at the tenpin bowling alley and thought she'd need to get me to call an ambulance. We saw Dad less and less.

Mum and Dad instituted a rotating roster of weekend custody. Schooldays were neutral territory; it was the weekend that was considered important family time. Mum and Dad would take turns, Dad taking us for every second weekend. But despite these weekends being technically Dad's, Mum insisted on coming with us, declaring boldly that it was her right as a mother.

Poor Dad. This really put pressure on him to make those four days a month memorable and worthwhile. At the same time, he was working as a chef in a hotel. He couldn't afford the luxury of time, so when it came to his designated weekends, Dad needed quick and convenient options.

He needed theme parks.

*

Let it be known: the Sunshine Coast hinterland is a haven for sad, miserable theme parks. In contrast to the Gold Coast's pleasure domes (Dreamworld, Movieworld, Seaworld), which are show-offy and grand, garish and decadent, theme parks on the Sunshine Coast are poor-cousiny, half-arsed and afterthought-ish. Come to Superbee, where our prime attraction is 'free honey tasting!' Also: you can buy honey! Look, here is a man, dressed as a bee! Here at the Hedge Maze, get lost! In a hedge! We also have scones!

On one of Dad's more disastrous weekends, we travelled to suburban Noosa to visit a deserted tourist attraction called the Big Bottle. It was, as its name implied, a giant bottle. You'd climb the stairs inside, which were made up of hundreds of empty beer bottles. Once you were at the top, a giant metal slippery slide curled around the bottle's exterior, and you'd slide down on a hessian sack. Inside the bottle, it smelled awful – like the piss of a hundred dehydrated men. Because the entire interior was made of beer bottles, you would never know which ones contained the urine. And because the bottles weren't exposed to the sun, the piss would never evaporate. It smelled so bad. We never went there again.

Another time, we visited Forest Glen Deer Sanctuary, a typically neglected drive-in wildlife preserve in Yandina. Despite its catchy television jingle, the place was starting to lose business to the reptile park a few kilometres away, which had recently renamed itself Australia Zoo. We bought bags of feed at the entrance, then slowly drove around the dirt track. The deer came up to the car in packs, and we fed them through the windows. There was also one single emu amongst all the deer and kangaroos. It started walking towards our car, pushing its way past the does and fawns.

'Are we even supposed to feed the emus?' my younger sister Tammy asked. 'Isn't this stuff just for deer?'

'Maybe it's developed a taste for it,' Dad said in Cantonese.

The emu proceeded to eat all the feed from my hand, then moved on to my youngest sister Michelle's open hand. Then, almost out of food, we wanted to move on. But then the emu spotted my paper bag – still full of feed, and reserved for the deer coming up around the bend – sitting next to me. It made a terrible, ungodly noise – an almost carnivorous, honking screech of excitement, not unlike the velociraptors in *Jurassic Park*. Its neck came the whole way in to the Honda as it continued to shriek. We screamed and screamed as feed pellets flew around the car.

'Drive faster, drive faster!' Michelle screamed.

Dad put his foot on the accelerator, and the emu squawked, trying to keep up the pace.

'Wind up the window!' Dad said.

What Dad didn't understand was that because most of the emu's head was in the car already, winding up the window would make the situation worse. But in my stammering panic, I reached out, grabbed the window winder and start winding up. The emu refused to retreat. Its head became stuck, and it croaked and coughed at us, spasming in panic, banging its head against the car ceiling in wild, spastic fits.

'Drive slower!' I said. 'We're going to rip its fucking head off.'

The whole time, Dad was creeping the Honda forwards a little at a time, but the emu was keeping up, walking alongside the car, screeching and honking.

'Stop the car, stop the car!'

We killed the engine and slowly wound down the window. Slowly, slowly. The emu gave the car's ceiling one last bang with its head, before sliding its neck out the window and stumbling away from the car in a daze.

We drove home in silence.

*

A fortnight later, Dad called me at Mum's place.

'So, what's the plan for this weekend?' he asked. 'You got any ideas?'

'I don't know,' I said. 'Haven't we done everything around here already?'

'How about the Ginger Factory? Or Underwater World? You guys like turtles. They're Tammy's favourite, right?'

'We did that last month,' I said, sighing. 'You know, we don't have to go somewhere special every weekend. We could just hang out.'

At that point, I detected a faint click over the telephone line. I coughed loudly – a clear message to Mum that I was aware she was on the other line, tuning in to my conversation with Dad.

'You know, I'm looking to invest in a new restaurant in Pacific Paradise,' Dad said. 'There's a theme park there we should check out. What do you reckon?'

*

Nostalgia Town's motto was 'A Laugh at the Past.' Its main attraction was a family cart-ride, a journey into an era when fibreglass brontosauruses roamed the earth alongside tableaus of Anzac diggers and plastic Aborigines. Slouching, I sat in the back of the cart with Mum, while Dad sat in the front with Tammy and Michelle. In the carts in front of us, mothers and fathers sat alongside each other with their children jammed in the middle. Obese as they were, they even held hands.

I wondered what they thought of our family, and whether they questioned why the Chinese family's parents sat so far away from one another. Maybe it was a cultural thing. I'd continue to watch them, wondering how, and why, their parents got along so well together, and how strange their families must have have been in private.

I'd watch them intently: like an outsider, like a tourist.

*

Nowadays, if you drive through Coomera, towards Dreamworld, you'll see the Thunderbolt has been dismantled. Nostalgia Town has long been torn down, and the deer at Forest Glen have disappeared, presumably having undergone a mysterious transformation into venison. (I don't know what happened to the emu.) That old wildlife sanctuary is now a luxury tourist resort. I can't find a trace of the Big Bottle on the internet, so I can only assume that the piss fumes proved a health hazard, and that it's been torn down too.

Right now, my family is planning to spend New Year's Eve together. (Everyone except Dad. He will be slaving away at a restaurant.) We're throwing around some ideas for what to do, since this will be the last time the family will be in the same place, at the same time, for quite a while.

Someone has suggested we go camping.

The Family Tree

Grandfather unfurled a yellowing scroll

with the calligraphy of the family tree
and twenty-eight generations rolled out

into the lounge room.

Only the male family members were there
the diamonds of the family

the ones who carry on the family name

the female family members cast off
to the blank scroll of oblivion

as if they were never born.

—KEN CHAU

The Firstborn

for Matthew

Ten thousand rivers flow into the sea;
the sea is never full.

—CHINESE PROVERB

Great-Great-Grandfather arrived
in 1897 by sea.

Great-Grandfather arrived
in 1931 by sea.

Grandfather arrived
in 1949 by sea.

I arrived
in 1961 an ABC.

You arrived
in 1996 by amniotic sea.

> *The sky*
> *is blue*
>
> *the earth*
> *is yellow:*
>
> *this is*
> *the Middle Kingdom*

this is
the sea

awash
with the unfathomable

Chinese
sons.

—KEN CHAU

Family Life

Diem Vo

My father owned a Vietnamese video store in Irving Street, in the working-class suburb of Footscray. The business is failing now, but during the days before home-pirating businesses took over, he was able to earn a decent enough income. Sandwiched between a Chinese hairdressers' and an Italian take-away shop and directly opposite the Footscray bottle shop, the video shop stood, rather oddly, with colourful, glossy Asian movie posters covering every inch of the glass windows outside. Over time, the posters faded from the constant exposure to sunlight.

The front of the shop was where the customers rented the Hong Kong serial movies (dubbed in Vietnamese), and the back of the shop was where both my father and mother sewed Country Road garments for eighty cents a piece (quite a high price in those days). Sometimes my parents would run long errands and leave us in charge. So there we were, two schoolgirls wearing our school uniforms running a video shop. We liked to think of ourselves as young businesswomen and took pride in the responsibility thrust upon us.

Customers came to the shop carrying plastic bags containing previously borrowed videotapes. They would inquire about the latest Hong Kong serials. Most popular at the time was one titled *King of Gamblers*, in which the characters fought and killed one another to become the top card-player. This involved a lot of fancy card acrobatics. In one scene, a skilled gambler slashed his opponent's throat by throwing a playing card from some distance away. The plastic card, expertly aimed and thrown like a boomerang, landed perfectly, slitting the man's throat. All very far-fetched and dramatic, and therefore extremely popular with Vietnamese people.

The customer would select his or her movies, choosing from the numerous coloured posters plastered on the walls. My sister would obtain their customer number and look it up in my father's handwritten filing system. I would fetch the movie from the piles of videotapes, which were stacked in rows and columns in no particular order, making searching difficult. The customer would hand us their money and we would give them change from the shoebox, kept in a drawer, which served as a cash register.

My sister and I would complain sometimes about having to work and having no life. However, we made up for it by using the coins from the cash-register shoebox to treat ourselves to hamburgers and take-away cappuccinos from the pizza shop next door.

*

When we weren't working at the shop or studying, our childhood and early teenage years were centred on our father's extended family. A weekend with the Vo family at St Albans was always a dramatic experience. It was like being on the set of the Vietnamese version of *Neighbours*, filled with drama and gossip. My dad's parents and his seven siblings owned two rows of double-storey houses on the same street, and family gatherings occurred regularly. Every child's birthday, Mother's Day, Father's Day, Grandparents' Day, New Year's Day, Ancestor's Death Commemoration Day, the weekend – any event was an excuse for the men to get pissed and the women to gossip.

However, unlike in Ramsay Street, there were never any cups of tea or bickies served. Instead, each family unit came armed with a slab of beer. VB – or, as my uncles liked to refer to it, 'Vietnamese Beer.' I can remember thinking that if I had collected all the beer cans from all those family gatherings, how rich I would be to this day.

An enormous amount of food would be served. Due to the large number of people, the dining table was useless. There would not have been enough space for everyone to sit down. Therefore, newspapers would be spread out on the floor and the food, brought out by the women, placed on top. The men would gather around the makeshift newspaper table; in front of each of them lay a little porcelain rice bowl, chopsticks and their beloved VB cans. Here they would contentedly eat and get pissed.

Meanwhile, the women would form their own group. These family gatherings were their chance to parade their newly purchased designer bags. They would show each other their latest Chanel or Louis Vuitton (always hot goods) and discuss the most flattering ways to carry the bags. Another popular topic of discussion was who had recently been to Vietnam to have plastic surgery. (Nearly all the women in my family have had plastic surgery). From the television in the background blared *Paris by Night*, a popular Vietnamese-American variety show. The female co-host, done up in her beauty-pageant finery and rumoured to have a brilliant plastic surgeon, always sparked keen interest. They also gossiped about pyramid schemes and who owed money to whom, and entertained themselves with gambling and karaoke. They tended to sing traditional songs, a form of Vietnamese opera, mostly melancholic stories about love or love for one's mother.

*

At family gatherings today, as our overweight, McDonalds-eating younger cousins struggle to eat their Vietnamese food, we tell them that they have it easy. We paved the way for them to have more freedom growing up. We tell them how our parents' discipline drove us to rebel. One of my cousins rebelled against her mother's strictness by leaving home and becoming a heroin user. She used to frighten her mother by saying, 'If you don't let Mai (her younger sister) go out with her friends, she will end up like me!' That was enough for her mother to loosen the reigns a notch.

We also remind our younger cousins that their parents came to Australia at a younger age than ours did, with at least a little English. Our younger cousins have not had to act as interpreters, translating at parent–teacher interviews, explaining every bill, forging their parents' signatures and writing their own school sick-leave certificates. They have not had to become masters of forgery and rebellion!

Like most migrant youth, we spoke English at school and our parents' language at home. This switch was made further complicated by our parents' use of 'Vietnamese-English': English words spoken with Vietnamese tones. When Vietnamese family or friends telephoned us, they expected to hear a tonal sounding

'Hello?' Answering the phone in an Australian accent would result in them hanging up, thinking they had called a Westerner's residence. On the other hand, answering with a Vietnamese-sounding 'Hello' would cause confusion among my non-Vietnamese school friends, who wouldn't recognise my voice.

All of these aspects of growing up Vietnamese in Australia were frustrating. Our younger cousins were spared some of these frustrations. On the other hand, we had the chance to witness our parents' struggles during their first years in Australia, and so to understand them better. Before they owned their own homes and obsessed over designer goods, our parents all lived in housing-commission flats and took public transport to work in various factories. Before they owned the video shop, my father earned a pittance picking fruit and working in shoe factories. My mother sewed in factories and at home. Sometimes she would sew until the early hours of the morning, working frantically towards delivery day. She developed chronic back pain from constantly bending over the sewing machine and sore eyes from squinting at the tiny stitches.

Having witnessed all this, we understood that our parents were struggling people who had recently left a war-torn country. Their old country was no longer theirs, and they were not equipped to participate fully in their new country. They found it far easier to deal with other Vietnamese-Australians than to learn English. However, this kept them alienated from the non-Vietnamese-speaking world; they lived in their own cultural bubble. This was problematic for them, and we too felt their uncertainty and awkwardness. Standing next to them, translating, we recognised their helplessness.

An Australian friend of mine used to speak about his experiences growing up as an only child. He lived with his mother and father in a middle-class suburb. His parents had a troubled marriage, often fighting and arguing. Feeling alone and miserable, he would set off on his bike, seeking refuge at the house of his grandmother, his only other relative. Hearing these stories made me realise that I would never be so isolated. Despite the chaotic and dysfunctional nature of my family, and the conflicts between my parents' generation and mine, loneliness was never a problem. We could always go and eat shrimp noodles at Aunty Hoang's place, or hang out with Aunty Thuy and her kids, or pester Unce Kiet to buy us icy poles. On Vo Street, life was far from dull.

Quarrel

Ken Chan

The children have bedded down, are edging into sleep in the cramped bedroom that they share with their parents. The older boy, Siu-Wing, doesn't know anyone else who lives like they do, overspilt in every direction. All his young life, he can only remember sleeping in the one room with his parents and his brother. There are two beds wedged side by side, two wardrobes and a dressing table. A narrow canal runs between the beds and the other furniture.

Voices, angry and confronting, pierce the closed door. Siu-Wing can identify his *yeh-yeh* and his *mah*, the two grandparents. There are other voices too, a backcloth of babble, an undefinable chorus, but it's hard to sift any meaning from them. The strident bellows of the grandparents block out any other words. They snap at each other in their Taishan dialect, that village vernacular that the Cantonese, in their odysseys, have carried halfway across the world. Siu-Wing likes its sound, its tones and cadences. It seems inappropriate that such a flowing dialect should be used to wound and scar.

'Don't give me your fistful of coins. You think that's enough?'

'What's wrong with my money? I earned every penny. It's honest cash.'

'You call what you do honest? Don't give me that rubbish. All those years I sweated to keep the family together, where was your honest then? Where was it when we needed it so badly, eh?'

'I always did the best that I could. Times were hard. I always sent you what I had.'

'Once every six or seven months. How did that help us?'

'Take the coins. I want you to have them.'

'No, never. They're no use now.'

Fully awake now, Siu-Wing climbs down from his bed and scampers to the door, turns the handle gently, pushes and stares into the lit hallway, sees an ensemble of his parents, aunts, uncles trying, futilely, to soothe the shouting couple. At the feet of the warring grandparents are scattered seven gold coins, English sovereigns. Siu-Wing wonders if they were knocked out of his yeh's hand or thrown aside by his mah in her anger. He looks at his mah. She is on the brink of tears.

'If you weren't so sick I'd throw you out of the house right this minute.'

'You think I need to recover here? Put up with your sneering all the time?'

'Where would you go? In the chill you'd collapse in five seconds.'

'I don't need to listen to this nonsense.'

*

Each Friday, his yeh comes to the small house in Maroubra for dinner. He arrives around six o'clock and at seven-fifteen everyone is seated around the table, which always seems to contract when confronted with so many adults. His yeh eats quietly and rarely injects his voice into the conversation. His children, all adults now, are tolerant but not deferential. He has not been a part of their day-to-day lives for such a long time that he long ago lost his position of authority within the family.

His contribution to the meal is generally some Chinese vegetables, gai choy or bak choy, together with a pound or so of roast meat – char siu or siu yuk or chu tow. There is little variation to the food he brings. He enters the house wearing his sagging dark-blue suit and plain-coloured tie, a felt hat covering his almost completely bald head. He is slightly built, though there is a kind of wiry strength to him. Before dinner he smokes a cigarette that he carefully rolls himself and reads a newspaper, usually the *Daily Mirror*, while Siu-Wing's mother and his mah prepare dinner. After dinner the family gathers round the radio and listens to the comic antics of Roy Rene's character Mo.

Except the grandparents, who don't understand a word of the quickfire repartee.

*

The house is orange brick, postwar suburban Sydney. It sits in a small block in a row of similar constructions with only minor variations in the colour of the bricks or the size. The family doesn't even own the house. It belongs to friends who have stayed in Darwin and prospered.

To Siu-Wing, the house is small; it feels as if the adults, all eight of them, fill every millimetre of space, so that there is never even a tiny nook that the kids can claim as their own. The logic of squeezing so many people into a minuscule three-bedroom suburban house is beyond him. Why don't his parents shift out? Some days he thinks it must be because of their poverty, but he has never known a day when they were not well fed. He and his brother have adequate clothes. They have never had to go to school in worn-out shoes like his friend Barry, whose shirt and pants are crisscrossed with patching and wafer-thin at the knees and elbows. Barry says that there are nights when his family doesn't eat and, at school, he's always happy to accept sandwiches others give him.

'So you've got eight grown-ups in your house? Where's everybody sleep?'

'The first bedroom, facing the street, is the largest. My mah, that's what we call my grandmother, and three aunts have that one. Then my mum and dad and me and my brother have the next bedroom and my two uncles have the third one.'

'You don't have a room you can share with your brother?'

'No, Barry, the house is too small.'

'Is it any fun living with all your relatives?'

'No, it's like having too many parents. We're always being yelled at. Especially in the mornings when you're washing your face and taking a leak. They're all banging and screaming at the door. How about at your place?'

'Well, we almost never see my old man. Mum says he's driving trucks but my sister told me she saw Dad with another sheila one day. I reckon he's shacked up in another place. Usually there's

161

just us four kids and Mum. Can I have that sandwich if you don't want it?'

'Sure, if you don't mind stir-fried beef and capsicum.'

'I've never tried one of those. Are they good?'

'No. I hate Chinese leftovers on bread.'

*

Wednesday afternoons are for sport. Siu-Wing plays soccer with the other kids and usually walks home by himself. On this particular Wednesday he is surprised to see his yeh in the house. He's wearing pyjamas and a dressing gown and is propped up on the sofa in the living room. His face is drawn and he is wheezing in between severe bouts of coughing. Siu-Wing's mother is ministering to the old man.

'Would you like to lie down? Would that make you more comfortable?'

'No, I'll just sit here. That's fine. When did the doctor say he'd come?'

'In half an hour. Do you want some more water?'

'Yes, please.'

When his grandmother comes home from shopping she hustles angrily into the living room. Siu-Wing has never seen her like this. Her rage threatens to shake apart the walls of the house.

'Who gave him permission to stay here? This is my house and I won't share it with that good-for-nothing.'

'He's not well, Mum, he's come down with a bad cold. Just let him rest here for a few days. He'll recover soon. Then he can go back to his own place. Right now he can't manage on his own.'

Siu-Wing tries but fails to match the purpling grandmother with the one who, from time to time, calmly and humorously tells him stories, like the legend of the swallow.

*

'There was once a kindly man who came upon an injured swallow. The bird's wings had been damaged and it was struggling on the ground, no longer able to fly. The man took the bird into his house and nurtured it back to good health. To show its appreciation, the swallow gave the man a seed. When planted it produced cucumbers that were the sweetest the man had ever eaten. But, more than this, each cucumber contained gold and silver and the man became wealthy. A neighbour, learning what had happened, hoped to do the same thing but could not find an injured swallow. One day he came upon a nest of swallows, took one and struck it hard. He nursed this bird back to health and was given a seed in return. The neighbour planted it eagerly but it never produced any cucumber. Instead its vine grew very quickly until it touched the moon. The man climbed and climbed expecting to get to the gold and silver at the end of the vine. When his feet touched the moon the vine vanished and he was left alone forever in the cold of the night.'

'Was there any gold or silver for him?'

'No, only the moon's surface.'

'What does the story mean?'

'That some forms of wealth are not ours to have.'

'I think it means that kindness is always rewarded. Don't you think?'

'Maybe, Siu-Wing, maybe.'

*

The doctor's booming, hearty voice cuts through the tension in the house.

'Hello, blossoms, what's happening with Grandpa? You've been smoking too much. I know it. Let's have a look. Take a deep breath. Good. Again. Again.'

Diligently, he prods and probes. He taps the sick man's chest in half-a-dozen places, then does the same on his back, listens with his stethoscope, checks himself, then listens again.

'You have severe pneumonia. I want you in bed immediately, resting. Here is a prescription for what you should take.'

It is one of the few times the two boys have had the company of their grandfather for a long period. Generally, when he comes on Fridays, he says a quick hello to them but that's about all. Now he sleeps in the bedroom normally occupied by his two sons, who have temporarily moved out of the house. Siu-Wing doesn't know for sure, but he assumes that they have gone to his yeh's place, a small apartment in the city.

'Are you getting better, Yeh-Yeh?'

'Slowly, Siu-Wing, slowly. The last time I was this sick was when I was working in Bendigo. In the market gardens there. The winters were so cold I never felt warm from morning to night.'

'Why did you go to Bendigo?'

'It was during the worst of the Depression. I tried to find work in Sydney but had no success. An acquaintance said there were jobs in Melbourne, in the markets selling fruit and vegetables, but that only lasted a few months. So I spent a lot of time chasing work: Stawell, Holbrook, Geelong, Ballarat. I'd go like a dog chasing his tail. Finally I ended up in Bendigo, on a small farm run by a couple who had lived in the district for many years. We grew bak choy and gai lan and fu gwah. Sales were always slow. No one had much cash in those years. Meat was scarce and expensive. I was practically a vegetarian for five or six years.

'When I came back to Sydney, just before the war, I scratched around for a while selling vegetables at Haymarket. But it was hard making a living from that. One day a man came by who looked like he'd never done a day's work in his life. He wore expensive clothes, silk shirt, brocade tie, highly polished black shoes. He smoked a cigarette on a holder. A bit of a dandy. He wanted a selection of Chinese vegetables for a big dinner.

'"How long have you been working at the markets, *Ah Bark*?" he said.

'"Maybe a year and a half," I replied. "Why?"

'"I want an honest man to work in my business."

'"What business is that?"

'"It's something in Dixon Street. Here's the address. Come and see me if you're interested."'

'Did you go?'

'Yes. I made some enquiries and learnt he wasn't a gangster or anything like that and I went to see him. He had a grocery store at the top end of Dixon Street, the Goulburn Street end, and behind the shopfront he ran a gambling establishment. He wanted me to be a stakeholder. He promised me a regular wage. It's been the steadiest job I've ever had. I've even been able to save a bit. Let me show you something. See these coins? Almost solid gold. Genuine English sovereigns. On this side you can see the profile of Queen Victoria. I bought them from a dealer.'

'I have gold coins, too. Want to see?'

'Those are fake, Siu-Wing.'

'No they're not. There's chocolate inside.'

*

Gradually Siu-Wing's grandfather gets better. By the end of the second week he has recovered enough to sit in the backyard on sunny afternoons and to resume eating solid foods. But he still tires easily and the wheezing has not disappeared. Barely a word is exchanged between him and Siu-Wing's grandmother. Siu-Wing is conscious of the arid atmosphere that has invaded the house. At night, when everyone has gone to their rooms, his mah can be heard reciting to her daughters her catechism of grievances.

'Could we have stayed in Alice Springs? Not after he gambled away most of our earnings from the shop. There was no money to pay for new supplies. We were in debt to so many people. Did he care? No, he went on gambling like the fool that he was, saying he'd win it back. In the end we had to sell up and leave. By the time we settled our debts around town we were no better off than beggars. I said we should go to Brisbane or Broome to make a new start. They were warm like Alice Springs and we knew a few families that had done all right there. Did he listen? Ever? No, he insisted we head to Sydney because he had brothers and cousins there. What a lot of no-hopers they were. Always dropping in to our place around dinnertime. He went off to Victoria to find work. Hah! He was like a hawker without anything to sell. What did he know how to do? He could barely speak English. He had no training. Never sent us enough to get by and now, here he is, in my house. Sponging.'

*

The Sunday of the quarrel begins in a promising fashion. As often happens, there is a large gathering of family and friends. Siu-Wing's grandmother enjoys company and frequently has an open house. People begin to arrive just before lunchtime. By mid-afternoon the house is ringing with laughter, the shouts of kids playing and the clack of tiles from several mahjong games. A team, mainly women, prepares food in the kitchen, chopping, stirring and washing. A car pulls up and Siu-Wing's uncles and several of their friends spill out wearing tennis whites and clutching their racquets.

When does the argument between the grandparents start? There is some sense of strain during dinner but Siu-Wing does not know its cause. He can see that his mah is displeased about something. Perhaps she is irritated because she has been losing at Russian poker, a game she loves to play. All he remembers, before he goes to bed, is his grandmother glaring across the room at his grandfather. Whether his yeh is aware of the stern looks Siu-Wing doesn't know. His grandfather doesn't gamble himself, is merely a bemused onlooker.

*

'I've had enough of this. You don't want the coins. Fine. Leave them there. I'm going.'

'Always the fool. In your condition you're mad to step outside.'

His daughters try to dissuade him, but there is little vigour in their protests. And anyway, Siu-Wing's grandfather is determined. He disappears into the bedroom and emerges some twenty-five minutes later wearing his familiar blue suit, his hat and an overcoat. He shuffles slowly past everyone without a word, opens the front door and steps into the bleakness of the winter cold. The wind seems to threaten to blow him back into the room. Perhaps it's only a pause as he steels himself for the lonely walk.

Siu-Wing wants to call out, to coax him back, but his voice, like that of everyone else in the house, is seized by silence. He slides back into his bedroom, glances across to his brother who has slept peacefully through the fracas. His grandmother's tale comes into his head. His grandfather is gingerly scaling the vine, on his way to the moon.

Ginseng Tea and a Pair of Thongs

HaiHa Le

Anh: Elder brother; also used by wives to address their husbands.
Em: Younger sister or younger brother; also used by husbands to address their wives.
Con: Child.

The Anh lamented the loss of his chicken farm to the communists and planned its revival in the backyard of their new Hoppers Crossing home.

He raised his head and glanced pensively over the packed boxes scattered around their $140-a-week government house.

'I came to this country not owning one thing but a pair of thongs and the clothes on my back.'

His Em was not coping well with pollen that season; in fact, she was a devout consumer of Sinex nose sprays and had been so since her arrival in this country. Her dull eyes, the white no longer white, the black lined with yellow, surveyed the cumulation of fourteen years, now crammed into big and small brown boxes.

'Now we have many things.'

Those many things had moved many times.

49 Corrigan Rd, rented from an elderly woman, was so dilapidated it was ordered by the council to be demolished the week after they moved out.

68 Millers Drive belonged to an alcoholic friend of the Anh whose young family remained in Vietnam. He drank to his loneliness and drank to his celibacy. The Anh was concerned for his Em. They decamped.

7 Athol Rd neighboured the Kingdom Hall of Jehovah's Witnesses and was leased out on condition of membership of their organisation. The Anh and his Em met the criteria. 7 Athol Rd was where Middle Con was conceived. When he was born, the Em was overjoyed to find that in Australia, hospitals allowed each mother a separate bed and provided enough food for her visiting family.

Youngest Con arrived at 10 Leunig Place. He was unplanned and unwanted for his first six months. They peered at him in his wooden cage, a living bundle of accident. But in time he grew on them like cancer and ate into their core, deep into their system.

The Youngest Con had immoral thoughts; they gnawed at his five-year-old conscience. He believed it was possible to expel them through his ear canal, so he knocked his head about.

I hate my brain.

I can't control my brain.

It has bad thinking.

What bad thinking?

It thinks of being a lady.

He once asked a girl who bathed with him if her dick had dropped off. And then he helped her search for it.

Youngest Con was abnormally curious about sex. When they shared the same bed, Oldest Con turned her back to him so his foot didn't dig into her crotch during the night. She slept on her front so her breasts weren't groped when morning came. He held her face and pressed his lips against hers.

'No!'

He did not remove his hand from his penis when he slept.

The Em said: 'No!'

She said: 'Jehovah is disgusted.'

So he whispered, 'Sorry, Jehovah'...

... each time.

*

Jehovah had been keeping a close eye on the Le residence ever since the Anh acknowledged his existence. Subsequently, Oldest Con served in the Theocratic Ministry for nearly ten years.

She would wake people up to the Good News of the Kingdom.

'Good morning, Aunty! Would you like to live in this paradise on earth?' she would say, and then she would flash a brochure at the householder to explain in plain Vietnamese how to arrive at this White Man's Utopia.

She couldn't recall how many times she'd heard 'I'm not interested,' or, 'I've got my own religion.'

But only one time was a door slammed in her face, and that was in English territory. Maybe they didn't like gooks with good news, maybe they didn't like Jehovah's Witnesses in general.

Waking up householders was unusual in Vietnamese territory. Even at nine o'clock in the morning the humming of industrial sewing machines could be heard and would continue being heard until the early hours of the next morning.

*

Preaching in the high-rise housing commissions was especially tedious in winter. The vile stench of urine, smackies shooting up in stairways, syringes scattered everywhere.

Nobody liked to open their doors in winter. It's too cold.

And people were afraid ... of white hooligans, of the Tax Commission ...

Old women were locked behind security bars, sponsored to Australia purely to watch their grandchildren – often because the parents were looking for easy money at the Crown Casino. These old women welcomed Jehovah's Witnesses with all the tea they had. Tea imported from Vietnam and India, China Jasmine tea, Ginseng tea ...

'Drink.'

'Very warm.'

'Very good for your liver.'

'Drink ...'

The old women wouldn't let them leave. They even listened to Bible discussions. It might be a long time before they had company again. Jehovah's Witnesses were often mistaken for charity workers.

*

When Old Con turned thirteen she decided to be an actor. The Anh and his Em went into hysterics.

'NO morals, NO respect.'

'NO employment, NO hope.'

'I will not watch my Con make love to a strange man!'

And, above all:

'What would Jehovah think?'

169

Oldest Con thought about that one, she thought long and hard. She wondered why the Anh and his Em were so impossible.

Was it their Vietnamese-ness?

Was it their Jehovah's Witness-ness?

Or a lethal concoction of Vietnamese-Jehovah's Witness-ness?

They economised a great deal more than the mainstream Vietnamese. They didn't support their ancestors financially in the spirit world with American spirit dollars, or spirit cars, or spirit clothes. They didn't sacrifice mangoes or bananas or cook lavish meals for fat, gigantic-earlobed gods. Their low income wasn't a bother come celebration time because they didn't celebrate.

Oldest Con was enclosed in the good news; it became a glass wall and distorted and magnified the splendour of the world. Through the glass the world looked sublime, its people extraordinary.

*

There was only one conclusion.

Oldest Con decided that although she respected his people, she could not be a witness for Jehovah. She stopped telling people the good news.

The Anh and his Em once again went into hysterics.

And now her spirituality was in ruins.

Her chances of surviving Armageddon were dismal.

Even so, the Anh and his Em still held hope. Oldest Con was an investment: she might prove to be profitable before her destruction.

The Anh and his Em had a mortgage to pay …

Legends

Teenage Dreamers

Phillip Tang

My father had a sixth sense. He knew when people would die.

We were watching a Leslie Cheung film together – a Wong Kar-Wai one with swollen colours, *Happy Together* – and my father was enthralled, totally outside himself, his small feet embracing the seat in front of us. In the dark of the Chinatown cinema, he massaged his wrists.

Leslie's character was bleeding in an old lover's doorway.

Without warning, the sound of sobbing leaked through the warm air of the cinema. At first, I thought it was one of the girls in school uniform, hugging each other in the front row. Their Leslie was hurt on screen. They had iPods in their ears, playing his hits, I guess.

But it was my father who made a sound like a ruined gate, his hands clamped to his cheeks.

I kept my eyes nailed straight ahead.

Ever since my mother had left him, my father had become obsessed with Leslie Cheung. I could picture him – a short ball of a man with grey-shot hair amongst the throng of girls, screaming at Leslie's concerts. He simply studied the singer on stage with the dreaming eyelids.

'He's a Solo Man like me,' my father said after one show, sprinkling in English he learnt from TV. 'So lonesome tonight.'

If he had been somebody else's father, I would have thought he was infatuated with Leslie.

While he continued crying in the cinema, I wondered if it would make me want to see him more often, or not again for another three months. Even though the rows of seats were mostly empty and I could hear a truck rumble in the outside world, I still flushed with embarrassment. One of the iPod girls turned to twist her face at me.

'Ba,' I said. 'Do you want a tissue?'

'He's going to die.'

'Come on, you've seen this film three times, he doesn't die.

Maybe emotionally, isolation, you know–'

'Suicide.'

'That doesn't happen. How do you even know that word? Take this tissue.'

He wouldn't stop crying.

'He was such an April fool.'

'Don't be stupid, he's still alive.'

He unmasked his face to me and looked more serious than I had ever seen him before. 'He's going to die next month,' he said with a metal sting to his words.

My mother always used to say, 'Too much drama. Your father is a victim.' Now I knew what she had seen all those years they were together.

I felt my chest flatten in the hot air of the cinema. I arranged my wandering limbs into the leather seat, and I believed him. The previous Spring Festival, my cousin, Fat Lydia, had emerged from hospital with a new lung blown into her. Everybody gave her red envelopes plumped with dollars, teased her about her first grey hairs, and laughed clumsily in chairs around her bed.

Except for my father. He said she'd be 'returning home' soon. Her lung didn't take and her funeral was two weeks later.

I hadn't believed him then, or cared about Fat Lydia, but the idea of no Leslie Cheung in the silver-screened world made my stomach tense. I was a fan too, though I didn't go to Kinko's to get posters of the star laminated, like my father did. I listened to him talking about Leslie's childhood. His story was recited into the air every other night. My father's voice was wet with pride for the other son he never had.

Sitting up in the aisle, waiting for my father to stop whimpering, I realised Leslie's childhood had become muddled with my own; I had reframed his history around mine. Was it me who loved *Gone with the Wind*? The problem was, some patches of our backstory overlapped. My parents were never at home – working in factories – just like Leslie's. Other things were obviously fantasy: just like my father had an imaginary Leslie son, I had an imaginary Leslie father. He was the tailor to Cary Grant and other A-list stars; he didn't work in a Hills Hoist factory. He didn't live in a weatherboard house in Footscray.

In the restaurant after the movie, my father seemed resigned to the fact of Leslie's death.

'Do you have enough money to pay for your own ticket? You should get a real job,' he said, ripping the crackled pork skin from the shell of bone.

'Ticket for what?'

'For Hong Kong, of course, that's where he was born and where he will die. Beautiful stories. Beautiful pictures.'

I plucked the soy sauce from a small plastic basket on the table for my father. His Kodak memories were making me even more muddled.

'Accountancy is a real job.' My face was filled with heat. My parents had pushed me into it. It wasn't my problem that the moment I actually found satisfaction in my work was the moment they lost pride in it as a profession.

'I'm not going. There's SARS,' I said. Hong Kong always had the fragrance of death, even before the disease came along. An old man shouldn't be going there. 'You wouldn't even come to my graduation.'

'We'll buy face masks.'

'Paper won't stop it. I'm staying here.' I was starving and put some plain rice in my bowl.

'Poor Leslie. If he wasn't a gay, he would be happy,' my father said, slipping his eyes from my gaze. 'It's not his fault.'

I never enquired about my father's private life, but in that pause, I felt I was compelled to do so. We were silent for a long time. The drawn sound of Vietnamese voices stretched from the kitchen. My noodles still hadn't arrived. The tiled floor felt cold, even through my runners. I dragged the plastic tablecloth between my fingers to keep my hand steady.

A question formed on my lips before I knew I was even asking it.

'Are you happy?'

My father's fingernails pressed crescent moons into his hand. A pause.

'Yes.'

'Right.' I pushed up a smile. 'Why don't I see if they'll play that Leslie song, like they did last time?' I went off and asked the woman to put it on.

Leslie's voice shone into the room. It was a narrow restaurant, slotted into the street like all the others, but in ours, his voice breathed through it. We both stared out the red neon-buzzed window to the street below.

'We'll have to make a sign to carry,' I said.

'What?'

'For his funeral.'

My father lifted his eyes to mine and swiftly back down. He picked up his chopsticks and wiped the oily ends on a tissue.

'You loved to draw when you were a boy.'

*

On 1 April 2003, Leslie Cheung jumped from the twenty-fourth floor of his hotel. In a note he said, 'In my life I did nothing bad.'

My father and I carried a big placard that read, 'In my life I did nothing as good as you, Leslie.'

Destiny

Shalini Akhil

I was very young when my obsession started; sparked by the cartoon version, it intensified with the television series. Every weekend I'd be rendered speechless from the first bars of the intro to the closing credits as I watched in awe, stretched out flat on my belly on the lounge-room floor. Every year, I'd get the show bag from the Royal Easter Show, and when we got home I'd sneak up onto the garage roof and fight off make-believe villains whose faces always ended up resembling those of my brothers. They were no match for me: my reflexes were lightning fast, my aim was true and my hair flowed like streamers, dark and glossy in the sunlight. It felt right, being her. A perfect fit. It was destiny.

When I grew up, I would be Wonder Woman.

Then one day, my grandmother came to stay with us. She

stayed for a while, and she watched *Wonder Woman* with me. After a few sittings, I thought she was ready to hear my secret. I told her about my destiny. Though she commended me for thinking about the future, it seemed she wasn't as sure about my choice as I was. As we discussed my plans, my grandmother reminded me that I was Indian. It was then I began to realise I could never grow up to be exactly like Wonder Woman.

My skin was the wrong colour, my eyes were the wrong colour, and my legs just weren't long enough. Not that it would have made a difference if they were, because my grandmother didn't like the way Wonder Woman dressed. I tried to explain to her that what Wonder Woman wore was a costume, a special costume to fight crime in. But my grandmother kept saying she thought it looked like she'd left the house in her underwear – like she'd forgotten to put her skirt on. You can fight all the crime in the world, she said, but if you leave the house without putting your skirt on, no one will take you seriously.

So we started to think about what an Indian-girl crime-fighter might wear. Truth be told, I wasn't too impressed with Wonder Woman's choice of outfit either; in the cartoons her pants had looked okay, but in the TV series they looked a lot like those plastic protector-pants they put over babies' nappies. Initially, I had tried to make up reasons why she'd wear them – maybe she needed the extra padding just in case she ever fell over, or maybe the seat in her invisible jet wasn't very comfortable. But no matter how I tried to explain it to myself, I couldn't really see why they thought putting Wonder Woman in a pair of sparkly nappies would make her better at fighting crime.

My grandmother suggested that Indian Wonder Woman could wear a lungi. That way she could run and kick and squat and jump, and still keep her honour. I wasn't so sure about that, so my grandmother made me a deal. She said that Indian Wonder Woman could wear a lungi over her sparkly pants, and that way if she ever needed seven yards of fabric in an emergency, she could just unwind it from around her waist. She could use the fabric to wrap the bad guys up in and then tie them up with her rope. I thought that sounded like a good idea. We sketched a lungi over Wonder Woman's legs.

My grandmother didn't really like Wonder Woman's top, either. She said that super heroes should have functional clothing, and that a strapless top just wasn't practical for a lady as active as Indian Wonder Woman would be. She liked the colours, though, so we kept the basic design and added some shoulder straps. I wanted them to cross over on the back, and my grandmother said she could sew me a top like that, so we drew it into the plan. Finally we moved on to her accessories. My grandmother thought that all of her accessories should be made of 24-carat gold, and that her earrings should be more than just two red studs. Maybe they could be crafted from rubies instead; that way they'd still be red, but better than before. I didn't really mind about the accessories; all I wanted was a red Wonder Woman top with criss-cross straps at the back.

At lunchtime, my grandmother mentioned that rolling rotis was like a magic power. I didn't really believe her. But then I watched her as she rolled them one after the other, and they all turned out perfectly round. I don't know how she did it, because when I tried, they looked more like blobs or squares. When my grandmother rolled her rotis, they spun slowly around and around underneath her rolling pin, and she didn't have to pick them up and stretch them out with her hands like I did. I was a little disappointed, but she said that it had taken her a while to learn, and that she'd train me. My grandmother said that the magic rotis were very good with super-hero eggs, so I asked her if she would make some for me.

My grandmother chopped up some onions and some chillies to add to the eggs. She said they would make me run faster and help me to see better in the dark. She fried them in a little oil and we both coughed; she said that was a good sign that the power in them was very strong. She beat some eggs and poured them into the frying pan and stirred them around till they were done. She sprinkled some salt over the eggs and divided them between two plates. My grandmother said I could pick the chillies out into her plate if they were too hot for me, but I managed to eat some of them. The eggs tasted good with the magic rotis.

I felt sorry for the old Wonder Woman. I imagined her eating her peanut-butter and jelly sandwiches alone, without a magical grandmother to suggest wearing a lungi over her embarrassing sparkly nappies. That day, I decided to change my destiny.

When I grew up, I was going to be Indian Wonder Woman.

Dancing Lessons

Cindy Pan

Daddy took my hand in his firm capacious one and we walked the cows' trail towards the dam. The water lilies were still open. Vibrant cerises and melting lemon yellows merged with the snowiest of whites in their crisp, sharp petals. How I would like to spend my days basking on those cool, emerald lilypads, nestling inside the lilies at night. The sun was going down and the breeze was cool.

'Yes, Liang Liang. You will be the first.'

'Do you think so, Daddy? Really?'

'Yes. No one has ever do *that* before. Many people can winning Nobels prizes, but no one has ever winning Nobels prize in *every single categories* before. No one!'

'But how?'

'What?'

'How will I do that?'

'You are genius! For you, you will have to working very hard but if you trying very hard, you can do it. I *know* you.'

'I *will* try hard, Daddy. I always try hard, but I don't know if ...'

'No, Liang Liang, I *know* you,' he paused and considered, adding suddenly: 'I've known you *all* your *life*!'

'Well ... I've known *you* all *my* life *too*,' I countered. I had hardly realised I had known him for so long.

'That's right! Liang Liang, you will make our Pan's family very proud one day.'

One day. While Daddy mended the fence, I sought a spot free of fresh cow pats. I lay back in the grass and thought about one day. What was my life going to be? I had wanted to be an artist, because I loved drawing, then an author, because I loved stories, then a teacher, because I loved my kindergarten teacher, Miss Yapp. Then Daddy told me that a school teacher was a stupid thing to want to be, because most teachers were stupid, that's why they became teachers. So I kept this shamefully modest aspiration to myself. Then I wanted to be a ballerina. Preferably Prima Ballerina Assoluta, like Dame Margot. I was shrewd enough to realise that even 'Prima Ballerina Assoluta' was likely to get just as cold a reception as 'school teacher,' so I held my tongue.

'Cindy, what do you want to be when you grow up?' Aunty Joan asked.

'A doctor. Or a scientist, like Daddy!'

This always got a good response.

In the library at lunchtimes I mooned over ballet books. Margot Fonteyn, Natalia Makarova, Gelsey Kirkland. They were my best friends. I knew them all intimately.

Natalia 'plays the piano and always makes a point of procuring the piano scores for all the ballets in which she dances so as to be able to acquaint herself thoroughly with the music,' wrote A.H. Franks in *The Girls' Book of Ballet*. Natalia 'took all the opportunities which presented themselves to see the Royal Ballet while she was in England and declared herself to be very impressed with what she saw,' Franks continued. Wondrous Natalia, 'her friends call her by the charming diminutive Natasha.'

I decided I would call my second daughter by the charming diminutive Natasha. There was little question as to the name of the first. 'One can talk and talk about Fonteyn and still not begin to describe or even indicate the reasons for her greatness.' So wrote A.H. Franks. I thoroughly concurred.

Margot grew up in Shanghai. Her original name was Peggy Hookham. She must have had it changed by deed poll, I nodded to myself. In her autobiography she described how Dame Ninette de Valois, artistic director and founder of the Royal Ballet Company, initially mistook her for a Chinese girl. Margot wondered if her time in Shanghai had made her look just a little Chinese. I vehemently hoped so.

Margot admitted that her *bête noire* was being photographed while performing on stage. She dreaded being caught in an awkward position and found the flashes put her off. She could not help wondering as each flash went off what image had been captured, and this ruined her concentration to the point that she had been known to walk off stage if insensitive photographers disregarded her wishes.

So it was with a certain guilty pleasure that I pored over each precious image. Most of the ballets I had never seen. They existed in my mind as a composite of all the photos and all the tidbits I had gleaned from innumerable ballet books from various libraries and classrooms. I didn't have any ballet books of my own but I started tracing and colouring in the pictures until I had my own lurid miniature photo library. My bedroom walls became a shrine. A shrine to Margot and her princely consort, Rudolf Nureyev.

I was sure Margot wouldn't mind. She might feel quite chuffed, in fact. Most of the original photographs were in black and white but I dressed Margot in golds and rich rubies, flashing with opulent oranges, searing scarlets and bleeding crimsons. Her hair was as black as mine. She did look a little Chinese.

'Who's the best dancer in the world?' I asked my dad.

'Margot Fonteyn.'

'I mean man dancer.'

'Well, depends what kind of dancing. Ballet, best one is Rudolf Nureyev. Oh he really can dance that one, jumping, *wah*, really good. Tap dancing ... be Fred Astaire, or Gene Kelly.'

'Who's Jeanne Kelly? Is that a man?'

'Yeah! You don't know Gene Kelly? "I'm singing in the rain ..." – that one, you know – "Singing in the rain ..."' Daddy improvised some odd-looking steps.

'Nuh. Never heard of it.'

'What, you mean you never see "Singing in the rain, I sing it in the rain!" That Gene Kelly, dancing like a wild bastard, jump in puddles. *Wah!* He really good can dance that little short bastard. Fred Astaire, I like that one better. Not so stumpy one. He more graceful, like you. He dance Ginger Roger. Yeah, that one I must say, very good, that one.' Dad waltzed around in a jerky fashion, seemingly trying to imitate both Fred and Ginger simultaneously.

'Can you ballroom dance, Daddy?' I asked cautiously, hoping to catch him out. Of course I already knew. He was a brilliant dancer. In secret, with my mum.

'Oh, Liang Liang, your daddy not like you, good dancer. Your daddy good at many thing,' he indicated the fence, for example, 'but dancing, your mummy will telling you, I am quite good at one time, but not my best ...'

'But you can do it ...'

'Oh, yes! Can doing it. When I am young, dancing, all the girls wanting to dancing with Pan! "Oh," they say, "Pan, you good dancer."' I am not bad.'

'Teach me!'

'Oh, I can teaching you some things I know. I know Foxy Trot. Slow, slow, quick quick slow ... slow, slow, quick quick slow ... that one easy.'

'Show me!'

'Tsk, ah! We got work to do, Liang Liang, got no time to be Foxy Trot!'

'*Please*, Daddyyyyyyyy ...' I bent over double, pleading.

'Okay. Okay you twisting my arms. I show you Okay? You holding on like this. You stepping on top my feet I dance with you. Showing you.'

I placed my two small rubber-booted feet on top of Daddy's big rubber-booted feet. Dad took off his thick leather fencing gloves and placed my right hand in his left. I put my left hand on his *pigou*, his buttock, and held on expectantly.

Slow, slow, quick quick slow. Slow, slow, quick quick slow ...

We siiinging in the rain, we siiing it in the rain!
What a glooorious feeeeling, we haaappy again.
We waalk-ing the lane, with a haaappy refrain,
The song in our heart and all reeady for love,
Let stormy cloud chain everyooone, to the plain,
Come on little rain, got a smiiile on my chin!
We laugh at the cloud, so daark up above,
We singing and dancing in the rain!

Daddy whirled me around the sloping paddock and my pony-tail fluttered in the dusk light. The rubber boots made a squelchy, whooshy percussive accompaniment. I held my breath and dared not blink; I didn't want to miss a thing.

The cows lifted their heads and chewed their cuds, bemused while the horses hung their heads over the fence and raised their upper lips, entranced.

Humans did funny things.

Papa Bear

Chin Shen

My dad grew up in Shanghai and was raised by his grandparents. His parents worked (and still do) for the Communist government. His dad had taught himself Japanese and plagiarised entire Japanese articles, translated them into Chinese and passed them off as his wife's work. She won some prestigious national award and dined with the political elite. They were shit parents. AND they had plastic fruit in their fruit bowls.

In primary school, my dad would coat his daily homework sheets in a thin layer of wax so he could scrape off the teacher's big tick and hand in the same sheet again another day.

He started smoking at about fourteen and sold cartons to his mates at school. (He became asthmatic a few years ago, but decided he didn't like the puffer so he quit cold turkey.)

He fought in street gangs until someone drove a six-inch blade into his left buttock. So he became a pacifist and a negotiator between gangs and bought off thugs with smokes and booze.

In the last year of high school, he had a relationship with one of his teachers and went to live with her in the countryside. (I don't know if this is actually true or the greatest rumor my mum has ever spread).

He made it to university on average marks. Mum was a genius and borderline Martian but she missed the last page of her exams and ended up at the same university as my dad.

Some crafty college slut was keen on Dad and gave him two movie tickets, naturally assuming that he'd take her. He took my mum instead. Burned.

Considering my dad looked like an anorexic Chinese mafia messenger, it's a wonder he pulled at all. Mum says she saw a kind heart. She wears glasses.

Four years later they got married.
Two years later they held hands.
I arrived in September of '86.

Dad says that when I was born they had just $200. He decided the best thing to do would be to leave their engineering jobs and start afresh in Australia, because obviously they'd have a better chance of success if they couldn't speak the language and had no recognised qualifications.

His right forearm was crushed in a machinery accident after a year down under. With micro-surgery and skin grafts from his foot and buttocks, they stitched it back together. He's got a metal rod in there but it still looks gimpy ... kind of like the 'strong hand' from *Scary Movie* except it's not strong, it's weak as balls. So he writes with his left hand now BUT ONLY IN CAPITALS. And he eats with a fork.

After calling himself John for a year, my dad realised he needed a name that symbolised something more than the average white Australian male. Something strong and heroic – something that embodied the promise and hope of his newly adopted home. But instead of looking through the phone book or a book of names for potential monikers, he took a trip to the local shopping complex. That's where he laid eyes on the brightest, reddest sign he'd ever seen:

TANDY ELECTRONICS

My father named himself after an electronics store.
Seriously, what hope did I have?

This is the same man who used to mix a little whiskey with my milk to pacify me.

The same man who recorded me snoring when I was six and played the audio every day like it was a Top 40 CD.

The same man who Googled Eva Green as soon as he got back from the cinema.

The same man who doesn't believe in power naps and can drive home asleep.

The same man who can play mahjong asleep. And win.

The same man who chirps, 'Honey! I'm hooooome' as soon as he steps in the front door.

The same man who can't wait to become senile so he can watch Tom and Jerry cartoons every day.

He's the same, yet he continues to surprise me.
He's my dad. And I want to grow up to be just like him.

Saturdays were always the strange day of the week.

It'd be the day that mum and the rest of the family would go to the shops at Cabra.

It was a weekly ritual; a day to run errands of all sorts...

...A day of haircuts...

...and congregation at the old Street Fighter machine.

STREET FIGHTER II

A New Challenger
Glenn Lieu · Matt Huynh

The old Street Fighter machine was in the complex that housed Woolies.

Just next to the butcher.

There used to be a shop behind the machine, but I didn't really care much about it at the time.

I was too busy, immersed in the game.

By 'immersed', I don't mean I was playing it.

No, me and Fatbody (my brother) never seemed to have enough change to play.

And when we did have change, our shit skills made ice creams and lollies appear the better investment.

We'd usually watch the other kids.

They had skills.

But on one fateful Saturday, that pretty much resembled any other Saturday, I learnt an important lesson about Street fighter machines.

I usually liked to mindlessly mash the control pad, I don't know why.

The other older kid was versing the computer at the time –

–not paying attention to what I was doing.

Suddenly, those yellow words ran across the screen –

HERE COMES A NEW CHALLENGER!

I jumped from the machine, trying to hide myself amongst the congregation.

Gimme a dollar!

The kid at the machine somehow thought my brother was responsible.

An argument broke out, my brother denying that he was the one to blame.

Under a barrage of accusations and denials—

IT WAS THAT LITTLE SHIT!

I realised my brother was still at the machine. Cautiously, I returned to find the previously hostile situation had been quelled.

They were all just watching the game as the kid played. They totally forgot about who owed who money.

Immersed, I rejoined them, completely forgetting about what just happened.

The Hots

Towards Manhood

Benjamin Law

There are some men in the world who are unambiguously male. Unquestionably, identifiably, inherently *male*. It's not uncommon for teenagers I encounter on public transport to be twice the size of me, twice as physically developed, even though I'm actually twice their age. These creatures – who apparently share the same XY chromosome pairing as my own – are tall and broad-shouldered. They have feet the size of concrete slabs, five o'clock shadows, legs like carved tree trunks, and sport hair on their chests and arses. One assumes their genitals swing between their legs like anvils, and their shit stinks like the wet earth. They are, undeniably, *men*.

When it came to me, it's as though my mother's uterus had several moments of hesitation in deciding what it'd produce. After coming up with Andrew – my veritable giant of a brother – then having to endure the horrors of a miscarriage in 1981, Mum's womb was exhausted and indecisive throughout 1982. 'Well, the baby should definitely have a penis,' the uterus thought. 'Yes: a penis. Slap one on. Should we put hair on its forearms? Maybe hold back on the forearm hair, I don't know. What about leg hair? Yes: leg hair. Actually, no: stop the leg hair. Oh no, wait: PUT IT BACK.'

The result of such indecisiveness was me: this Asian hybrid man-child thing. Someone with a 27-inch waistline, hands like a well-manicured woman, unsightly and improvised leg-hair growth and – inexplicably – a baritone voice which can sometimes sound like a gay James Earl Jones with a cold. Despite my skinny frame and Asiatic eyes, I also have sensual full-bodied lips, not unlike those of an African-American woman. It is a confused and strange body to inhabit.

For the majority of my life, I've worked against the outcome of this genetic lottery. I've tried bashing shit, listening to different music, gaining weight, building muscle, slouching, pretending to like girls – but nothing's really worked. Now, at the age of twenty-five, I've given up trying. Yes, I'll swear like a stevedore, but I refuse to heckle; I'll belch in public, but will refrain from farting; I grow hair on my abdomen, but not on my calves; I'll eat your meat pie, but not your vagina. I'm a compromised failure of a man.

*

My siblings are fond of reminding me that the signs were there from the start. There is an infamous family video we sometimes bring out at Christmas. It shows my four siblings and me, between the ages of two (Michelle) and fifteen (Candy), holding an improvised fashion parade through the living room. My mother never got rid of clothes back then. Pantyhose, old bath-robes, hideous socks with ruined elastic – she kept them all. They simply went into a massive plastic tub, and *voilà*: Jenny's Bucket of Fun was ready. When you're a mother of five, you need cheap entertainment.

Much of the home video simply contains incomprehensible screaming and shrieking; we were laughing so hard the whole time. At one point, Candy – dressed like an abomination from a medieval fete – comes close to the video camera and crosses her eyes. 'I'm a lesbian!' she declares. Delighted, six-year-old Tammy screams with laughter, and starts calling after her: 'Darling! Darling! Darling!'

My older brother Andrew and I refuse to be outdone. We know we can be more entertaining than a medieval dyke in rainbow glasses. We find old, saggy brown pantyhose, and pull them tight over our genitals, past our navels, and into our armpits. We strut down the makeshift catwalk made of sofa cushions and headrests, hands on our arses, blowing kisses to the camera. Tammy laughs, scandalised and confused. Two-year-old Michelle, not really understanding what is going on, simply screams and screams and screams.

Things get out of hand, and Andrew cruelly tries pulling off my shorts, laughing as I stumble over the cushions, still in pantyhose and high-heels. Siblings start running into each other like idiots. Costume changes behind the sliding doors become more violent and frenzied. We scream and scream. Dad, who works hid-

196

eously long nights at the restaurant, comes into the scene, looking disoriented. 'Darling, darling!' Tammy screams at Dad. 'I'm a lars-bian!' screams Candy again. Inexplicably, I spontaneously start humping the cushioned catwalk violently, moaning, pretending I'm a woman orgasming. 'Urgh, urgh, urgh!' I grunt. It is chaos. Then Andrew comes bursting out of the doors –

The video camera cuts out to black.

When we return, Andrew is on the floor, bent over and howling in pain. Someone has kicked him in the balls. Actually, from what we gather watching the video, it mightn't have been a kick, but a punch. It seems Tammy had just balled her fists, aimed, and – without reason – cushioned them straight into his testicles.

Andrew crouches, keeled over, crying his guts out.

Behind the camera, Mum sighs. 'Michelle, give your brother a tissue.'

Andrew continues crying, and Michelle waddles over and gives him a Kleenex. It's a touching moment. The mood has definitely changed from unhinged frivolity to sobriety. But watching the video now, I know that without a doubt, somewhere in the background, my ten-year-old self is sitting around, out of frame, happily oblivious, still wearing his dress and pantyhose, examining his nails in the sunlight.

*

Around the time of the fashion parade, I'd been having a successful run in childhood gymnastics, and was featured in the newspaper several times for my sporting prowess. After a while, however, the bars started hurting my hands. The exercises and demands became increasingly excruciating: 180-degree, full-circle rotations on the high bar; supporting my entire body-weight in a 90-degree L-shape on the rings; spinning my legs around a pommel the size of a shetland pony. I was experiencing the painful transitionary period where male gymnastics suddenly became less about nimbleness and agility, and more about brute strength and courage. Lacking both of those qualities, I quit. People told me it was a girly pursuit anyway.

Andrew recruited me into the decidedly more manly sport he was pursuing: karate. None of this cartwheel, leg-splitting crap.

Now I was moving on to a sport that involved bashing the living shit out of people, which was as manly as it got. During one of my first lessons, our *sensei* – a white dude called Eddie – told us how in shopping centres, he always kept an eye out for potential attackers by watching his reflection in glass store entrances and shopping-centre window displays. He always kept his hands in fists, just in case.

'You just *never* know,' Eddie told us. 'One of the main ways people get attacked is from behind. They never see what's coming. Sure, you might call those attackers cowards. But calling them names won't make any difference when they've slit your throat and you've got blood all over your shirt. Newsflash: you are now *dead*. So do what I do: watch for people in reflective surfaces. Stay alert. And when those bastards attack, be ready to smash their faces in.' He punched the air in front of him. Everyone nodded sagely.

Eddie's presence made karate a more frightening prospect than it had to be. Even though I was fond of the *kata* routines, which seemed like a choreographed dance, I sucked hard at the actual bashing component of the sport. My gymnastics training afforded me the flexibility to kick a fully grown man in the head, but there was no strength behind my knocks. My frail little boy-bones meant that you could probably have broken my collarbone by tapping me on the shoulder. The freestyle sparring sessions were the worst. 'Green-belt,' an orange-belted girl said to me one night, beckoning me with her finger. 'You're with me.' One well-aimed kick to the gut later, and I was winded. I may have wept.

Even though Andrew and I walked to and from karate class together every week, I'm not convinced we bonded during that period. We were just too different. He was the boy of the family: a monosyllabic, grunting champion tennis player who smelled weird and punched holes in the walls to vent his frustration. I was on the primary-school debating team, jumped rope during recess, and had a defence mechanism that involved a unique combination of scratching and spitting.

'What are you?' Andrew asked one night, withdrawing from a fight after I had repeatedly spat in his face and clawed at his eyes, squealing like a pig. He wiped away the soup of saliva and phlegm that marinated his face, and looked at me with utter disgust.

'I mean, really, Ben: what *are* you? Fight back properly. Be a man.'

*

Our music tastes were irreconcilable. It was 1993, and Nirvana had just released *In Utero*. Andrew would listen to the fourth track, 'Rape Me,' over and over again. He didn't have a personal stereo, so Kurt Cobain's ironic plea for someone to sexually abuse him droned in from the living room into everyone's bedrooms, and even into the kitchen where Mum was cooking dinner. Apparently, it was what guys listened to. But even as an eleven-year-old, I thought the song was pretentious and embarrassing. Why would anyone want to rape Kurt Cobain? He was greasy, married to Courtney Love, wore flannel and clearly did not look after himself.

Instead, I immersed myself in another seminal album that was released the same year: Mariah Carey's *Music Box*, a serious and studied meditation on love ('Dreamlover'), bravery ('Hero'), loyalty ('Anytime You Need a Friend') and profound loss ('Without You'). I ordered it on the back of a *TV Week* catalogue, alongside Bryan Adams's *So Far So Good* and Billy Joel's *River of Dreams*. I would listen to *Music Box* endlessly on my Sony Walkman, for which I'd saved an entire sixty-five dollars. Because I wasn't at the stage where I could discern what was cool or not, I tentatively asked my best friend James about Carey's album, and whether he also loved it as much as I did.

'Mariah fucking Carey?' There was pity in his eyes. 'What are you, a fucking homo?' I shuffled in my spot, unsure of the appropriate response. 'And what are those shorts you're wearing, by the way?' James said. 'Are they fucking *Mango*?' I looked down at the imitation Mambo-brand shorts my mother had bought me from Best 'n' Less – the ones I reserved for special occasions, like the Fridays James and I went tenpin bowling. What I had thought was cool – Mariah Carey, my imitation brand-label shorts – I now realised was actually supposed to be a source of deep, deep shame. At least I was feeling it now.

'Listen, you can't go on listening to that shit,' James said, not unkindly, spraying Brut-33 deodorant into his eleven-year-old armpits. (I made a mental note: use deodorant.) Driving to the tenpin bowling alley, James told his mother to put on several CDs for me: The Twelfth Man's *Wired World of Sports II* and Denis Leary's 'I'm an Asshole.' Denis Leary's song I could understand and enjoy – you would have to have been retarded not to. But being raised in a non-cricket household, the Twelfth Man went right over my head. He was boring. But because it was spoken word, all I needed to do was block it out, by privately looping Mariah Carey through my head.

*

Needless to say, there was an answer once I, as Mariah suggested, 'reached into my soul.' All of these things – the fashion parade; the gymnastics lessons; Mariah Carey; my lack of body hair; my almost religious commitment to mid-90s gameshow *Man 'O' Man*, the male beauty pageant hosted by *Phantom of the Opera*'s Rob Guest – pointed towards a particularly aggressive form of homosexuality.

When puberty eventually hit, all the teenage schoolyard boys – reeking of armpits, various penis odours and locker-room Lynx – were on the hunt for anyone remotely queer to exercise their knuckles on. God knows how, but I apparently passed the test. I learned which girls were supposedly attractive; I perfected my man-walk; and I had that rich baritone voice to hide behind. For whatever reason, my peers chose to look beyond my involvement in the all-female clarinet ensemble, and my art-class assignment submissions of semi-naked, muscled Christ figures. Being Asian helped. People never suspected you could be a racial minority *and* gay. Of course you're not gay; you're *foreign*.

In any case, I was busy convincing myself that I was infatuated with Kate, a girl from my extracurricular acting class. She was misanthropic, liked Radiohead, was obsessed with Jonny Greenwood and smelled nice. She had lovely feet. I had severe scoliosis and a Tori Amos rarities collection. In our area, and in this era, this was as close as the youth got to cutting-edge. A few months into our friendship, I sent Kate an anonymous Valentine's Day card with Elliott Smith lyrics scrawled all over it. She called my bluff and asked me out on a date during an online chat.

I became flustered, confused, and – somehow knowing in my gut that this would be wrong – typed something like 'Uhmnoth-anksokaybye.'

Then I made my online profile invisible.

(Knowing my teenage self, it's very likely I then spent the next few hours looking at homosexual pornography.)

The next time I saw her, Kate had put on weight and scowled a lot. Later, she would email me to tell me her misanthropy and weight gain had more to do with a chemical imbalance in her brain than anything I did. But being self-obsessed goes hand in hand with being young and gay, and I couldn't help but feel partially to blame.

'What's the problem?' Mum asked one night, after she found me heaving and dripping snot all over her sofa. I was crying so hard that I couldn't breathe, and sounded like I was caught in a strange combination of having sex and shitting myself from food poisoning.

I couldn't even speak. 'I-HAH-AVE-SUH-UH-UM-THING ...' I gasped.

'Yes?'

'SU-UHM-TH-ING ... TO-OO ... TE-EHL ... YO-OO.'

Mum patted my shoulder comfortingly and smiled.

'I have no idea what you just said.'

'I ha-ave sum-thi-ing,' I choked, 'to tell you.'

'Hmmm,' my mother said, concerned. 'Is it bad? Are you on drugs?'

I shook my head.

'You've gotten Rebecca pregnant.'

'Oh go-oh-od – no!' I continued sobbing.

'Um...' Mum said, as though she was on a gameshow. 'You're *gay*.'

Tentatively, I nodded, still blubbering.

'Okay. Well, what's wrong with that?' Mum asked. 'There's nothing wrong with being gay.'

I looked up at her. 'Ree-heh-ly?'

'Gay people can't help it,' she said. Her reaction surprised me. 'It's just that something went wrong in the womb, that's all.'

*

After I came out, it was strange not having something to be constantly anxious about. So I chose to focus again on my body. A moment from high school was still haunting me, from Moreton Island on Year 12 camp, when a girl called out to me as I got out of the ocean: 'Ben! Oh my god: if you had tits, you'd have my ideal body.'

Having hovered around the 49-kilogram mark for most of my postpubescent life, I was sick of it. I hadn't grown taller or put on any weight since I'd left high school. My aim was to build some biceps, stack on some muscle and stop looking like someone had draped skin over a skeleton. My metabolism was like a furnace. I would devour veritable troughs of food, only to crap it all out minutes later. It made weight gain extremely difficult.

However, my friend Daniel (so aggressively heterosexual that he once shat *on* a toilet seat by mistake) had recently become noticeably beefier. When I went to hug him each time I saw him, it became increasingly difficult. He was becoming a truck. Daniel's advice was simple: go to the gym; invest in protein shakes. So I did exactly as he said: I joined the gym, worked out like a demon and swam laps every other day. If my life were a movie, this period would be a montage of protein shakes, scrambled eggs, bacon, bananas, bench presses, swimming laps and grunting. Sweat would trickle down my face.

About a month later, I'd put on five kilos. On a body size like mine, this was conspicuous and noticeable. Then I put on another two. Encouraged and exhilarated, I decided to be adventurous with the protein shakes. Into the mix went: protein mix, milk, bananas, Milo, a tub of Milo dairy dessert, Weet Bix and two raw eggs. But Asians aren't known for having a strong tolerance to lactose. Five hours later, the resulting farts were indescribably rancid.

'Jesus,' said my sister Tammy that night, choking. 'Dear fucking god, what is that smell?' The farts would not stop.

Later, when my boyfriend Scott had marched back from work, sleep-deprived and tired, the farts had still not subsided. Tammy had opened all the windows and doors, gasping. By bedtime, my bowels were still putting on a musical, one with both an auditory and olfactory score. Sighing, Scott endeavoured to 'massage them out' of me, rather than having me leak gas throughout the night. He was tired and needed to sleep.

A few hours later, it was still going.

'Benjamin,' Scott finally said. 'This is a new low. Even for you.' He said this firmly but gently, as he lovingly guided the gas from my bloated abdomen towards my anus.

In the dark, I nodded. Then I farted. Groaning and waving his hands, Scott got up and opened windows and doors. Tammy screamed – she could smell it from the next room. It was official: I was repulsive. But while my bowels continued to spasm, expand, then lazily yawn out sulphurous gas into the night, I couldn't help but think, 'Being disgusting. That's manly, isn't it?'

The Lover in the Fish Sauce

Chi Vu

In the darkness the only thing visible was the glow of Trung's watch. Then a sudden change of light and loudness. Trung turned and watched the way Diep tucked her hair behind her ear with a small, efficient movement. Her blue loose-fitting dress looked white in the brightness from the screen. Trung got her to skip afternoon classes to see this.

They were almost alone in the cinema. Another couple sat right in the centre, and an old guy sat in the third row, his arms outstretched over the two seats on either side of him. Trung put his arm around Diep's shoulders. Warmth and dampness. His arm was heavy given his slight build.

The air con was dry, the velvet curtains dusty, there was a little bit of rubbish around on the seats. Popcorn, cardboard containers. Small plastic wrappers especially crinkled up, hiding under seats.

Diep took Trung's arm off her shoulder. In that moment she felt his body tense up, so she held his hand. The touch of two palms, smooth and light. They smiled and their teeth glistened in each other's peripheral vision, but neither of them looked at the other.

Later the titles on the screen had a more adventurous appearance – jungle and bamboo font, with diacritics on them.

'This is a funny movie,' Diep puzzled.

'It's not a movie,' Trung said, 'It's an advert.'

Diep leaned forward. 'Oh, it's a Viet company.' She squinted harder at the screen.

'It's my father's company,' Trung said finally.

'That's why you took me here …'

'Do you like it?' Trung realised his voice was hard as soon as he said it.

'Yeah, sure I do,' Diep smiled and looked downwards.

*

Twenty minutes into the promo Trung got quite sick. He ran away from the seat while the movie was still playing. Diep sat there not knowing what to do. She looked at the nearly empty cinema. She watched the men on the screen; a buff businessman was dashing across the pedestrian crossing with his tie fluttering about his engorged neck, slashing his pale chiselled jawline.

Then cut to an interview of another man, older but also well built, talking about what he loved about his job and his company. He said to camera: 'It is a cutthroat industry, but supportive.' High-powered keywords spun across the screen before landing on the front middle of the frame. What were the words? Diep involuntarily turned her head sideways to catch the spinning words, but could not read them.

Trung returned to the seat, moving slowly. His footsteps were unsure on the plush multicoloured carpet. Diep immediately stood up and put her arms around him, helping him sit down. He had an acrid smell about him.

She cradled him in the diamond of her crossed legs, his head at her knee. Diep leaned forward, looking at his feverish temple. Trung was trembling as though to shake off the beads of sweat on his skin. Diep thought that they were not familiar enough for her to be holding him this way. She was falling for him as he lay semiconscious in her lap.

Trung looked up, unfocused, towards her small breasts. And he was shrinking back into a little boy. His hair seemed to melt into his head. The eyeballs beneath his eyelids were getting bigger and protuberant. His skin turned a translucent orange-pinky colour, so thin and succulent that it revealed his blood vessels and the tiny bones of his web-like hands.

When he shrank so small, he went and crawled into a plastic Vietnamese take-away container and lay there. Like an embryo in the fish-sauce bag. The liquid through the light looked like amber with trapped flecks of chilli.

Diep poked gently at the plastic bag with her finger. The embryo bobbed silently inside the sac, suspended in the tangy, soured amniotic fluid. The embryo seemed to curl tighter in response, sucking on one of its webbed fingers.

Diep thought this was rather strange but didn't say anything.

*

A few days later he rang Diep up.

'Hi …'

'Trung?'

'Yeah. Do you want to get some food later?'

'All right. Whereabouts?' She sounded pleased to hear from him.

'Maybe the city.'

'Are you all right?' Diep asked him.

'Yes, of course I am.' He deepened his voice. 'I'll pick you up from school.'

Diep hesitated. 'I want to go home and change first.'

'Okay.'

She told him to pick her up from the Victoria Street shops. They set a time.

*

Trung was given his white sports car as a present for completing Year 12 with such a high mark. It was a very expensive car with P-plates on it. His parents celebrated his results at a Chinese restaurant in the city. They ordered two crabs and a very large crayfish. They spent much time taking photos of their son with the cooked crayfish.

Diep was waiting on the bench at the bus stop on the busy

shopping strip. She wore a light beige skirt and T-shirt, with thin sandals. Trung opened the car door for her. Diep sat with her arms folded and her pointy knees close together in the plush moulded interior of Trung's car. The air-freshener in the car overpowered her small, dark scent. Trung took corners too fast but kept within the speed limit the entire time.

'We'll drop by my place,' Trung said. 'I've just got to get a jacket.'

'Oh,' Diep said.

'Won't be long.'

They got off the freeway and turned down streets with round-abouts and wider and wider lawns.

*

It was a house with a sweeping concrete driveway, neat lawn and some indistinctive shrubs. The entrance was high with columns on each side. Two marble lion-dogs guarded the front entrance. Above was a balcony with cream-coloured tiles. The house reminded Diep of the houses she saw in Vietnam when she visited her relatives, but wider, fatter and whiter.

'Are your parents home?'

'It'll be okay. Want to say hi?'

*

Inside the house, Trung's parents were watching *Phim Tap*, a serialised video. Trung's mother had jade earrings, immaculately carved eyebrows and pale soft hands with shimmery-pink nail polish. His father, Mr Cuong, looked older, but still had strong powerful shoulders. Trung addressed his father first, then his mother.

'Bo, Me, I'm home.'

'Con,' his father said, not glancing at him.

'This is my friend Diep,' Trung continued.

Diep was introduced to Trung's father, Mr Cuong, and Trung's mother, Mrs Cuong. Diep held her arms in a pose that could pass for politeness or nervousness. She noticed that Mr Cuong was watching her, even when she stood up to look at the black and white photo on the mantle, of a simple-looking man in a traditional *ao dai*.

'Are you getting a jacket?' she asked Trung, who then disappeared. Diep turned around to see Mr Cuong's eyes were still on her. Diep sat down next to Mrs Cuong.

Trung was back in the room, wearing a faded sports jumper. Mrs Cuong saw the jumper and exclaimed in mock horror, 'Our son the doctor.'

'Med student, Mum,' Trung teased.

'Doctor to be,' she corrected herself.

'Where do you study?' Mrs Cuong asked Diep.

'Richmond Girls.'

'What do you want to be?' the woman continued.

'A nurse,' Diep said, looking at Trung with half a smile.

Across the lounge room, Diep noticed three large black lacquer panels on the white wall. She saw flecks of red on one of the panels, the one with the peasant riding an ox that was tilling the soil. It was unusual to see red flecks on a black and white *son mai*. It was very pretty and vivid.

*

There were lounge seats with thick cushions, a cane armchair with a high back, tropical plants in brass pots sitting on small tables, and on a wall were black lacquer *son mai* panels depicting village life – a boy blowing a flute while balanced casually on a happy ox. It was a room several stories above street level. In the middle of the room was a wide coffee table with a large crystal ashtray. A cigar was smouldering away in the ashtray, its blue-grey plume lifting up slowly until it reached the movement of the ceiling fan, which chopped up the smoke into a pale haze.

The dark, skinny man tried to make out the pulsating light on the shiny, beige floor. Its rhythm matched the throbbing in his back, head and hands. The man recognised it was the reflection of the overhead fan. He continued to crawl.

There was another man standing over him, the owner, wearing a white short-sleeved shirt, leather belt with a gold buckle, and a French watch. The owner made the discovery a week ago. He had talked to his suppliers and found out that the amount going in was considerably greater than the products produced.

The man on the floor reached up the wicker armchair. The

owner struck down again on the foreman's shoulders. Air rushed through the bamboo stick, making a shrieking, whistling sound.

It wasn't so much the money, it was the betrayal and the foreman's boasting. The owner could call on his underlings, his *dan em*, to do the job, but this was more of a humiliation.

Still on the floor, the foreman could *hear* a hint of perfume. Slowly he could make out her long black hair, her dark, horrified eyes in the doorway watching the two men.

*

It was the first time he did this. Trung left the house abruptly, without saying to his parents, 'Father, mother, I'm going.' Trung's mother was shocked and looked at Diep accusingly.

Diep ran after him. Trung was already in the car, and reached over to open the door for her from the driver's seat. They drove away from his parents' white, tiered wedding-cake home. Trung and Diep sat with their silent, separate inheritances of fear and guilt.

Diep sat back into the leather seat. They were protected by moulded plastic and the plushness of the car interior. Diep closed her eyes and dreamt of kissing the boy in the fish sauce.

The Embarrassments of the Gods

Xerxes Matza

Philandering is the sin of the Gonzales men. This, and their obsession with their penises. After years of attending these obligatory family Christmas parties, listening to their jokes, I can now rattle off each uncle's pet name for his penis as surely as I can recite the Ten Commandments. My father, Enrico Gonzales, Chairman of G Freights, calls his thing Junior, or sometimes Humpty Dumpty, a nickname that offends the sensibilities of his new wife, Katie, a kindergarten teacher.

Uncle Christopher calls his thing Pipo, or, most of the time, '*My* Pipo.' Although he only has one name for it, he himself has gone through several name changes. His given name was Benjamin Christopher and everyone used to call him Benjie. Discovering in his late teens that Benjie was the name of two granduncles, and always wanting to be *original*, he insisted on being called Christopher. He also made us drop the *Tio, Tio* being 'a product of the old world.' 'We're all Aussies now, so call me Uncle,' he corrected me once on our way to a footy match. I was nine then, newly arrived in Australia. My father had sponsored me to come after my mum died in Manila. *New country, new expressions*, I thought then. *But same old values where the Gonzales blokes are concerned*, I would come to realise. By deed poll Uncle Chris dropped Benjamin and added James, making him James Christopher Gonzales. 'James for James Bond,' Katie informed me conspiratorially years later. That explained the extensive 007 memorabilia and complete DVD collection of Bond movies in his lounge room. Uncle Chris claims that Connery and Brosnan are the best Bonds because they can epitomise male coolness simply by slicking back their hair, a style he often imitates. He even talks in a well-modulated voice and smiles the Bond smile – moving only one side of his mouth, simultaneously half-raising an eyebrow.

As if those aliases were not enough for my multi-handled uncle, his American wife Barbara, whom he met while doing his masters at Harvard Business School, calls him Thopie, one of those silly pet names couples call each other. But when she calls him Thopie, I suspect she's wanting Pipo. Vanessa, Chris's grown-up daughter from his first marriage, confirmed this while playing Scrabble with me one summer night when all the cousins rented a cottage at Ulladulla. 'That blonde is a nympho, let me tell you, Cous. Thopie-this and Thopie-that and Dad is under her spell. And you know what? She's a screamer. It's so embarrassing when Alfie spends the night. I can't compete.' We sniggered as we finished off the chardonnay.

'You behave down there, Patrick. Finish your food,' Barbara commands her seven-year-old, who is holding a drumstick in one hand and is about to bowl a cricket ball with the other to Alfred, Dad's eldest by Katie. Barbara's massive breasts are on display while she breastfeeds baby Thaddeus on the terrace.

'Let them have fun, Barbara,' snaps Uncle Terence, youngest

of my father's siblings. I've heard that Uncle Terence has finally cured his smelly feet. The women in his life left him over those feet, or so I was told. But a relative of a relative said it was his gambling that drove Auntie Laura and Auntie Bessie away.

'Your wife is still in very good shape for her age, Chris.'

'Exercise, diet and a good root keep your missus young, Terry.'

'Teddy agrees with that, brother. Cheers.' They lift their beers in a toast.

Terence, an accountant who makes a lot of money financing porn sites on the web, calls his thing Teddy, while his son Benedict calls his Kiko. Benedict, who hadn't yet had a love-child with his then girlfriend, Alicia, wasn't included in the conversation last year. Now that he's a father at seventeen, he is an official member of the dick club.

'*Dios mio*, these men have nothing better to do,' quips Auntie Amanda, who is sitting next to me.

'My new girlfriend always makes my Teddy red,' boasts Terence to no one in particular.

'*Por Dios, por Santo*, Terence, I hope it isn't as red as it was when I used to clean it after you were circumcised,' my favourite aunt interrupts.

'Not quite, *Até*. Teddy experiences a different kind of sore now.' The men roll with laughter.

'I'm sure. Richard, go and play with Patrick and Alfred. And stay away from your uncles,' she calls to her six-year-old adopted son, who is standing by and looking inquiringly at his uncles. Auntie Amanda is a director of an IT company. She carries her bossy, do-it-now tone everywhere – even at home as she feeds her cat or when talking to Richard. 'So where were we, Emilio ... Oh, your thesis. How's it going?'

'Progressing.'

'Oh good. Glad to hear– Richard, no! Put that down. It's an antique from India, Grandma will be mad at you. What is it about, Emil?'

'Semiotics in Nick Cave's lyrics. But my tutor suggested I write a childhood account instead, then apply semiotics.'

'So which is it to be? Richard, don't make me get up. God, I seriously need a nanny for this boy! But babysitters are hard to find in this city now. The memoir sounds good, but if you've started the other one, stick with it. Don't waste time. Prove to your father that your course is as valuable as a business course. You know how this family measures success – how much money you make, how many brats you produce. One more time, Richard, and–'

The vase crashes. Auntie stands and barks at Richard. The boy cries.

'Our sister needs a new husband,' I hear my old man say from the next table.

'No I don't, Enrico. I don't need *hombre, purisima*, you know that,' she snaps back and carries the bawling Richard into the lounge room. 'Emil, we'll talk later, sweetie.' I smile at her. She's pushing fifty yet looks at least ten years younger. She entered a Jenny Craig program after her husband of twenty years left her for – cliché of clichés – his secretary, two years ago. Uncle Ron, as I recall, calls his thing Ronron. He used to be a part of my father's and uncles' conversation circle at family parties. Despite divorcing Auntie Amanda, he's still my father's best mate and solicitor, and one of the directors of the family firm.

'Emil, *hijo*, where's your girlfriend?'

'I don't have one at the moment, Uncle Chris,' I reply without looking at them.

'Boy, you've got to have fun sometimes. All work and no play makes *my* Pipo decay,' he says, laughing at his own joke.

'Shut up down there, Thopie,' teases Barbara from the terrace, still breastfeeding.

'Leave him alone, Chris. Emilio needs time to finish his thesis ... so he can graduate,' my father says dryly. He told me once that my degree would not put food on the table. He said I should be studying business management and was critical of my bar work. He criticises my foreign-film-going and even my flat in New-town, which I share with an often-unemployed filmmaker.

'Look who's here,' Uncle Terence says excitedly, as if seeing a movie star. '*Muy guwapito*, Miguelito.'

Uncle Chris pauses from lighting his cigar then exclaims, 'Our big boy Miguel and his muse.'

My father stands and opens his arms to Miguelito, my half-brother, born on the feast day of Archangel Michael. 'Ah, Miguelito, how are you, champion?'

'Good, Dad. How are you playboys?' He is shaking hands and hugging my uncles and Benedict. 'Everyone, this is Charmaine.' The Gonzales men, in mock chivalry, take turns kissing the girl's hand.

'Make yourself at home, *hija*,' says Uncle Chris, flashing his 007 smile.

'Emil, good to see you, bro,' Miguelito says. I shake his hand. 'Charmaine, this is my big brother.'

'Hi,' I say. Charmaine smiles and stands awkwardly, wondering whether I'm going to give her a hug or kiss her hand too. I finally offer my hand. 'Pleased to meet you, Charmaine.' She nods silently. *She looks familiar.*

'Have something to eat,' my father offers, directing them to the long buffet table full of greasy meat dishes.

As he returns to the group he says, 'What a boy. Let's ask him later how Charmaine takes care of his *titi*.' The men laugh in unison once more as I wolf down my food, trying to block out my father's joke.

My brother is going from table to table, introducing Charmaine to the aunties and other relatives. As usual, Miguel is a bit overdressed for the occasion, not to mention the season. He's wearing a suit, probably by Cerruti. His heels, loud as gunfire on the stone floor, proclaim 'shoes by Bally.' Miguel drives a dark-blue BMW which he bought with his own money when he was just twenty-three, another achievement to make our already-proud father prouder still.

Although I am my father's first and so-called legitimate child, which places me in a very crucial position as a *jeredero* in the Gonzales clan, I feel I'm the bastard son, a distant second to Miguelito, two years younger than me but with significant financial achievements under his belt already.

He made my father proud the day he became captain of the school football team, and even more so when he impregnated his girlfriend in Year 11. My father raved to his brothers that Miguelito was following in his footsteps. When Dad was losing money on

the stock market, Miguelito, newly graduated from uni and starting out as a broker, advised him to invest more in *blue chip shares*
and sell off his *ordinaries* (whatever that means), which turned
around Dad's fortunes. When G Freights was collapsing, he developed a 'brilliant' marketing strategy (overpricing goods and services) that saved our father from bankruptcy and humiliation. Dad
told me all this over the phone while I was in Europe, staying in a
smelly backpackers' hostel and biting him for a loan. Why didn't
I come home soon and finish uni instead of waiting tables to
stretch out my travel? he barked down the line. My brother was
doing very well in his career, he reiterated, the gospel for the day.
And now, at the family reunion, an occasion for discussing penises
and careers, my brother parades his new girlfriend (underdressed
in her designer outfit), proving once again that he is worthy of the
clan name. This must be what he means by a win-win situation,
jargon I hear him use quite often. He will complete his all-impor-
tant MBA next year.

'Did you see that dress, Emil?' asks Vanessa. 'Shocker. And
the metallic nail polish is just appalling, doesn't even match the
dress. Pretty sure my father was in awe. By the way, Cous, Maxine, my yoga instructor, needs a date on the twenty-eighth. Are
you free?'

'Nope, I'm going to a buck's night,' I lie.

'Bugger. Maybe I'll ask Miguelito to take her. Maxine definitely has a better fashion sense than this one.'

'I'm pretty sure I've seen Charmaine's face somewhere,
Vanessa.'

'A face and a dress like that belong up the Cross. Who's getting married, anyway? Oh shit, here come Nan and the ladies.
Charmaine, Charmaine …' She leaves the table. A woman of contradictions!

Grandma's chihuahua greets me first, circling and licking,
wanting to be picked up. I nudge it with my foot. I'm a cat person.
Nan grimaces. My grandmother's excessive affection for her dog
could be compared to her sons' extreme regard for their dicks.
Nan Diling, the great Doña Delilah to generations of corn-
harvesters in the old country, Lilah to her Eastern Suburbs and
North Shore friends, has names for the little bitch: Henri, short

for Henrietta, or sometimes Little Treasure; or, when she's drunk, *Putang aso* – the translation is close to the 'c' word.

'And this is Enrico's son Emilio. *Hijo*, you've met Mrs Cutler and Lady Bray, haven't you?'

'Of course, Nan.' I stand and shake their hands. Their aroma, a mixture of antiseptic and old perfume, makes me think of ancient film sirens.

'You have your father's handsome smile, Emilio,' compliments Mrs Cutler, whose hip-replacement surgery was all over the social pages a couple of months ago. It almost got more column inches than the privatisation of Telstra.

'He is a scholar at the university,' my grandma brags through her permanent smile, a result of lip surgery. Every time she introduces me to people she emphasises the word *scholar*, the way Chris stresses *'my'* in *'my* Pipo.' Being a scholar I guess is what makes me worthy of the Gonzales name. 'Emil's going to be a writer and help me with my biography.'

'That's wonderful, Lilah,' says Lady Bray, whose philanthropy probably makes her worthier of a biography. 'Your eyes twinkle like your father's, young man.'

'Thanks, Lady Bray,' I chuckle self-consciously. *This pair must have the hots for Dad. I wonder if knowing that would get his Junior excited.*

'Hu-llo, Grandma,' my brother embraces Grandma from behind, then kisses her on the cheek.

'Oh stop it, Miguelito, you're tickling me,' Lilah laughs like a giggly schoolgirl. 'Ladies, you remember Miguelito, don't you? Faye, he made your assistant cry once when he lifted her skirt, remember?'

'Oh yes, the naughty child!' Lady Bray is all smiles. Miguelito gives both women a European kiss – the old biddies offering both cheeks indulgently to the football hero. 'And who is this beautiful young lady?' Charmaine smiles and tosses her hair seductively, a familiar gesture. Now I know where I've seen her face. A shampoo commercial.

My brother introduces his girlfriend. In Miguel's presence, I become as invisible as an unlighted post on a freeway; even with my father's 'twinkling eyes,' I can't compete with my brother's oily charm. I make my way through the lounge room as the ladies hang off Miguelito's update on the redecoration of his Rushcutters Bay penthouse.

The lounge room is full of familiar faces – relatives who are dressed to kill, my cousin's mates from Cranbrook (Double Bay wankers), Lady Bray's entourage, Father Charlie and some of the local nuns, and Mrs Cummings from next door, already drunk, staring blankly at the unlit fireplace. Little cousins are running around everywhere. Someone cries. Henri chases one of the nuns. An occasional 'Hello' interrupts my progress to the Red Room.

As I pour whisky at the bar, I spot the Virgin Mary in the corner. I have never understood this Filipino thing for altars and life-sized statues of saints. The richer they are the bigger the statues in their homes. My father was opposed to paying costly freight to bring the Virgin from overseas. Upon hearing this, Grandma signed a blank cheque to cover the transport costs and had her solicitor personally deliver it to my father's office. Lilah didn't speak to him until the statue was delivered and installed. Now the Virgin stands, largely ignored, between Grandma's portrait and the white baby grand, a mute eavesdropper on the Gonzales men's annual penis conversation.

The whisky tastes good after all that oily food. I pour another as I stare at Grandma's portrait by a famous Filipino artist with whom she had a torrid affair. She looks regal in her nineteenth-century Spanish-style gown; her eyes sparkle as brightly as her gems, her head tilts slightly to the right like Ava Gardner in a movie pose. She smiles radiantly, the high-profile widow of a political crony of the former dictator. A renowned concert pianist, Grandma was a society matron in the old country, friends with the flamboyant former First Lady. Her affair with the artist, who was young enough to be her son, had scandalised the strongly Catholic nation. In that and the subsequent rumoured affairs, Doña Delilah Gonzales easily matched her philandering late husband, who had fathered children the length and breadth of the country. Her sons Enrico, Christopher and Terence Gonzales at this very moment are discussing their penises and their own philandering. They have always excluded me from their conversation because I have yet to demonstrate any prowess with either dick or dollars.

I gulp down my drink. Guess I have to be controversial, too. I'm a Gonzales, after all. I reach for the mobile in my pocket and dial Craig's number. He's on his way here now but I'll tell him not to come. Not today. He'll be pissed off, I'm sure. I'll just tease him about his *Craigee*. Then, I hope, everything will be fine.

My First Kiss

Lian Low

Kuala Lumpur, Malaysia, 1991. When I was growing up, I never saw people share mouth-to-mouth kisses. Malaysia's censorship laws snipped out tongue kisses, homosexuals, anti-government sentiment and anything else it deemed offensive. There were no explicit laws against non-Muslim Malaysians kissing and hugging romantically in public, but local by-laws forbidding 'indecent behaviour' could be interpreted to include public displays of affection. For queers the repercussions were even worse: homosexuality is still a criminal offence in Malaysia.

Maybe it's every other little girl's dream to grow up and have breasts so that they can fill out their frocks. Not me. I envied my father's flat chest and how he could go topless without being self-conscious. Becoming more 'womanly,' I suddenly lost footing in my tomboy world. The dynamics of my friendships with my male playmates changed. I retreated into my own private attic, literally and symbolically; this space existed at the top of my house, away from everyone else. In the first two years of high school, I would spend most of my lunchtime in the library, nose in a book, away from the chatter and gossip in the canteen. I was the quiet type who was part of the school chess team, who read *The Hobbit* and *The Lord of the Rings* trilogy all in one go. I didn't contribute to the 'Oh, he's sooo hot!' conversations about New Kids on the Block, Jason Priestley and Luke Perry. Instead, I fancied Mary Stuart Masterson and fantasised about flying like Superman so that I could whisk away the popular girl I had a crush on.

We moved to Australia the year I turned fourteen. On my first day at my Australian high school, the only students who approached me were the other overseas-born Asians. One was a Hong Kong Chinese and the other was Vietnamese. None of the white kids really took an interest in me. I had been placed in the English as a Second Language (ESL) class, based on the fact that I'd just arrived in Melbourne. This despite the fact that I'd spoken English all my life and had always done well in English at school. In Malaysia, for two years I had attended a private school at which English was the main written and spoken language. Although there were good things about ESL – the classes were small and I made some good friends – I resented being in a class where I wasn't challenged.

I only started to make friends with the non-Asian kids later, after I enrolled in Year 11 literature class. I was the only Asian and the only ESL student in the class; one of the highlights of high school for me was walking up to the stage at the end-of-year ceremony to accept the joint award for the highest marks in Year 12 literature.

Throughout this time, despite my little friendship posse, I still could not shake my shyness. Although English was the language I spoke in, dreamt in and created my reality in, I felt a foreigner whenever I opened my mouth. Whenever I spoke, my accent betrayed my origins. It was a mix of a Malaysian-lilt, Manglish, TV-influenced Americanisms, the Queen's English and Australian. Most times the Malaysian-lilt was dominant; the Manglish somehow faded away without my notice. I never said 'mate' or 'how ya going?' or 'g'day' in a 'Strine' enough way. I always spoke diffidently. And when I did speak, a barrage of questions would follow: 'Where are you from?' and 'How long have you been here?' My attempts to blend in failed as soon as I opened my mouth.

Like most teenage girls, I had long hair, pimples and too many crushes. Unlike any other girl I knew, my secret crushes were on Linda Hamilton from the *Terminator* series and Amanda Keller from the Australian science show *Beyond 2000*. I had no one to share these feelings with, and my journal became my best friend:

I once met a beautiful girl in a camera shop: I wanted to drown in her almond brown eyes. I couldn't listen as she explained the technicalities of the camera to me. She went on about f-stops, shutter speeds and depths of focus – while I got very unfocused. All I saw were her animated hands, her beautiful slender fingers, the way her mouth moved. Inside I was aching.

I couldn't imagine feeling this way for a man. It just didn't feel natural. Everyone wants romance in their life, but it's always the same boring guy-meets-girl Hollywood love formula. I wondered where my story was in these narratives? Where was my fairytale ending? 'Oh dear Lord Buddha,' I prayed, 'where can I go to find answers?'

When I told another girl how much I loved kd lang, she asked, 'You're not the L-word, are you?' Of course I denied it. I guessed my Malaysian badminton buddies wouldn't take so well to it either, or my Malaysian Christian friends.

When I was sixteen, my brother's friend Ken, from the chess club we both belonged to, teased, 'Sweet sixteen and never been kissed.' Ken was the stereotypical nerd – thick eye-glasses and greasy hair, which was thinning on the crown of his head. Being a bit of a nerd myself, finding a fellow nerd could be quite charming. Unfortunately, Ken was boring. And he wasn't such a crash-hot chess player. Ken took my brother and me out to the Astor Theatre once, and then asked if he could give me a kiss on the cheek when he dropped us home. I said yes, but that was the last time I went out with Ken.

Four years later, at university, I orchestrated my first real kiss. I had a short-film project to do and I wanted to have a kissing scene in it. My short film was to be set in the cavernous toilets in the basement of the Menzies building at Monash University. My star was a tall, skinny, gorgeous woman; I used to spy on her sitting in the front row of the Melbourne Cinematheque. By fate, she was also a Monash student, and we had met through a coalescence of coincidences – the Women's Room, the student newspaper and student theatre. Sitting ourselves by the staircase outside the toilets just before the shoot, I confessed to her, 'I've never kissed anyone before.' She didn't blink. 'Really?' was all she said. And then we kissed. I closed my eyes, bent towards her and felt her lips on my mouth. When I started to rush the kiss, she said, 'Slow down' and guided me. Her lips left a waxy taste in my mouth. Coming out of the kiss, I was spinning, and the lenses of my eye-glasses had oil-skin smudges on them. We rehearsed kissing a number of times before the actual take. It was bliss.

Creativity and my personal growth have gone hand in hand. Thanks to my writing and performing, the big private turning points in my life have become very memorable public events. The year before my first kiss, I came out to my parents, my uncle, my grandmother, my brother and a packed theatre. I was the Under-25 winner of a prestigious inaugural short-play competition.

The afternoon of the performance I was a mix of nerves and worries. What would my family think? What would the audience think? My parents had some idea what the monologue was about and my brother had been taping kd lang videos for me. All my uncle and grandmother knew was that I had won a playwriting competition. I sank low in my seat as an actor began to perform my monologue:

> *I dreamed of kd lang and her girlfriend in a dark place underneath a big busty table, but I don't know what they're doing down there. Dear Lord Buddha, what does the dream mean?...*

After the performance, my brother exclaimed, 'That was so funny! Mum was gripping my arm so hard.' My mother smiled tightly, but then beamed and told me she was very proud. My father rolled his eyes and asked, 'Why so vulgar?' but I knew he too was proud of me. My uncle and grandmother congratulated me, and so did so many other people. The day had ended well.

Writing and performance have been outlets. They have let me be myself, express myself and explore my multiple identities: Asian, woman, queer, migrant, Chinese-Malaysian-Australian. And within the framework of performances, sides of me that were suppressed or ridiculed throughout my school years have been accepted and applauded.

A Big Life

Jenny Kee

Nineteen-fifty-eight was my last year at Bondi Beach Public. I was a champion runner and captain of the school captain-ball team that year. On my final day in primary school my teacher said to Mum, 'Mrs Kee, Jenny's such a good little girl – but watch her.' I think she'd had a premonition that the devil in me would emerge.

Mum tried to convince me to go to Sydney Church of England Girls' Grammar School because the local high school, Dover Heights, was a huge concrete jungle and she thought it was rough. That made it all the more attractive as far as I was concerned. I also didn't want to be separated from my friends.

I didn't go to school to learn. It was where I met my friends. It was where I continued my popularity project. Even as a self-conscious teenager with Clearasil and pancake make-up concealing my pimples, I concentrated on the survival strategy. But gradually my technique changed. In Forms One and Two I still had a bit of the princess about me, but by Form Three I'd become a full-blown rebel. My greatest strengths were art, jazz ballet and athletics – I loved to move my body. In Form Two I came second in art, but in Form Three Mum insisted I do maths instead of art, and that was the beginning of the end for me educationally.

Once art, my only creative outlet at school, was closed to me, I rebelled. At twelve or thirteen I was secretly reading *Peyton Place*, which I'd found hidden in Dad's wardrobe. Sexuality became my chosen form of expression in the years that followed. I became sex-obsessed. I had recurring dreams of being a slave girl, imprisoned in a cage in ancient, torch-lit catacombs, doing the Dance of the Seven Veils while surrounded by hordes of Victor Mature types clawing at the bars. They could look but not touch.

I discovered that boys liked me, and that entirely changed my self-image. Right up until I turned thirteen I'd wanted to be Jennifer Ackroyd. Then came spin the bottle and the teen pashing parties. I knew instinctively what to do and the boys responded. It was a revelation. For the first time in my life I began to feel comfortable about my Chinese appearance. Indeed, I was coming to see being Asian as an asset. Boys, I learnt, found 'exotic' girls 'sexy.'

Suddenly I had the confidence to cope with troublesome teachers, bullies, racists. Going up to Bondi Junction I'd always been conscious of being part of a minority. I'd always looked over my shoulder, prepared for a racist taunt. Now I was ready to hurl a jibe back, or a punch. If anyone tried to mess with me they'd get a rock in their face. Along with my father's will, I'd inherited his temper. My attitude was: I'll show you – I'm going to go out and get it all. I wasn't going to be like most of my Chinese family: sedate, pious, conservative. I was going to break free, and I wasn't going to do it by halves. Nothing, ever, by halves.

The first boys I hung out with were the Jewish ones at Bondi. I'd sit with them on the steps below the Bondi Pavilion in the middle of the beach. My close neighbourhood friend Margaret Peard and the surfies hung out at south Bondi, by the baths. That was too blond for me. I went to surf-club dances but I felt like a bit of an outsider there. They played early surfer music such as the Ventures and the Beach Boys, and some of the crowd were already dropping tabs of acid, which came via the Californian surfing circuit. I preferred the Jewish kids, and the Hungarians, because they had rich cultures and traditions.

I wore a tiny leopard-skin one-piece cossie, which came up to my collarbone at the front but had a low back. As soon as I got to the beach I put the make-up on: foundation to conceal the pimples, thick black Cleopatra eyeliner and pink lipstick. Mum came down to the beach one day and freaked out when she saw me. In front of everyone she shouted, 'Get into the change-room and take that make-up off this instant!' I was so humiliated I ran home.

In the afternoons we'd hang out in the small pavilions on the grass above the beach. Bobby Steinberg (my first kiss) and his friends played cards there. The Jewish boys had dark, greasy rocker haircuts and stovepipe jeans like the Jets in *West Side Story*. They had a rocker manner about them as well. Robert Symonds was my favourite. We pashed on the cliffs at Dover Heights and I would have gone all the way with him but he was too scared. The boys I knew were big on kissing but not much else, including dating. They'd pash the night away on the sand, then the next day walk right past without a second glance, which felt awful. When I got moody and depressed about it I'd walk along the water's edge at Rose Bay with my trannie, listening to the Drifters' 'Save the Last Dance for Me' or the Shirelles' 'Will You Still Love Me Tomorrow?'.

After the beach we'd move on to the home of anyone whose parents weren't there and throw parties. There were steamy afternoons in Bondi flats with Del Shannon's 'Runaway,' Chubby Checker's 'The Hucklebuck' and 'Let's Twist Again,' and Wanda Jackson's 'Let's Have a Party' on the turntables. I was the best dancer and I knew it. I had the body beat and animal magnetism to match. Even King Kong, Taronga's newly acquired gorilla, felt it. On a school excursion he went absolutely ape for me – throwing grass in the air, beating his chest at me and showing off. He didn't do it for any of the other girls, much to everyone's amusement.

*

November 1962 was the Form Four formal. My dress was made by Ariane of Double Bay in white organza with huge mauve-pink cabbage roses. It had a tight bodice, a bell-shaped skirt and a scooped, shoulder-skimming Audrey Hepburn neckline. I wore matching fabric stiletto slingbacks and my hair was teased into a bouffant by John from Carita's (Carita's of Edgecliff was *the* place to have your hair done). I was a Chinese Annette Funicello.

I'd been nagging Mum for a year to let me leave school. I was determined to study dress design at East Sydney Technical College. Mum wouldn't hear a word of it until I deliberately failed my fourth-year exams, scoring 11 out of 100 in biology. She realised then that I was as willful as her and my father put together, and relented. I twisted the night away at the formal, ecstatic that I was never coming back.

This is an edited extract from *A Big Life* by Jenny Kee (Penguin Books, 2006).

UnAustralian?

Be Good, Little Migrants

Be good, little migrants
We've saved you from starvation
war, landlessness, oppression
Just display your gratitude
but don't be heard, don't be seen

Be good, little migrants
Give us your faithful service
sweep factories, clean mansions
prepare cheap exotic food
pay taxes, feed the mainstream

Be good, little migrants
Use leisure with prudence
sew costumes, paint murals
write music, and dance to our tune
Our culture must not be dull

Be good, little migrants
We've given you opportunity
for family reunion
equality, and status, though
your colour could be wrong

Be good, little migrants
Learn English to distinguish
ESL from RSL
avoid unions, and teach children
respect for institutions

Be good, little migrants
You may fight one another, but
attend Sunday School, learn manners
keep violence within your culture
save industry from criminals

Be good, little migrants
Intelligence means obedience
just follow ASIO, CIA
spy on your fellow countrymen
hunt commies for Americans

Be good, little migrants
Museums are built for your low arts
for your multiculturalism
in time, you'll reach excellence
Just waste a few generations.

—UYEN LOEWALD

How to Be Japanese

Leanne Hall

The view from the car park is amazing. Once you're past the rag-gedy asphalt and the clumps of dry grass, the vista explodes into layers of white and blue. A long arc of powdery white sand extends to the left and right, further than my eyes can reach; beyond that is the kind of deep blue sea that creates instant contemplation. The sun burns so brightly overhead we all have our hands perma-nently shielding our eyes.

But we're not looking at the blinding sand or the sparkling water or the far-off horizon; we're looking at Emma's breasts. She's wearing a hot-pink bikini and the effect, to say the least, is impressive.

The stylist is the first to speak.

'Wow. An Asian with boobs.'

'It's a miracle.' The make-up artist reverently sponges bronzer across Emma's cleavage.

'I'm half-Aussie,' says Emma. 'It doesn't really count.' She smokes lazily while women cluck around her, pulling at threads, smoothing down stray hairs and wrangling her breasts.

Almost everyone on the shoot is Asian in some way. The styl-ist is half-Malaysian; the make-up artist, the woman organising the shoot and one of the models are Japanese. Emma and I are both half-Chinese and half-Australian, but to very different effect. Emma's Anglo blood has given her boobs, while I have inherited my Australian father's beanpole gene. My bikini top is crammed so full of rubbery 'chicken fillets' I'd probably bounce if you threw me.

These Clayton's breasts jiggle realistically when I jump up and down on the spot. It's a strange but pleasant feeling having weight up top; I'm not sure I'll be able to hand the fillets back at the end of the day. I've always derided other women for wearing push-up bras and padding; now I'm feeling temptation pull at me like a rip.

The shoot is for a famous Japanese beer brand that wants to

make a greater impact in the Australian market. The idea of the campaign is to mimic the Japanese 'image girl' look. The image girl is kind of like the Japanese version of the Big M girl of the seventies and eighties, with the difference that she is created to be infinitely more innocent than her antipodean counterpart. It's a big deal in Japan to be picked as the image girl for a well-known brand and it is often the launching pad for an acting or singing career.

The photographer shows us examples of Japanese advertisements that he's using as reference shots. The ads walk the thin line between virginal and sexy. The girls are young, their smiles are coy and the fashion is a few years out of date. The models look as if they've never held a beer in their lives, let alone drunk one. The Japanese are deadly serious but we are aiming for coolly ironic and kitsch. It's difficult to judge whether what we're doing is homage or just making fun of a different cultural aesthetic.

When it's time to shoot I camp it up, making my eyes and teeth sparkle with fake delight. I wear an outmoded bikini and hold a glass of warm beer in one hand. I can't drink the beer because alcohol makes my cheeks flush bright red, and I'm not allowed to take a dip in the sea because my make-up will wash off. I've never felt more decorative in my life. An assistant follows me around with a large golden reflector, making sure the sunlight is always pinging off my face. I yell out nonsensical Japanese phrases and aim for an ultra-*kawaii* look.

Although I never anticipated this when I accepted the job, the photo shoot turns into an exorcism. I get to act out my worst nightmare: the cutesy, Hello Kitty-loving Asian manga-girl people sometimes mistake me to be, before I open my mouth and they hear my unmistakably Australian voice. It's surprisingly cathartic to let myself become the enemy, the stereotype I have always tried to avoid. The pleasure I get from this is unexpected and slightly puzzling. There's something seductive in acting out a stereotype; life would be simpler if I only had to exist in one dimension.

*

When I look at the finished advertisement I don't recognise myself nestled amid the beer logos and Japanese text. I smile toothlessly as I recline on the sand, toasting an unseen person, tossing my manufactured beach-hair off my face. I look blandly sexy and completely unlike myself. The photographer has altered my already-augmented breasts even further with Photoshop, inflating them to incredible proportions. If I were built like that in the flesh, I would have been face down in the pristine white sand, unable to get up.

I get a text message from a male friend who spots the ad on the back of a magazine: *Congratulations on setting feminism back seventy years*. And then five minutes later my phone beeps again, the same friend: *You look hot*. I try not to think about these two competing concepts. Instead I think of how the money I was paid will finally get me out of the debt I racked up on an overseas holiday.

My two best friends kindly wallpaper my house with the ad, posting the torn magazine covers in the most unlikely places. Months later I am still finding them in my sock drawer, in the freezer and behind the washing machine. The longer I look at the photo, the less able I am to see myself accurately. Is that me? Do I really look like that?

The worst encounter with myself comes when I invite a man back to my house for a late-night cup of tea. This is the first time he's been in my house and we're both a little nervous. While I set out mugs and wait for the kettle to boil he idly prowls the kitchen, looking at the family photos blu-tacked to the fridge and the under-utilised cookbooks crammed onto our shelves. When, for some unfathomable reason, he springs open the door to the microwave, I am laying in wait inside, with a smile on my face and a beer in my hand. *Cheers. Bit hot in here, isn't it?*

Three weeks later the boy dumps me for a Japanese saxophonist who can't speak a word of English. I think of all the wasted conversations I had with him; I feel so spurned I wish I could take all my words back and use them on someone else.

*

I wonder what my late Chinese grandfather would have thought of his granddaughter pimping Japanese beer. It's fair to say Grandpa did not like the Japanese. He was born too late for political correctness and had no interest in softening his opinions for public consumption.

Every year his grandchildren brought their school report cards to Christmas lunch for Grandpa to read. He would gradually leaf through the stack in the sleepy lull between turkey and pudding, while my sisters, my cousins and I hovered around like mozzies, waiting for his words of approval.

Every year that I studied Japanese at high school, from Year 9 onwards, my mum would remove the slip of paper showing my Japanese grades before giving my report card to my grandpa.

'It's easier this way,' she said.

And it probably was. The behaviour of the Japanese while occupying China featured heavily in the informal history lessons Grandpa delivered from his favourite armchair after Sunday lunches. He would start calmly enough, leaning forward sagely as he plodded through dates and places, in every way the wise and benevolent grandfather. But his oratory quickly gathered force and speed and spittle; whoever sat closest to him would get sucked in like an unwilling game-show contestant pulled from a studio audience. Grandpa would stab his finger in the air, spit out his words and eventually work himself into such a state that he was unable to speak anymore.

The lectures were largely incomprehensible; I managed to grasp only key words: *Manchuria, Kuomintang, Chang Kai-Shek, Nanking.* I would try to pay attention but invariably wound up straightening the laces in my sneakers, pulling at split ends and rolling my eyes in despair. I was always impatient for dessert, which might be angel's food cake or sweet red-bean buns, or rainbow jelly and ice-cream.

I couldn't understand Grandpa's anger, and his mania made me uncomfortable. War was something that happened a long way away, to other people, a long time ago. So far I had led a happy and sheltered life, and I had no experiences that came close to helping me understand the killing and treachery he described.

It was only later, after Grandpa passed away, when I began to read about Chinese history, that I began to appreciate what it was that he had been trying to communicate. I understood finally that he didn't want the world to forget, but I could also see that remembering too much made it difficult for Grandpa to forgive.

Through my reading I also realised that Grandpa had long left China for Australia when most of these events happened. His passion had been so great, and my grasp of history so poor, that I always assumed that he had actually been there. But Grandpa came to Australia in 1920, when he was just ten years old, before the Japanese occupation of Manchuria. He was so young when he emigrated that he spoke with a broad Australian accent. His assimilation into Australian life was so complete that neither my mother nor any of her four siblings can speak a word of Cantonese.

In Grandpa's later years he wore an Australian flag pinned to his jacket lapel every day. I don't know what had happened to him in Australia that he felt he had to display his allegiance so prominently. I don't know how this allegiance to his adopted country fitted with the strong connection he obviously still felt to his homeland.

Grandpa underwent a strange transformation as he went through his eighties; he began to look less and less Chinese. His hair grew pure white like all the Anglo men his age, and cataracts gradually turned his eyes milky blue.

*

I often wonder in what ways life would be different if I looked less Chinese. I am the youngest of three daughters and the most Chinese-looking. Both of my older sisters have the same dark hair and eyes, but the overall effect in them is diluted and racially ambiguous. From a very young age I was used to people not realising that the white man next to me was my dad. In shops we would get treated as if we were there separately. Now that I'm older, if just the two of us go out to dinner together, I can see the other diners looking at me as if I've landed myself another sort of daddy, the sugary kind.

I once told a Chinese high-school friend that I really wasn't *that Chinese*. 'You're probably more Chinese than you think,' she replied. I agreed with her to be polite, but I wasn't convinced. Even you've been fooled by my exterior, I thought. If I was Chinese I would feel it inside – and I don't. When I racked my brains for all the Chinese things in my life, the list I came up with was far from convincing: red packets at Chinese New Year, stir-fry for dinner, a wooden chest full of my grandmother's old cheongsams.

*

The band room is crowded and dark, lit fleetingly by dim blue and red lights sweeping across our heads. I'm here with a work friend, Naz, to see an obscure Japanese avant-garde psychedelic-rock band we read about in the street press. Naz is Singaporean so I know she'll laugh when I describe the crowd as being mostly 'graphic designers with yellow fever.' There's a large Japanese contingent here as well, pressed to the front of the room, against the stage. They're the real fans, as opposed to the culturally curious; they own the albums and know all the words to the songs.

I get the feeling the rest of us are here purely on the hunch that if it's Japanese and rock, it must be cool. It was a relief when all things Asian became trendy sometime during the '90s while I was at university. We had been unfashionable for so long. In high school the coveted look was icy blonde, the clothes were from Country Road and Esprit; everyone was trying to look like they rode ponies and skied. When mainstream Australian culture decided to champion anime and sushi, when every T-shirt had to feature Chinese characters, I couldn't help but gloat: our time had come. I was willing to forgive the murky catch-all 'Asian' branding just to finally be cool.

The crowd waits restlessly for the band to come on. Smoking bans have only recently come into place in Melbourne venues and I'm not sure people know what to do anymore with their hands when they're at the pub, or how to have conversations without cigarettes to punctuate them. We sip our beers and Naz tells me battle stories from her former days as a teenage groupie in Singapore.

After a few minutes I notice three guys huddled to our right, conferring quietly and moving closer to us, like they're playing a primary-school game of statues. They whisper frantically amongst themselves, then turn to stone when I look directly at them. The tallest guy, in a red T-shirt, appears to be receiving a pre-match motivational speech from his friends.

Don't do it.

He does.

Red T-shirt breaks away from his pack and marches up to us with purpose. I feel the sense of doom that comes with already knowing what he's going to say. It's like watching someone trip over their own feet in slow motion.

'Are you Japanese?' he asks me politely. 'My friends and I have been having an argument about it.'

He is earnest, smiling and looking me in the eye, genuinely seeking guidance.

'No, I'm not,' I reply, slowly and carefully. 'The Japanese girls are shorter and better dressed than me.'

Red T-shirt nods quite seriously, making a mental note of my valuable insider information. He still looks baffled. 'We just can't tell which ones are the Japanese chicks.'

There are other things I want to say on this subject, but I don't. I'm still not over the saxophonist incident and I'm brimming with prejudices of my own. I turn my back on Red T-shirt. Naz looks like she might want to punch him; I just roll my eyes. It's a relief when the band finally walks on stage.

*

If I sound bitter or paranoid, then it's because I am. I've heard most of it before, in venues across Melbourne, from men in varying states of drunkenness.

'I love Asian women.'

'You're really exotic.'

'Are you on the Malaysian swimming team?'

'Where are you from?'

I live in perpetual fear that I'll get caught out by a serial Asian fetishist. I snoop through photo albums to find out if lovers have dated many Asian women before me.

I don't know why I expect others to immediately understand who I am from my appearance, when I have never been able to draw the connection myself. I'm like a perpetual toddler batting away at my reflection in the mirror, unable to comprehend that what I see is myself. I have little hope of understanding who I am by looking at photos of myself as a Japanese pin-up.

*

A very odd thing happened to me when I visited China for the first time: I felt at home. It wasn't a homecoming of the soaring-violin-soundtrack sort, but a sense of quiet comfort that I felt as I walked the streets of Shanghai and Beijing. I don't speak a word of Chinese, but everywhere I went I could make myself understood. After months of travelling on my own in India it was a relief at least to look the same as the throngs of people around me.

It was a surprise and a contradiction. To feel at home in a place because of my appearance, without being able to feel the connection between the person I am and the way I look. It was the strangest thing.

Silence

Tony Ayres

Robert and I had an hour before the film started to find something to eat. Our favourite Italian restaurant was packed, so we drifted with the sidewalk crowd down Russell Street, past buzzing games arcades and hooded-eyed junkies. Across the road, teenagers were queuing for Billboard, where some band I'd never heard of was playing. A huge fluctuating insignia cast neon blues and reds onto shiny faces.

We passed a little Chinese café where a few people sat mournfully over bowls of steaming noodles. My first ten years in Australia were spent in the backs of places like this, and a rush of sentimentality prompted me to stop.

'Let's eat here.'

Robert looked dubiously at the filthy laminex tables, the plastic Hong Kong lanterns, the window display of headless and roasted red ducks hung on coat-hanger wire. How many times in the many years we'd been together had I insisted on eating at places like this, hoping to rediscover some elusive memory of childhood? How many times had he good-naturedly conceded, preferring the threat of salmonella to my ill-tempered pout?

A girl led us to a window seat, tucking a stray edge of lanky black hair behind her ear, her teenage face shiny with perspiration. She placed two plastic-coated tomes on the crimson laminex. I was dismayed by the size of the menu. From previous experience I knew that too much choice was not a promising sign.

The girl set a teapot, two small teacups, two bowls and two sets of chopsticks before us.

'We'd like to order. Something fast, we're going to the movies,' I said in precise Australian-accented English. I always made a point of speaking first in Chinese restaurants, to avoid the embarrassment of having to explain that I didn't speak Chinese.

'All fast.'

I nodded. Another bad omen. I glanced at Robert, already apologetic. Was it too late to go to McDonalds?

We ordered roast pork, roast duck and Chinese broccoli, which is about as imaginative as asking for spaghetti bolognaise at an Italian restaurant. But after a lifetime of reckless gambling on ducks' tongues, pigs' ears and every variation of offal imaginable in the mistaken belief that it was my cultural heritage, I had finally learned some circumspection. At least on the first outing.

The waitress scribbled in her notebook without glancing at either of us, then hurried back to the kitchen, where she barked out our order in high-pitched and dissonant Cantonese. Someone in the kitchen answered back, and said something that made her laugh. For a moment, her face became animated, and I realised that she was really quite pretty.

Adjacent to us were three young Chinese men speaking in staccato Cantonese. They were in their early twenties, and each bore some mark of imperfection. One had big buckteeth. Another had raging acne scars, which he tried to cover with wisps of half-formed beard. The third was plump, with an auburn-coloured perm. They wore a mismatch of loud designer rip-offs with labels such as Versace and Dolce and Gabbana prominently featured. My guess was that these were restaurant boys, probably from Hong Kong, possibly illegal. They worked slavish hours cleaning dishes and chopping vegetables in Chinese restaurant kitchens, or hauled crates at 5 a.m. at the Victoria or Footscray markets. In their spare time, I imagined, they learnt martial arts, drove hire-purchased cars, drank cheap brandy and gambled at the casino, desperate to grasp some vestige of their own potency, to feel, through the drudgery of spattering oil and endless labour, the shiny promise of their youth.

One of them, the bucktoothed one, caught me looking and I turned away, embarrassed, wondering what he saw in return.

Meanwhile, Robert was watching the gathering crowd outside Billboard. He glanced at me, and indicated with his eyes to two handsome skinhead boys sauntering along our side of the street.

I watched them swagger past the restaurant, with their matching crew cuts, bovver boots, tight jeans, braces and tattoos glowing on oily forearms, arrogant and charismatic in a loin-stirring way.

'Very cute. I think we've got their movie,' I laughed, referring to a recent porno we were both particularly enamoured with.

I turned for one final ogle, only to see the taller, more muscular one staring at me angrily. A thick gob of mucous landed with a smack and oozed down the front of the restaurant window.

'Fucking poofter!' he yelled, leering into the glass. I blew him a kiss and immediately regretted it. It was the kind of thing I used to do when I was younger, mistaking it for some kind of gay activism.

The skinhead's face turned a low, angry mauve colour as he swung open the restaurant door, letting in a rude blast of summer-night heat. His equally indignant but somewhat mystified companion stomped in behind. Before he could reach our table, though, he was intercepted by the waitress.

'You want table?'

'I want to talk to that *poof* over there!' he said loudly, pointing to me.

Robert, who had not seen the kiss, was ready to spring to my defence, but I grabbed his wrist protectively. His smaller, office-bound frame didn't stand much chance against the two skinhead thugs, whose physical charms were diminishing by the moment.

'If you don't want a table, you have to go,' the waitress said defiantly and calmly.

'Don't fucking order me, *slope*.' The tall skinhead loomed over her.

'If you don't want a table, you have to go.'

She repeated each word slowly, as if to a child, as the skinhead puffed out his chest inches from her face. Without flinching, she pointed to the door.

'Go!'

The commotion had attracted the attention of everyone in the restaurant, and some of the kitchen staff had come out to join her. Outnumbered, the skinheads backed down.

'Come on,' the taller one said, grabbing his mate awkwardly by the elbow.

With a parting stab of hatred, the skinhead glared at the waitress.

'Bitch!'

She stood her ground until they were out of sight. Then her shoulders sagged, she sighed into her chest and began to tremble. She turned towards our table. My attempt at a smile of solidarity was cut dead by her stare. I felt a flush of shame. For inciting the incident. For not standing up for myself. For letting a teenage girl defend me.

Without anyone's comfort she pulled herself up, straightened her spine stiffly and held her head erect. She saw the mess on the front window, angrily grabbed a handful of napkins and went outside. On the pavement, she wiped furiously at the spit, smearing it into a slimy film, then rubbing and rubbing until her intensity scorched the taint away. Watching her from across the road were a couple of bored, curious teenage punk girls.

'What happened?' Robert asked.

'I don't know,' I lied.

'Those idiots—' he said angrily, and was about to continue when I snapped.

'Don't go on.'

'What do you mean?' he asked, offended.

'Nothing happened. She handled them better than we could. Let's not *moralise*.'

The waitress returned with our meal and plonked it in front of us. We avoided looking at each other. Her tired eyes, her precocious maturity, the slump in her shoulders, gave her away as a first-born daughter. I tried to imagine her life – working at the restaurant at least twelve hours a day, six days a week, looking after her parents and younger siblings. Did she have a boyfriend?

Did she go to school?

Robert played with his food while I tentatively poked at the dry, inedible roast pork.

'Sorry I snapped at you. I was tense.'

'I wasn't moralising.'

'I know you weren't. I'm sorry.'

Robert ate his meal in the methodical, measured way that he did everything. Sipping our tea, we fell into silence. I guess Robert was thinking about all the things he had to do. The ironing he would do before bed. The phone calls he'd have to make first thing in the morning. I stared at my chopsticks, trying to remember when I first learned to use them. A long time ago, in a restaurant just like this.

'We should ask for the bill,' Robert said, looking down at his watch. I nodded in agreement, although I felt shy about facing the waitress again.

She came back to our table, took out her notepad and absently began to add numbers. I was trying to work out her age. I'm sure she couldn't have been more than twenty. As she waited for us to pay, her gaze drifted dreamily across the road to Billboard. The doors had opened, and a wave of youngsters surged into the venue, flushed with the possibilities of the night ahead. It occurred to me that our waitress must have to watch that door night after night.

She caught me looking at her, and this time it was her turn to be embarrassed, as if I had caught her out. I had an impulse to say something, to touch her, but realised how ridiculously inappropriate that would be.

'Thank you for before,' I said.

She didn't answer. I left her a ten-dollar tip, and spent the rest of that night feeling inexplicably melancholy.

Afterwards, I realised that what lay between the waitress and me was the silence that is the gap between two cultures. It is neither misunderstanding nor hostility, just the empty noise of two frequencies out of alignment. Perhaps it is possible to be attuned to both, but it was my fate to cross a threshold from one culture and class into another. Once that is done, there is no going back. That other world becomes a series of imaginary conjectures and 'what ifs,' a land you can only see if you close your eyes and squint.

Anzac Day

James Chong

'He [John Simpson Kirkpatrick, of Simpson and his donkey fame] represents everything at the heart of what it means to be Australian.' —Dr BRENDAN NELSON, then federal minister for education, August 2005

In high school I learned to play the bagpipes and went on to lead my band as the pipe-major. Every Anzac Day during high school I would march in the Sydney city street parade with my school's pipe band. It was always a big and proud day, with regiments of decorated veterans marching, some of whom had fought in the country where I was born. I was proud to be a part of this heritage and to pay respect to the soldiers who had served their country in the most difficult of circumstances. I felt at times, though, that because of my heritage and the colour of my skin, I was not allowed to be part of the Anzac tradition, which to many people defines what it is to be Australian. Maybe this was mostly adolescent angst. One year, however, I encountered it in a very public and unmistakeable way. In 1992, a friend of my father gave us a video tape of an episode of the ABC current affairs program *Lateline*. The episode had aired just after Anzac Day, and opened with footage of the Sydney march. The camera focused on a kilt-clad piper in full highland regimental dress before zooming in on his Asian face – mine! I was intrigued and excited to see myself on television. Then the theme of the show appeared, flashed across the screen in big letters:

TRUE BLUE?

I didn't watch the rest of the show. I was confused and a little hurt. I wasn't sure what it meant (maybe I should have watched it), but I remember a lonely feeling of exclusion.

Special Menu

APPETISERS
Eight cold cuts & assortment of pickled hurts
Crap sticks on a bed of lattice

MAIN COURSE
Twice-cooked bear paw braised in a cauldron of silence,
red hot to touch
Fish lips in soup of secrecy, gelatinous and tender to taste
Tongues sautéed in myths and stories, garnished with
little white lies
Bean curd stuffed with inaccuracies, served scalding in a
casserole pot

DESSERT
Dainty spoonfuls of rainbow jelly of hope curdling in a
swirl of gossip traps
Sliced jack and star fruits to cool heated foreheads and
temperamental palates

SPECIALS OF THE DAY
Wild hog knuckles red-cooked with hearts of spoiled
children, drizzled with blackbean sauce
Hundred-year-old hens drenched in brine of sages, chilled
and tossed with jellyfish

CHEF'S SERVING SUGGESTIONS

Insulted platters of cold cuts laid out on a bed of steel
Migrants steamed with a pinch of cultural enhancer
In a bamboo boat of hopefulness
Sailing towards candied shores
Mother tongues coated over with sesame-seed oil
Deep fried in batter, swimming in a sea of forgetfulness
Married to a marinade of otherness
Sticky in mouth with aftertaste of bitterness
Glutinous rice sticking to roof palates
Gluggy and hard to remove from between teeth
Proceed to pick away at teeth with toothpick with some
discretion.

—Mei Yen Chua

A Call to Arms

Michelle Law

'You shave your arms!'

'Sorry?'

It was a particularly humid late afternoon in sixth grade and I had been left for dead at school. Teachers, maintenance staff, even the sanitary-disposal van had left the grounds, leaving me in the company of a peer that I had spoken to only once throughout the entire year (and that was only to ask if she could please stop using my treasured connector pens). She was a prematurely developed, buxom girl who spoke in a deep, husky voice and had sun-bleached hair from over-tanning.

Let's just say she was the antithesis of me.

She repeated her revelation, this time with more gusto.

'You shave them! That's *so* gross ... I can't believe you'd do that!'

'I don't shave them!'

I tried to explain that I was just born that way, and that most Chinese girls don't have much hair on their arms, save for a fine fuzz. However, she had already lost herself in a state of cackling delirium – clearly overwhelmed by her own hilarity and the freakish nature of my body.

I crossed my arms in defiance, but after realising this would probably expose their hairlessness more, made to hide them under my Lion King swimming bag, which contained chlorine-soaked hand-me-down togs that literally hung off me if I didn't knot them up at the back. It had not been a good sports lesson; once again I was isolated in the sixth lane with a pair of flippers and a kick-board, while my friends mastered tumble-turns and learnt to open their eyes underwater. I watched them through my blurry, steamed-up, over-sized goggles, and saw their hair floating around them with an ethereal quality that mine, tightly contained in a cap full of baby powder, simply could not achieve. I had pleaded for hours with my mum about the cap, but she had remained adamant:

'When you put the powder in, it makes the cap come off so much easier! Like magic!' she explained.

'But it looks like dandruff ... or nits.'

'*Ai-ya*! You know what herbalists say. You'll get a headache with wet hair. Do you want to get sick from having a wet head all day?'

'If it's normal, yeah!'

'What is normal, eh?'

Normal was not my swimming cap. Normal was not my hairless arms, scoliosis, myopia, severe middle part, scrawny frame, inability to play sports, excellence in the string ensemble or childhood idolisation of Fa Mulan. Now that I thought about it, everything up to that point in my life seemed so incredibly abnormal compared to everyone else I knew.

At lunchtimes, my friends chose from a selection of neat and colourful packaged foods, an apple, or a vegemite sandwich cut into little soldiers. I had soymilk, cheong-fun and flavoured seaweed. Don't get me wrong, I loved my lunches; I just resented the reactions my so-called exotic foods provoked, such as: 'Yuck! What is that stuff?' and (this, to the seaweed) 'Are you eating a piece of burnt rubber?' While I loosened my wobbly teeth by gnawing on a preserved sea plant, my friends suctioned theirs off with Rollups and Spacebars.

For Christmas, my teachers would receive boxes of chocolates or bottles of champagne from my friends' parents. From mine they would receive a traditional Chinese teapot or (if they were lucky) an electronic coffee mug that sang 'Silent Night' on nonstop cycle and flashed tiny neon lights until the cup was entirely drained of liquid ... or, alternatively, until it was smashed against the wall. The teachers never seemed to care; in fact, they couldn't get enough of them. But I cared. How could anyone see something as tacky and useless as a carolling cup as quaint and adorable? Surely the novelty would have worn off by the time the flashing baubles began to induce epileptic fits.

The differences did not stop there. While my friends drank Coca-Cola at home, my siblings and I were provided with a suspicious black-coloured concoction my mum branded 'homemade coke.' We would guzzle these treats down happily and never once questioned what exactly the ingredients were. It was not until my mid-teens that I discovered homemade coke was an infusion of various toxic-looking herbs packed with a ton of brown sugar. I felt gypped by years of lost obesity-inducing and teeth-rotting sugar trips; the fact that the herb drink was absolutely delicious was beside the point. My siblings and I seemed to be working alone together, teetering between our Chinese heritage and our incredibly Australian upbringing. I had never felt alienated by Australian culture, but I was certainly aware of not fitting in.

These cultural differences were only reinforced by a trip made to Hong Kong some years later. I had been to Hong Kong once when I was four, but nothing could have prepared me for the cultural revelation I was about to experience. It was as if I had stumbled into a kind of extended Chinatown. Everyone behaved the way my family and I did (washing cups, plates and chopsticks with boiling tea at yum cha, and, like my father, spitting phlegm balls and shooting hardened snot into gutters and rubbish bins), meaning these actions no longer incited automatic embarrassment. Instead, I felt something I had never experienced before, and something I had certainly never consciously been seeking: acceptance. I could completely lose myself in a giant swarm of people; the anonymity, which was something I had never dreamed I might value, made me feel euphoric. The 'stand out from the crowd' mentality had hitherto been deeply ingrained in my mind, but for the first time I was happy just to disappear ... to be invisible. However, it was purely physical appearance that allowed this; my Western side still exposed itself in the most mortifying forms possible.

Let it be known that I am terrible at Cantonese. I can understand it for the most part when spoken to; it's just the responding aspect I'm particularly shocking at. Considering I once asked my grandmother for a glass of spicy water (how was I to know that in Cantonese there are two words for 'hot'?), it came as no surprise that when I tried to order at a McDonalds in Hong Kong, things were destined to end horribly. I asked the person serving me if I could please have an ice-cream and something unexpected happened: she asked me something back. I was not anticipating this and began to panic.

'No, just an ice-cream please,' I reiterated.

She repeated her question ('Cone or cup?'), this time visibly confused.

Thank god my mother intervened.

'She wants a cone, thanks,' she answered for me.

I wondered if my mum was embarrassed by me like I had so often been by her. In Hong Kong she was in her element and for once I was able to see things from a less self-centered perspective. The locals could probably smell my foreignness and in some bizarre, ironic twist I began to feel self-conscious about being Australian. I felt ashamed that I did not know more about my heritage, and even more ashamed at being embarrassed of my Australian upbringing, something that has significantly shaped my identity. I began wondering what life would have been like if I had been raised in a place like Hong Kong. Perhaps my natural talents would have flowered and rendered me popular among my peers, rather than securing my reputation as one of the token Asian girls in the class, interested in reading club and drama.

To this day I am to some extent confused … am I more Asian or Australian? I am still taken aback when addressed by an Asian-Australian who speaks and acts like me. Following these types of encounters is a mixed sense of shame (at having been surprised) and curiosity (about whether they felt the same way). Nonetheless, having just graduated from high school and being on the brink of entering the 'real world,' I have become acutely aware of two things when it comes to being Asian-Australian: first, that I count myself incredibly lucky to have grown up with, and been influenced and enriched by, the best (and worst) parts of two cultures and second, that at age seventeen my arms still remain hairless, eating seaweed has now become chic, and I still cannot master a tumble-turn – a fact that I've finally learnt to embrace.

Chinese Dancing, Bendigo Style

Joo-Inn Chew

The hall was silent. Two hundred blond and brunette heads angled attentively, ready to hear us play. Four hundred round eyes blinked expectantly. My little sister and I sat on the unfamiliar piano stool, our feet not quite touching the ground. I adjusted the sheet music that had been chosen for us. We raised our sweaty hands and launched into our duet, 'The Asian Waif.' Plaintive notes filled the room, along with some clumsy plonking from my sister's left hand. The audience seemed rapt, gazing at our bent black heads, our small brown hands. They applauded warmly at the end, smiling and nodding at each other. *How cute!* the smiles seemed to say, as they took in our dark eyes and straight-cut fringes. A faint wave of humiliation broke over me. We had played badly but they loved us. I didn't know exactly what an Asian waif was, but I realised it was something to do with a Chinese kid everyone felt sorry for. And that that was why it fell to us, the only Asians in the competition. We shuffled off stage. In the hallway mirror I caught a glimpse of my poo-brown eyes and flat yellow nose; then I just looked down at my feet as they slunk away.

We were half-Chinese, growing up in a paddock in central Victoria, surrounded by fifth-generation Australian farmers. My parents had moved to the country to live out a counter-culture dream. They had met at uni, married despite the dismay of both their families, and given their kids Chinese names that only Dad knew how to pronounce. Dad had stopped hanging out with overseas students, and Mum had stopped going to church. They had new friends who talked politics and drank red wine, who experimented with nudity and curry and communal living. In this spirit Mum and Dad decided to give up their city jobs and move to the country to make a living from the land, growing organic vegetables and selling them on the highway. We moved into a mud-brick house twenty kilometres out of Bendigo. Goats were bought but escaped; the tractor failed to start; rabbits and slugs ate the vegetables. When the veggie plan fell through, Dad started importing crafts from South-East Asia and selling them at local markets. Over time he built up a jewellery business, cheap plastic earring by cheap plastic earring; Mum sold them in a shop in Bendigo, and in this way there was brown rice and curry on the table.

We didn't seem to belong anywhere. The kids in my country primary school had sandy hair, pale freckly skin and blue eyes that could read the board from the back of the room without corrective lenses. They drank red cordial and ate white-bread sandwiches. The girls played Barbies and netball and had names like Debbie and Michelle. The boys rode BMXs and kicked footballs and were called Craig and Derrick. All of them knew the difference between the Hawks and the Magpies, and between a Ford and a Holden. They got pocket money, watched commercial TV, and had parents who made chocolate crackles for the school fete.

My siblings and I had dull black home-cut hair and glasses that got broken when we failed to catch balls that were thrown at us. We ate wholegrain bread and drank boiled tank-water. We lurked at the edge of the playground and ate our lunch in the library, where we read the *Guinness Book of Records* for the tenth time. We sometimes forgot to wear shoes or undies. We drooled over everyone else's lollies, and were perplexed by TV references, given we only watched the ABC and SBS. We dreaded school sports day, when we knocked over multiple hurdles in a row and were the only kids not sunburned at the end of the day. At the school fete we tried to bargain with the other kids, like Dad encouraged us to, but at the end of the day we took home our plate of organic fruitcake. It would be untouched, except for the missing three slices where each Chew child had dutifully eaten one before bingeing on fairy bread and toffee.

It was hard to know if we were the odd ones out at school because we were half-Chinese, or because we had middle-class urban-hippie parents. Did we feel grimy next to the clean white girls because we had olive skin, or because during the drought we only had a bath once a week in water from the dam? Were we hopeless at sport because we were Asian, or because our family thought it was competitive and meaningless?

We were peculiar hybrids, all three of us different blends of Eurasian, with Aussie accents and Chinese names. 'Where are you from?' people would ask, and it was hard to know how to answer. Melbourne? Malaysia? Here? I remember meeting Dad's family from Malaysia. My cousins lined up, neatly dressed and fully Chinese-looking, chattering together in Mandarin and Hokkien (and possibly other languages I didn't know), switching politely to English when they remembered us. They all pronounced my name the correct Chinese way, which I couldn't do. At dinner they speared slithery noodles and ferociously hot chilli with expert swivels of their chopsticks. They had aced their concert-piano exams and it was clear they were going to be cardiologists or very good accountants. I sprawled on my chair with my spoon, my scabby knees poking out of faded shorts, and my woefully inadequate single mother-tongue. I suddenly remembered how I'd messed up my piano rendition of 'Run, Sheep, Run!' at the Bendigo piano competition. There was no way I was Chinese.

Not only was it disorienting in the wider world, it was also confusing inside our family. Differences between my parents were often put down to cultural factors. Dad valued education, had business sense, was calm and hard-working – because he was Chinese. Mum was sociable and creative, an idealist, easy with money – because she was Anglo-Australian. Dad was the only Chinese person I knew for a long time, so I thought everything he did must be Chinese. His bargain-hunting, his work ethic and his expectations that we should top the class. His shyness, his bad jokes, his Labor politics, his love of peanut butter and his morning ablutions. It wasn't until I grew up and met lots of other Chinese people that I realised a lot of 'Chinese' things were just Dad things. And that actually Dad was not stereotypically Chinese at all, that in moving away from his origins, he had evolved into his own peculiar species. But at the time, these racial characteristics seemed absolute. I applied them to myself as well: when I was being thrifty and studious I was being Chinese; when I played games and left food on my plate I was being Australian.

We were half-half, and for a long time we didn't belong anywhere. But in our third year in the country we found somewhere that felt a bit like home. A place that was as half-half, as kooky and contradictory, as we were. Just when we were getting used to feeling mostly Australian while looking somewhat exotic, we met the blue-eyed Tans and brown-haired Wongs from the Bendigo Chinese Association. It was like climbing onto a made-in-Australia dragon-shaped life-raft in a sea of cultural contradictions.

The Chinese Association was left over from the gold-rush days, when migrants flocked to central Victoria to seek their fortune. Most of them went home to China after the gold rush, leaving faded silk costumes and joss houses. A few stayed and married locals, and their descendants still lived in Bendigo. No one had spoken Mandarin for generations, but there was still a proud affiliation with the Chinese Association and its hall of relics. Anyone with Chinese ancestry, however distant, could join. Every year the association marched in the Bendigo Easter procession, following bagpipe bands and monster trucks with lion dancers, lantern-bearers, costumed children on ponies and finally the star of the procession: Sun Loong, the longest dragon in the southern hemisphere.

We joined the association, and my sister and I put our names down to learn 'Chinese dancing.' We were soon practising steps choreographed by a local ballet teacher, who wasn't even remotely Chinese, but had lots of ideas about what oriental dancing was. We twirled ribbons and fluttered fans, and sashayed back and forth with parasols and lanterns to Asian-sounding music. When we performed at Easter we were dressed in fake silk costumes and had slanted oriental eyes drawn boldly onto our faces with black eyeliner. We were a hit. We performed in RSL clubs in nearby drought-stricken towns; prawn crackers were served before the performance to set the atmosphere. We danced in windy car parks, in school halls, and even in front of Prime Minister Bob Hawke. We instinctively affected a mysterious Eastern reserve during the performance, which fell away the moment we stepped backstage and could run off and find a pie before getting back on the bus. We weren't all friends, but when we stepped out together to the music we were a tribe. It wasn't something any of us could articulate then, but everyone in the group knew what it was like to suffer under a Chinky surname, to look a little different, and perhaps to have a Chinese parent who would stay too long at parent–teacher night discussing our marks. And we knew how good it felt to have these differences go from being liabilities to being assets, reasons to go on stage, to dress up and dance and be applauded.

We marched each year in the procession, surrounded by drums and dancing lions, fire crackers and silk banners covered in characters none of us could read. My little brother, dressed in his pyjamas from Malaysia, rode in the children's float, waving at the crowd. One year I rode a horse and wore the gold silk Chinese princess costume with its embroidered flags and heavy crown. I smiled magnanimously and myopically at the crowd (having left my glasses with Mum in an effort to look beautiful), not able to see anyone's face but sure all the pink blurs were cheering me on.

We did Chinese dancing and walked in the procession for years. It was glorious to march before the cheering city, to smile and wave like royalty, to dance and be applauded by classmates – all for being Chinese. Most importantly, for being the kind of Chinese that we really were – not Asian waifs, but Australian Chinese, half-halfs; part-Chinese but mostly Australian, same and different, just a little bit special.

Tall Poppies

Quan Yeomans

Quan Yeomans was born in Sydney in 1972 to a Vietnamese mum and an Australian dad. He is well known as the lead singer and guitarist for the Australian rock band Regurgitator. Regurgitator has been a major contributor to the indie pop scene in Australia since the release of their debut album, *Tu Plang*, in 1996. The band is also well known for their 3D animated videos, most of which were created by Quan himself. Quan is currently based in Hong Kong working on solo projects.

*

What did you want to be when you were growing up?
I can't remember ever being that interested in any type of career at any particular age. Profession seemed to destroy family relationships as far as I could tell. I recall more wanting to be in love. Perhaps I had innate leanings towards being a fireman or an astronaut but I'm sure it was only because those jobs seemed wreathed in the romance of fire and the stars.

How did you end up becoming a musician?
I never studied music academically with any conviction but I loved trying to play like Hendrix, Jimmy Page and Slash. My passion for the guitar came from a hatred of the piano, which my mother had tried to get me into at the age of seven. She finally gave up and bought me an acoustic guitar at thirteen. Fortunately I was terribly bored at art school. Fine art was completely the wrong choice for me. I should have taken up graphic arts but it was just before

computers had become indispensable in the field and I was far too messy a draftsman. It took music show me the dumb, 'Fuck you' beauty of punk, pop and sweaty hands.

What were the first days on the job like?
They were like taking my id to an ego-Disneyland everyday and making it ride the biggest rollercoaster in the park.

How has your family responded to what you do?
Despite my mother and father's completely disparate personalities they were, as most good parents are, two perfect halves of the one brilliant, dirty beast. My mother was the giant dumb heart and my father the perfect self-possessed brain. Mum had a bit more of an intimate relationship with my music in the sense that in the early days she would have to pick it out of her hair on a regular basis. Her tolerance for it still astounds me to this day. When the band first started becoming quite well known, I knew the mouth on me was a cause of some dismay. Admitting to being the source from which this river of profanity seemed to flow made her question her skills momentarily, but I think she loved a challenge. She was an independent Asian woman floating in an Occidental ocean and I was yet another strange twist in the cocktail. I remember going to the Women's Museum in Hanoi, staring up at a statue of a woman staring defiantly into the skies with a rifle under one arm and a baby in the other and thinking – this is my mother's bloodline. She still attends every one of my concerts in her hometown and charms my friends and embarrasses me in front of them in equal amounts.

My father was the planter of seeds. He showed me how to step back and watch how the world worked, and made me interested enough in its hypocrisies and inequities to want to write irreverent shit about it. He taught me to be proud of my unique ethnicity and encouraged me to dabble and fuse other musics and instruments into what I was doing with the rock band. He was at the very first Regurgitator show. I remember him smiling. He's still the most intellectually interesting and truly eccentric man I have ever known. He taught me about the profundity of the absurd and the absurdity of the profound and that 'a job worth doing is worth doing badly,' which is perfect advice for an artist whose job is to continually fail and keep smiling.

I think they were both relieved that I turned out almost, if not quite, as odd as them.

Who is your inspiration?
Einstein. Apparently he said something like, 'The secret to creativity is knowing how to hide your sources.' So I'll refuse to elaborate on that question on the grounds that I may reveal my inadequacy.

Can you tell us one important lesson that has changed your life?
I've said this before but in the end sometimes the only thing left in the whole world that can make you smile is blowing gas out of your arse. I learnt that from my father when he was high on morphine dying from cancer.

One memorable person who has changed your life?
Everyone I meet changes my life. I couldn't really narrow it down. It doesn't seem fair.

Khoa Do

Khoa Do is a film-director, screenwriter and teacher who has worked extensively with disadvantaged youth. In 2003, he directed and produced *The Finished People*, which was nominated for three AFI Awards, three Film Critics' Circle Awards and an Australian Writers' Guild Award. His most recent feature film is *Footy Legends*, starring Claudia Karvan and Anh Do. He was Young Australian of the Year in 2005.

*

What did you want to be when you were growing up?
I wanted to be a vet. I used to love animals when I was a kid. At lunchtimes, I used to catch grasshoppers, praying mantises and spiders rather than play handball. At home, we kept birds, dogs, fish, mice and even a blue-tongued lizard once. But then one day, I noticed that every animal I kept either got sick, ran away, died or just didn't like me. That's when I realised that perhaps I shouldn't become a vet.

How did you end up becoming a film director?
I've always loved telling stories. When I was in Year 5, my primary school teacher got us all to come up to the front of the class and tell everyone what we did on our weekends. I got up and told the class about being chased by a Rottweiler. The whole class laughed. My teacher said it was the best story anyone had ever made up about their weekend. I said, 'But it's true!' They said, 'Yeah, good one!' From then on, he made me come up every

Monday to tell everyone about my weekend. I've never told anyone this, but seriously – apart from the weekend where I got locked up inside a supermarket freezer and had to eat frozen fish fingers to survive, everything else was heaps true.

Since then, I've always loved telling stories. When I was at university, I found myself sitting in a commerce lecture about the law of diminishing returns, realising that my life would follow the law of diminishing returns if I didn't follow my true calling. That winter, I auditioned for a part in a local community theatre show called *Running in Circles*, won the part, and have been in film and theatre ever since.

What were the first days on the job like?
Before working as a writer and director, I worked as an actor. One of my first roles in a feature film was on the set of *The Quiet American*, acting opposite Michael Caine. I was cast in the opening scene of the film. The scene involved me arresting Michael Caine, speaking French. I had to intimidate and arrest one of the world's best actors, speaking a language that I had failed at school.

The first day started off really badly. Apparently I spoke French with an Australian accent. In between takes, a little French lady kept running up to tell me that my French was incomprehensible. To make matters worse, the cinematographer kept telling me I was falling out of the frame (I wanted to say to him – why don't you move the camera, then?), and the director kept yelling, 'Louder!'

Later on, I discovered that I was cut out of the film completely. That's when I realised that perhaps I was better off behind the camera than in front of it.

Can you recall one memorable or funny incident in your career?
In my career as a writer and film-director, there have been many memorable moments. It's because I have to constantly make decisions. Sometimes you get it totally right – and sometimes, you get it totally wrong. Sometimes they're small decisions (the colour of the curtains in the hospital scene should be green rather than blue), and sometimes they're massive decisions (should we go for Julia Roberts or Cate Blanchett for our film? Okay, I'm kidding,

I've never had to make that decision). But sometimes, they are life-and-death decisions. I'll give you one example.

A few years ago, I made a film with a group of young people from at-risk backgrounds. With few resources, we were trying to make a feature film. I was directing it. One day, a few weeks before our film shoot begins, I get a phone call from the girlfriend of one of our actors.

'Khoa,' she says, 'I think Eddie is going to kill someone today. Everyone's tried to talk him out of it, but he won't listen. Can you talk to him?'

Now, this is the type of phone call you dread the most. Let me tell you a bit about Eddie. Eddie was on parole at the time, he was charged with slashing someone's arm during an armed robbery, in a stolen car.

When he was fifteen, he went out to the corner store to buy some lollies and he came back – to find out that his best friend had been shot and was lying in intensive care.

So when Cathy told me that Eddie was going to kill someone, I believed her. Eddie was capable of anything.

Now, I had the task of trying to talk him out of it. But what do you say to someone who's so volatile, so angry, that he won't listen to all those who are closest to him?

So I get in the car and I drive out to meet him. And as I'm driving, I think to myself – should I even be doing this? I'm just a writer, a film-director – what do I know? Maybe I should call the police?

As I drive past Kmart, I think to myself – does Kmart sell bulletproof vests?

Should I ring my brother now to tell him that just in case something happens to me, he can have my stamp collection?

But then I realise that in the past few weeks, I had become his friend and I knew he trusted me – as his director, his mentor and teacher. And I knew that deep inside, Eddie was a good person, who had lost his way.

So I meet up with him, and there he is – fired up and angry. He had planned it out – how he was going to slash Terry with a samurai sword, because Terry was telling everyone all these bad things about him.

So I sit in front of Eddie, and I think – what am I going to say?

Never have I had to choose my words more carefully – I say the wrong thing and anything can happen.

So at first, I try fear as a tactic – the fear of losing your freedom if you're locked up. I tell him, 'Eddie, if you do this, you're going to get life in jail, man.' But he doesn't care. See, to Eddie, life is a prison already.

I then tell him, 'Eddie, if you do this, you're never going to see the beach or the Opera House again.' I don't know why, but there's something really nostalgic about the Opera House that I thought might just work.

'I don't care, Khoa,' he says. 'I've seen enough.'

I then tell him, 'Look man, if you go to jail, they're going to rape you.'

He then tells me, 'Khoa, you think anyone's going to touch *me* in jail?' Good point.

Eddie then looks at me and says, 'I'm gonna kill him. I don't want to do this, but I have to.'

By now, I'm out of solutions. I mean, what else is there left to say? I've said everything. So I rack my brains ... and nothing comes out.

Eventually, I just look at him and I say, 'Eddie, if you get locked up for life, who's going to replace you in the movie we're making? You're the only person who knows this role. You were made for it ... and we need you. If you get locked up – all this hard work, all this preparation, it's all going to go to waste because we're going to have to cancel our film.' I pause for a moment, then I say, 'Eddie, we need to make this film to show people the truth. We can change people's lives if they watch this film.'

I see him begin to light up slowly, and I say, 'You can change their lives, with your performance and your story. Making this film is my dream. Help me realise my dream, man. I need you.'

Eddie takes a moment. He looks up, he looks left, he looks right. Then, he looks at me. And finally he says, 'All right, I'm not going to kill him. But just for you, man.'

Two years later, Eddie is nominated for an AFI Award and walks the red carpet for his work in the film.

He's been in several films since then, and has a bright future ahead of him.

That's when I realised the power of creativity to change lives.

How has your family responded to what you do?
They ask me when I'm going to apply to study pharmacy.

Can you tell us one important lesson that has changed your life?
Everything always works out in the end.

Hoa Pham

Hoa Pham is a psychologist, mentor and award-winning author. Her children's books include *49 Ghosts* and *No One Like Me*, and her novels include *Vixen* and *Quicksilver*. In 2001, she won the *Sydney Morning Herald*'s Young Writer of the Year Award. She also writes for theatre and film, and is the founding editor of *Peril*, an online journal focusing specifically on Asian-Australian issues.

*

What did you want to be when you were growing up?
A writer! I became a writer because my parents forbade me to write creatively when I was in high school. So I hid it under the blankets when I was a teenager and started sending things to magazines and journals when I was twenty-one.

What were your first years as a writer like?
Writing was a release for me, and an important escape. My first books were children's books for kids from non-English-speaking backgrounds like my own – so that they would have books they could relate to. My Vietnamese background was now valuable in Australia in a way I had not seen before.

Can you tell us one important lesson that has changed your life?
When I was six I remember drawing myself with blonde hair and blue eyes, because that was how I wanted myself to be. That was what I thought was pretty. Now I know that was whitewashing

from the Australian mass media, making me blind to my own beauty.

I went to a middle-class primary school in a predominantly white neighbourhood where the only other Asians were one Chinese boy and my brother. My blonde friends giggled and said the Chinese boy was my boyfriend. The one Greek boy in the school would call me a Chink then smile at me as if it was a joke. In my secondary school there were more Asian students but I still didn't totally fit in with them. They were Chinese or overseas students and I felt awkward and clumsy next to their chic haircuts and cute Hello Kitty hairclips.

When I first started going out with boys, I tried Asian guys first. After sussing out that I was Australian, they would ask me if I knew how to cook. Then I tried Anglo guys, who would nickname me spring roll and had mothers who wished their sons would go out with a nice Irish-Australian girl. I had so much anger in me, not fitting in anywhere. I only accepted that I could be considered beautiful after going out with a photographer who asked me to be a model for him.

How would I draw myself now? It's hard to tell. There is the me in photos, squinting, red-eyed and sometimes double-chinned. I think there would be a smile in my self-portrait – not the passive Asian smile that says everything is good and wonderful, but a grin that says I'm ready to take on the world and anything that is projected onto me.

I went to my first Asian club-night this year and was astounded. I had never been surrounded by so many Asian faces, happy, sleek and cool. They weren't bad dancers, either, and the only white faces were the club staff. I envy the Vietnamese-Australian girls growing up now, their self-confidence, hanging around in self-contained groups.

I would say I am a Vietnamese-Australian girl, but there is a struggle in that hyphen. I used to say I was Australian, defiantly. I was born here, don't speak Vietnamese, and the generation before me insists that I am not Vietnamese. But lately, having gotten to know other Vietnamese-Australian girls and having embraced Vietnamese Buddhism, I can say I'm of Vietnamese origin and proud of it.

That's after my younger years of wishing that I wasn't. I cannot speak Vietnamese. I stopped speaking it when my beloved grandmother moved to America when I was ten. Then I was raped by an uncle, and the ensuing silence and trauma made me hate extended family events when he was there. The Vietnamese pressure to save face and not tell anyone was ground into me and I could not seek help for what had happened until I was nineteen. Back then, I thought being Vietnamese was a curse.

Then university exposed me to feminism and I gradually learned that all cultures had difficulty with incest – it was not just traditional Vietnamese face-saving that oppressed women's experiences.

The anger that used to drive me has gone. Instead, I find that I am calm and accept who I am. In Thich Nhat Hanh's Buddhist concept of the world, all places are home. You need to find the place within yourself that is home, an island of peace. After many years I have found this peace, accepting who I am and what I can be. I can draw on Vietnamese Zen Buddhism as a source of strength, and not blame Asian or Australian culture solely for what happened to me and to others. As the teachings go, our enemies are not other humans, but the hatred and anger that drive human actions.

One memorable person who has changed your life?
My partner, Alister Air. He is supportive of all my artistic endeavours, including me being in Vietnam for four months without him. To find someone who loves you enough to support your full potential and not feel threatened by it is amazing – and an essential thing if you want to be a partner for an artist.

How has your family responded to what you do?
My mother and father are now really proud of me – which is great, as they've had to handle some confronting material in some of my stories and plays.

Jason Yat-Sen Li

Jason Yat-Sen Li worked for the United Nations International Criminal Tribunal for the former Yugoslavia from 1996–98 on a number of pioneering cases in genocide and war crimes. Jason is currently the managing director of a private equity, investment banking and advisory firm. He is also vice-chair of the Australia–China Chamber of Commerce in Beijing, a director of the George Institute for Public Health, and a governor of the Smith Family, one of Australia's largest charities.

*

What did you want to be when you were growing up?
Apart from the usual boyhood dreams of becoming a policeman, a jet-fighter pilot and a martial arts hero, my first real memory of having a 'professional' ambition was when I wanted to be a child psychologist. As a child myself, I loved the company of other children and felt I could understand them far better than the adults around me could. My father thought it was a marvellous idea. But more broadly, throughout my childhood, I very much wanted to belong. I grew up in Australia in the 1970s when the community was less diverse than it is now. I wanted to fit in.

How did you end up doing what you do now?
It is hard to describe what I do now. I wear a number of hats. I run an investment banking, private equity and strategy firm in China. I am involved in community politics and social issues and give a great number of speeches in Australia about leadership, diversity,

Australia's future. I am the director of a number of not-for-profit organisations involved in medical research and public health, volunteerism and public affairs. I still describe myself as an international lawyer. I want always to be known as a political activist and a change agent.

What were the first days on the job like?
I'm not sure when my first days on the job were. I've always worked. My mother's family ran restaurants when they migrated to New Zealand. I worked as a waiter and loved the interaction with customers. I worked throughout university as a research assistant to various professors and lawyers. My first serious job was as a legal assistant in one of Sydney's law firms when I was still studying at university. What I remember about this time is feeling hopelessly out of my depth. My work would come back with red lines through eighty per cent of it. I had a wonderful mentor, though, who steered me through with a kind but firm hand. There was one night when I was working late, helping to write the prospectus for a large Australian company that was going public. I had long hair and a real 'student' look at that time. A senior executive from that company came to see the partner who was supervising me and saw me in the office. He asked the partner, 'Are you sure that fellow's English is good enough?' My supervising partner responded, 'He topped the state in English in the HSC several years ago, so I don't think you need to worry.'

How has your family responded to what you do?
My family have always supported me in what I do. I owe them a great deal. I remember the sacrifices my parents, who were never wealthy, made for my education and so that I could have access to opportunities never available to them. I remember asking my father once how I could repay what they had done for me. He replied that I could simply treat my children in the same way as he and my mother had treated me. These Confucian values were strong in my family: the attention to education, the generational thinking, the centrality of the family unit. Our family's story is a typical immigrant's story: one of parents who came to Australia with nothing and worked hard to build foundations in

a community where they had no real friends, no networks, no history. Second-generation migrants owe our parents a great debt for the paths they paved for us.

When I was heavily involved in political campaigns for the republic and for anti-racism in Australia, my parents were always behind me, quite in spite of them being quiet people. My father, who fears nothing more than public speaking but who is one of the most authentically naturally brilliant public speakers I have ever heard, gave a talk on my behalf once when I was unavailable for a campaign commitment. My sister remembers the beads of sweat on his forehead as he was waiting to be cued. I am still very deeply touched by the sacrifices both my parents made and continue to make for my sister and me.

Who is your inspiration?
There are many people who have inspired me through my life. Some are famous and important and powerful but most are not. I think often the most inspiring people are just ordinary individuals who do extraordinary things; things that are not splashed across the pages of newspapers but instead are very private and mostly go publicly unrecognised.

Can you tell us one important lesson that has changed your life?
In my younger days, I didn't much participate in things. Throughout high school, I didn't really take part in the life of the school or the community. Part of that was out of laziness, but also out of a lack of confidence about the contribution I could make. It was the issue of racism in Australia and my belief in an Australian republic that drove me, finally, to participate and to get involved in public life and community affairs. This changed my life and gave me tremendous confidence that ordinary people can achieve significant social change by the force of their convictions, through effective organisation, and by making the decision to participate with confidence. This is the essence of social capital and I try to do as much public speaking to audiences of young people as possible to encourage them to get involved in the issues that matter to them. It will change their lives for the better too.

One memorable person who has changed your life?

I worked with Sir Ninian Stephen at the International Criminal Tribunal for the Former Yugoslavia in the Hague between 1996 and 1997. What struck me about Sir Ninian was his humility and his care to treat all those around him with dignity and genuine interest. I compared this at the time with the arrogance of many who had achieved not even a fraction of what he had. This taught me the importance of humility and that arrogance is inexcusable, particularly in those who claim to be leaders.

'Dad and Me' by Shaun Tan

Shaun Tan

Shaun Tan became known as the 'good drawer' while he was at school in Perth, which partly compensated for always being the shortest kid in class. Now an internationally renowned, multi-award-winning artist and author, he has also worked for Blue Sky Studios and Pixar, providing artwork for forthcoming films. He was named Best Artist at the World Fantasy Awards in Montreal in 2001, and won the 2007 Australian Book Industry Award for his book *The Arrival*.

*

What did you want to be when you were growing up?
An astronaut. When told that this was a very narrow career opportunity, I wanted to be an artist from about age six. But when saying so to grown-ups, even this did not seem to be taken entirely seriously. As a teenager I guessed the reason: it might be quite difficult to make a living as an artist, and it was generally not regarded as a real profession at school or in suburban Perth. I also became increasingly interested in science, particularly biotechnology, which I came close to studying at university. I was also interested in the idea of being a writer. So I've always had three main interests: visual art, science and writing. I think all three are very similar as kinds of inquiry and ways of making meaning.

How did you end up becoming an artist?
I did not really plan on being a 'picture-book illustrator'; in fact, it was not an area of expression that I took very seriously until I

actually started doing it. At the end of my arts degree at the University of Western Australia, I realised I was not really qualified for anything beyond illustration, something I had practised semi-professionally as a student, producing regular work for science-fiction magazines, music posters, campus brochures and newspapers, as well as my own landscape and portrait paintings. I decided to try working for a year as a freelance illustrator and artist, and contacted anyone I thought might commission such work – museums, publishers, design studios, magazines. The biggest response to both my writing and painting came from children's publishers, which may well explain why I spend so much time with picture books, as opposed to any number of other possible careers. I have seldom illustrated books specifically for children; it's just that children's publishers are the ones that most often deal with illustrated books.

What were the first days on the job like?
Quite vague and isolated; my first professional commission was a fantasy-novel cover, and I figured out how to do this by visiting the newsagency at my local suburban shopping centre and examining all of the covers on the small fantasy-novel stand at the back. I then went to the library next door and got out some books on castles, Antarctica and polo. I replaced the polo sticks with swords, elaborated the castle and worked on a wintery mountain backdrop: the result was a convincing cover that inspired further commissions and marked the beginning of a bill-paying career as an illustrator.

How has your family responded to what you do?
Always positively, and keenly interested, without knowing too much about the world of art and literature. My dad is an architect, from a family in Malaysia that ran a biscuit factory; my mother was always very interested in drawing, living in a working-class Australian family where this was very much an oddity. So both my parents have a good visual sensibility. My brother, a geologist, is very down-to-earth and a good test audience for paintings and stories, being somewhat outside of the fine arts and literary culture. I think he can best recognise the sincerity in my work, as well as any falseness or pretension.

Who is your inspiration?
Not so much who as what: it would be a combination of nature and something like 'artificial nature.' That is, the way human structures tend towards a semi-conscious, jungle-like growth, best seen in old industrial sites and rambling urban landscapes. I tend to draw these a lot, alongside animals, plants, skies and natural landscapes. I'm interested in their commonalities, through pattern and shape, beyond their obvious differences.

Can you tell us one important lesson that has changed your life?
Accepting mistakes as something useful rather than regrettable. This is something I've learnt primarily through drawing over many years, which seems more and more to be an act of 'guided accidents' than some kind of controlled mastery of knowledge and tools (as I used to think when I was younger). It's all about adaptability, and trusting unconscious intelligence as much as conscious calculation. This seems to also apply to real life, but it's an ongoing lesson – I don't think I've learnt it entirely, and possibly never will!

One memorable person who has changed your life?
Well, Inari, my partner, obviously! She is a designer and artist, so a lot of our aesthetic observations are shared rather than solitary.

John So

John So is the first Lord Mayor of Melbourne to have been directly elected by the people; previously, Lord Mayors were elected by the councillors. In office since 2001, Lord Mayor So is currently the longest-serving Lord Mayor of Melbourne, and was voted World Mayor in 2006. He is also one of Melbourne's longest-serving councillors, having won four consecutive elections since 1991. He has a science degree and diploma of education from the University of Melbourne.

*

What did you want to be when you were growing up?
I had aspirations towards becoming a great scientist when I was growing up. Two Asian-Americans, Tsung-Dao Lee and Chen Ning Yang, had won the Nobel Prize in physics in 1957, so I came to Melbourne in 1965 as a young student with the dream of following in their footsteps.

But when I came here at seventeen, I got a big shock. I had not realised that the White Australia Policy was still in place. I was bewildered when I found out about this, because as a teenager in Hong Kong, the two prominent scientists I had looked up to had achieved their success in a Western country. I thought that if I had known before I arrived that people like us were not welcome, perhaps I should have chosen another country to complete my studies.

At first it was very lonely being in Australia, particularly adapting to a different culture. I missed my friends, family and homeland terribly. But I completed my science degree at the University of Melbourne, and stayed at a residential college called International House. International House had a policy of accepting at least fifty per cent of its students from international backgrounds – so I lived with students from Africa, Asia and Europe. I encountered diversity as I never had before, and learned about cultural harmony. I did not end up becoming a scientist, but completed a diploma in education and worked for a number of years as a science teacher in Victorian schools.

What brought you to your current career path?
When I was finishing my matriculation, I lived with some Hong Kong friends, and we formed an association of Hong Kong students. We discussed politics and got involved in debates about the Immigration Restriction Act. I was the youngest member of the group because I was still in high school back then, but we really wanted to help the local Chinese community. My early experiences working with committees, ensuring consensus and speaking out probably had a significant influence later in my life.

I was appointed Ethnic Affairs Commissioner by the Victorian government in the 1980s. It was unimaginable how little support there was for immigrants in Australia then, particularly in aged care and ethnic schooling. The young and the old have very little opportunity to be heard, I realised – even less so when they lacked language skills. So I assisted in developing one of the very first Chinese aged-care homes in Victoria, and also became principal of a Melbourne Chinese-language school.

How did you become Lord Mayor of Melbourne?
My role as a councillor for the City of Melbourne came about after I opened a restaurant in Melbourne. The local Chamber of Commerce didn't seem to be representing the interests of the business as well as I thought they should, so I decided I should do something about this. Unfortunately, I was told they already had candidates to participate in the next round of council elections. But friends told me not to be daunted, and to stand on my own, because I already had a background in committee and community

work. So four days before the nominations were closed, my nomination was put in!

Who is your inspiration?
Many people have inspired me throughout different stages of my life. When I was younger, it was the great Chinese-American scientists; but as I got older I admired others who had dedication, passion and vision – people who were proactive in making things happen.

One important lesson you have learnt that has changed your life?
Life is strange, and what you least expect to happen sometimes happens! I never thought I would be involved in local politics! But I did things as community needs arose. Since 1991, I have served three terms as a councillor, and two terms as the Lord Mayor.

Joy Hopwood

Joy Hopwood has over ten years' experience in children's education and the arts, and was the first regular Asian-Australian presenter on *Play School*. She studied education at Edith Cowan University and now lives in Sydney, where she runs her own production company. She writes, illustrates and produces the *Fairy Joy* animation series and is also a painter and musician.

*

What did you want to be when you were growing up?
When I was about five years old I went to England with my parents and we went to a fun park in Blackpool. There were donkeys, bumper cars, rowing boats and, best of all, a competition to win a giant Blackpool rock lollypop! To win it, I had to go up on stage and perform a song. I sang a nursery rhyme. I loved the thrill of being on stage and seeing people smile and clap. To my surprise I won the giant lollypop. From that moment on I thought that I would like to be a singer, or to get up on stage and perform knock-knock jokes.

In high school, some teachers said to me, 'Oh, you should be doing as well as the other Chinese girls.' There was a lot of competition, and a lot of pressure to achieve high results. I decided that if I always did averagely, there'd be no high expectations of me. The only two subjects in which I was able to score quite high marks without trying too hard were English literature and art. By Year 12, I knew that I wanted to work in the arts.

My parents had different plans. Once, when my class went to

the school library, the librarian handed me some information about the Perth stock exchange.

'What's this?' I asked.

'Don't you want to work at the stock exchange?' she replied.

'No!' I quickly retorted.

'Oh ... but your mum told me you did!'

How did you become an actor?

After Year 12, I did work experience at ABC TV in Perth. I loved it. I was inspired and wrote to a children's television presenter and asked for her advice about what university courses I should take. To my surprise she wrote back and advised me to study either media or education. And so I enrolled in an education degree.

During my teaching placement, an Aboriginal child said he wanted to be on TV but never saw anyone like himself on screen. I told him I'd try to change all that. I don't think he believed me.

After university, I worked in various casual jobs and modelled for several months in Perth and Singapore before making my way to Sydney. I auditioned for an actors' agency and while waiting to hear whether I had been accepted, I worked as a telemarketer. I figured telemarketing was kind of like acting – I could use my voice to try to convince people.

Once, a caller complained that they had spoke to a person with an 'Asian' accent. My supervisor automatically thought of me and I was reprimanded. I said, 'I don't work during the day, and I don't have an Asian accent.'

'Yes, but you look Asian,' he replied, 'so it must be you!'

At the time, I felt extremely low. Another telemarketer told me not to worry. 'You'll be stronger for this,' she reassured me, 'Even if you don't feel it yet.' Her name was Michelle Joyce (now Baine), and she became a lifelong friend and inspiration.

A month passed and I finally received 'The Call' – I had been accepted by the agency! I was ecstatic. I could quit my casual jobs. But it took a while. I had to do the 'go sees' – rounds and rounds of auditions – before any acting work came my way.

During these auditions, I noticed that my friends who were Caucasian in appearance had auditions every week. Mine came only every few weeks, and I was always sent for medical roles, doctors or nurses, karate type roles, and once a concubine role. I was also asked to put on an 'Asian' accent instead of my broad Australian one.

I remembered the Aboriginal boy back in Perth, and my promise to change things. I started to write my own material, composing songs and recording demos, and I started to paint. I saved up for a video camera and filmed myself performing a script similar to ABC TV's *Play School*. I sent the producers of *Play School* a copy.

When I telephoned them, they told me they were looking for 'actors, NIDA graduates, not teachers.' I didn't hear any more from them, so I gave up on the gig. Months later, however, I was invited to audition. But as soon as I arrived, I was told that I looked too young; they wanted somebody more 'mother-like,' with life experiences.

I was devastated. I had brought along my ET doll as a prop. On my way out, I accidentally slammed the door on my poor ET. His blue eyes now scratched, and my eyes blood-shot red from crying, we caught the bus back home. I felt that I had failed that little Aboriginal boy.

Eventually, my agent called to say that *Play School* wanted me to audition again. They sent me a script the day before my audition and I had to remember it all. Before I went in, I thought of the boy and said a prayer. I had ET with me again and they remembered him and me. I remembered all my lines and performed from my heart. At the end, the producer said, 'That was a good audition.' Two or three weeks later, I got a call to say I had the gig. It was one of my proudest moments.

Play School was a tremendous learning experience for me. I learnt so much from the other actors, especially George Spartells, a generous, natural actor, and Monica Trapica, a down-to-earth actress who gave me words of wisdom. I loved the experience. And I loved those *Play School* toys.

After a few years on *Play School*, my contract was up and I wanted to get my own cartoon series going. I had started writing children's books, and a cartoon series was a great opportunity to combine my art, music, writing and acting. I have now published my children's books, exhibited my artwork and had my music played on radio. I am not motivated by money but my making a difference, educating and entertaining people through my music, art, books, acting and cartoons. Creativity is my secret to freedom.

How has your family responded to what you do?
My parents were not really enthused when I moved to Sydney to become an actor. They hated the thought of me giving up my university degree. Things changed when I became the first regular Asian *Play School* presenter, though. To see me on television made it all sink in for them, and they used to tell all the neighbours. It wasn't until this moment that they felt proud of me. These days, now that I run my own business, they are happy that I'm happy.

Can you tell us one important lesson that has changed your life?
When I was in primary school, my mum started volunteering in the school canteen. I thought it was a good idea until I heard some older kids say, 'We can't understand your mum. Can't bloody understand what she's saying. You don't speak Chinese, do you?'

'Of course not,' I said, and I never wanted to.

I started to feel ashamed of my mum and stopped visiting her in the canteen. When kids came up to me and said, 'That's not your mum, I hope,' I started replying, 'No, it isn't.'

I started to notice that when Mum and I went shopping together, some people, like the local butcher, either imitated her accent or served other people before her even though she was there first. Every Friday, I'd go with Dad (who is English) to the fish and chips shop. I noticed that no one imitated him or ignored him. Mum was brave and always said, 'Ignore it. You know we are better off than a lot of people in this world.'

Those words have stayed with me, as have the wise words of my friend Jan Edmunds, which I will treasure for life: 'Racism reflects the person who has said the racist remarks, not the recipient. It reveals the racist's ignorance and lack of intelligence and by no means is it a reflection of the receiver.'

I wish I had understood this as a child.

One memorable person who has changed your life?
Last year, my mum was diagnosed with colon cancer. I also heard from my high-school drama teacher for the first time in over twenty years. Unfortunately, she is also battling cancer. These two women have taught me to embrace life. You don't know what is around the corner or when your time will be up.

Anh Do

Anh Do is a Vietnamese-Australian actor, film-producer and stand-up comedian. Perhaps best known for his appearances on television programs such as *Thank God You're Here* and *Dancing with the Stars*, he turned his back on a career in law to pursue one in the performing arts. He has acted in a number of films, including *Footy Legends*, and has been voted Comedian of the Year.

*

What did you want to be when you were growing up?
I wanted to be a martial arts champion, like many young Asian kids. I once signed up for a ninjitsu class. One day I bumped into the instructor on the street and he said, 'It's been seven weeks since I've seen you in camouflage class!' I said to him, 'That's because I'm getting really good.'

How did you end up becoming a comedian?
I was at the end of a five-year law degree and went for an interview with a big prestigious law firm. The guy reached across and congratulated me, and told me to expect a sixty-hour working week. I then asked a comedian friend, 'How many hours a week do you work?' He said, 'Four.' So I switched out of laziness.

What were the first days on the job like?
I got fifty dollars for my first stand-up show – and all I had to do was five minutes. I thought to myself: 'I just earned ten dollars a minute – how good's that!' Of course, for the next six months

I only got to do about five minutes of work per week.

Can you recall one memorable or funny incident in your career?
Hopefully in my career every day is funny – so I'll tell you about an unfunny incident.

I rocked up to a diggers' club in a country town. I thought, 'This should be sweet – country folk love to laugh.' Then I walk in and there are 500 blokes. No worries – just do the blokey material and I'll be right. Then I realise they're all drunken old blokes. 'Sweet,' I thought, 'Drunken old blokes laugh at just about anything.'

Just before they bring me on, the MC does a minute's silence for all the fallen brothers who fought against the Japanese in the Second World War, in the Korean War and in the Vietnam War. Five hundred old guys close to tears remembering their comrades who were killed by Asians. Then the MC introduces me. It was a hard gig.

How has your family responded to what you do?
They laughed at me.

Can you tell us one important lesson that has changed your life?
Enjoy the journey, because the destination is never as satisfying as you think.

One memorable person who has changed your life?
My two sons have taught me that nothing is important other than the health and happiness of the people you love.

Caroline Tran

Caroline Tran presents 'Home and Hosed,' the Australian music program on Triple J, the national youth radio network. On completing her radio broadcasting course at Macquarie University, she landed a job at 2SM as a part-time receptionist and production assistant. Since then, she has presented Triple J's 'Super Request' and lunch and weekend-breakfast programs. She has presented 'Home and Hosed' for the last three years, listening to mountains of new music and uncovering gems to share with the nation and the world.

*

How did you end up getting involved in radio?
After a run of boring office jobs and flitting about I reached the grand old age of twenty-five and thought, 'Holy Moley! I'd better get cracking and find some type of serious proper job.' I surmised that the two things I loved the most were writing and music, so being a music journalist was an early idea. But then I came upon the genius idea of incorporating radio as the ultimate medium that could fulfil both of these things. That idea has really stuck well!

What were the first days on the job like?
Frightening as all buggery! My first radio job was at 2SM, a make-or-break station in its heyday, these days a golden-oldies station. I answered the phone and did administration stuff on reception. I got to be on the production team for the Breakfast Show, which was hosted at the time by Clive Robertson, who used to call me

'Madam' and chastise me for being late and holding his coffee mug on the rim of the cup: 'I don't want my lips touching your fingers, Madam!' He could be so funny and grumpy and narrow-minded! Prior to getting the job at 2SM I had sent a demo tape to Triple J as well – 'Hey, might as well have a shot,' I thought! Lo and behold I get a phone call saying they were interested in meeting me. Little did they know, once I got in the building, there was no leaving!

How has your family responded to what you do?
Initially, when I told them I wanted to go to radio school, they were like, 'What? What for?' They didn't think it was a serious or an easy path to follow. The industry is very small and competitive. They are quite happy though with where I'm at now, especially because Mum got her mug on the telly for a little cooking segment I did for Triple-J TV!

Who is your inspiration?
Here's a secret ... I was inspired a lot by Kasey Casem, who used to host the American Top 40 on one of the commercial radio stations. He had an ability to draw the listener into each song, and you really felt as though he was speaking just to you. That's what every decent radio broadcaster aims to do! He had loads of cheesy segments and love-song dedications, which I wouldn't be able to endure these days, but his presentation and style of delivery made you think, 'This guy really cares!'

Can you tell us one important lesson that has changed your life?
I aim to learn important (at times difficult) things about myself all the time. By working to stay open and aware, life and the universe provide constant insights into how to keep changing my life for the better. So awareness and trying to live consciously are huge goals and continue to be so.

One memorable person who has changed your life?
My son. Everyone says it because it's absolutely undeniable the impact a child has on your life. It's a huge privilege and responsibility and its rewards are unmatched.

Leaving Home

Five Ways to Disappoint Your Vietnamese Mother

Diana Nguyen

Step One: Become an Actor

Like many Asian parents, my mum bought me a piano when I was three years old. So from early on in life, I was a performer. I danced, sang and acted in primary school. My mum was proud of me. I know she was proud because I heard her gossip:

'Oh, Diana, she sings. She is having her piano exam tomorrow. I put so much money into her piano and ballet classes.'

In secondary school, I continued to perform. It was in my blood. But by Year 11, my mother's support started to alter:

'Why you singing?'

'Why you watch video clips?'

'They sluts, you want to be slut?'

'Why you not studying?'

My mother's dream was for me to be rich, successful and healthy. She wanted me to be a doctor. But I didn't pick the right subjects in high school to become a doctor. Instead, I did drama and all the humanities subjects and joined school charity groups to fill in my time. I was in a band. I had the lead roles in my school productions. My mum got frustrated:

'When I gif you piano lessons supposed to be hobby, not a job. Stop this stupidness. If you school leader how you go to concentrate on studies?'

When I received my university entrance score, I was happy. I finished top of my drama class and I had had a fulfilling school experience. But when I told my mum my results, the first thing she said was, 'What did your friend get?'

I told her.

'How come you didn't get higher than her?'

In her eyes I was a disappointment – I had made her lose face.

My mum has made me lose face, too. When I had a lead role in a school production, I invited my family to come and watch. I was so excited that my mum would see me shine, that she would see the love and energy of my performance. During interval, I saw her car driving away. I can still see it today. I was shattered. When she came to pick me up that afternoon, I didn't talk to her. I let the hurt sink deeper into my soul.

Maybe I should have told her how I felt, because it happened again. During one of my university performances, I looked out into the crowd during the interval and saw an Asian woman walking out. For the past two years I have been a working actor in Melbourne, and not once has she come to see me perform. I don't invite her any more.

Step Two: Work Four Jobs – But What Career?
I have four jobs. Three of them support the fourth: my acting career.

I used to work at Coles in Springvale and I saw all the ethnic groups come through. I saw the waves of refugees pass through my register: the Greeks and Italians with their pasta and cheeses; the Vietnamese and Cambodians with their rice and carefully selected fruit; the Afghanis and Sudanese with their new-found freedom. And they all had something in common when they came through my register. When I finished the transaction, I would turn to them with a smile:

'Okay, that's $10.45. Do you have any Fly-Buys?'

Pause.

'Huh?'

I would look them in the eyes and say very slowly, my hand imitating a Fly-Buys card, 'Fly ... Buys ...'

Another pause, and a lost look in their eyes.

'Ah, it's okay,' I'd say with a shrug.

Some customers devised a beautiful plan to get out of this game.

'Oh, I left it at home,' they'd laugh. 'Okay, see you later.'

They also loved to get rid of their change. No matter how much they had or how long the queue was.

'How much?'

'That comes to $14.85.'

'Okay, I got change.'

Groan.

'Two dollar, two dollar, five dollar, five dollar fifty-sen, twenty-sen, tin-sen, fi-sen. See you later.'

One day, I was serving a customer who bought nappies. I put her transaction through and said, 'Have a nice day!'

She looked at me and said, 'Bag, bag, bag,' pointing at the nappies.

I showed her that the nappy bag had a handle, so she didn't need a bag.

'Gif me bag!' she demanded. 'You Chinese all the same.'

I felt like I had been slapped in the face. With my best angry-on-the-inside customer-service voice I said, 'I am not Chinese, I am Vietnamese.'

She finished off with, 'You Asians are all the same.' She grabbed her nappies and went on her merry way, leaving me angry and frustrated.

In the entertainment industry, being Asian was daunting at first. I had a Bert Newton face with Bart Simpson skin; I had Chinese eyes and huge black hair. At least I could never be stereotyped as a bimbo.

Step Three: Become a Viet-school Drop-out

I am Australian. I am a second-generation Australian Vietnamese. My mum would stress that I am Vietnamese-Australian. All my life I've had this mixed idea of who I am and what my role is.

When I was in Year 7 my mother forced me to go to Vietnamese school for the first time. After coming back from a three-month family trip to Vietnam, she realised she had better send her eldest daughter to Vietnamese school.

So there I was, a Year 7 student in a Grade One Vietnamese class, my little peers staring up at me. I cried so much before every Sunday-morning class that family friends asked if I was being bullied by my tiny classmates! Being a dutiful Vietnamese girl, I went to Viet school for another three years, until I finally quit, telling my mother I needed to focus on my schoolwork.

My lack of interest in learning her language created a lasting communication barrier between me and my mother.

Step Four: The Boyfriend

I was ugly when I was in high school; I'm not scared to admit it. I was an Asian bookworm, with big owl-eyed glasses and a brown school uniform two sizes too large. I hung out with my Asian crew of girls and did Vietnamese daughter chores: after school, I looked after my two little sisters and attempted to teach them piano to save my mum money. But this all changed the summer after I finished high school. I discovered the internet. There, in a chatroom full of Asian teenagers, I met my boyfriend.

Big no-no. Number one rule in the *Asian Mother's Handbook*: no boyfriend until after university. This rule encompasses all the other rules in the book. If you don't have a boyfriend, you will still be dependent on your family and stay at home. You will concentrate on your studies. And your virginity will be intact.

By having a boyfriend, I created a lot of fear for my mother. It didn't help that my boyfriend was Chinese. Soon after finding out, my mum decided she hated Chinese people.

'They are too tight with money, always family first. Why can't you go out with an Italian boy, you like pizza?'

Once I overheard her gossiping to her friends:

'She can date anyone other than a Chinese. I don't care if he's Iraqi or Indian, but not Chinese.'

So, how about a nice Vietnamese boy?

'No Vietnamese. He will cheat on you and gamble all your money.'

Step Five: Get Kicked Out of the Cuckoo Nest

When my mother kicked me out of home at the ripe old age of eighteen, I found a freedom that I had never known before. My mother forced wings on me and pushed me out of the nest, and I know she regrets it. At first I was scared. I was the first and only Asian girl in my group of friends to be kicked out of home. I became known as the girl with no home, the girl who had brought shame to her family.

What was my shameful act? I had a boyfriend before I finished university ... and she found him in my wardrobe. My mum is Vietnamese, and no way was her daughter not a virgin. That afternoon, I got home from uni and saw all my belongings in the backyard. Everything. I was stunned. She had threatened to kick me out before but never acted on it. I collected my essential belongings and moved in with my first ever boyfriend. We slept on a foam mattress on the floor. My friends were supportive, but they couldn't understand: we were all conditioned to depend on our Asian parents, and now I couldn't.

To my mother, I was the slut daughter. I am still with my boyfriend after five years and I'm still a slut in her eyes. I guess I will be for the rest of my life.

So, there you have it: five simple ways to disappoint your Vietnamese mother.

The Courage of Soldiers

Pauline Nguyen

Like his peers, my father wanted desperately to raise four high achievers, believing that the sacrifices he and my mother had made were far too great for us not to be. We aimed high because we had no choice. We were made acutely aware that he and my mother had fled Vietnam not for their own future but for ours – to ensure that we could lead a prosperous life and have a better education. 'You are like cars with no direction,' my father would say, 'and I am your steering wheel, leading you in the right direction.'

My father feared that his children would lose the old culture. At home, we spoke Vietnamese to our parents and English to each other. We practised all the formal traditions and lived the pious Vietnamese way. We upheld filial obedience and dutifully worshipped our long-lost ancestors.

My father had hoped that the two very different cultures could blend into one well-adjusted whole. In theory, this sounded better than when it was put into practice. We worked at the restaurant seven days a week before and after school, stopping only to finish our homework and complete household chores. Outside activities included maths school, Vietnamese school, cooking school, debating and martial arts. We did all this and had to get top grades as well.

My father placed tremendous pressure on us from an early age – any average result was a failure in his eyes. The knowledge of this lingered over our heads like a cheerless cloud that never lifted. He sent us to strict same-sex private Catholic schools, which was a challenge in itself. But report time was the worst. Twice a year, from the age of seven until thirteen, we would bring home our school reports with total fear and loathing. Assisted by his favourite billiard stick, the stiffest, shiniest one, my father would cane us once for every 'B' grade. For every 'C,' he caned us twice. This ritual required us to lie flat on our stomachs and not budge a millimetre as we waited for our father to deliver his wrath. Our polished floorboards, as hard and shiny as they were, offered no support as my father's stick sliced the skin of our buttocks and hacked at the flesh of our thighs. When my father was done, and as we lay there in a bloody heap, he threw us a dollar for every 'A.'

With teeth clenched and fists squeezed until the knuckles turned white, I sometimes stared out the window and wondered what the neighbours would think if they ever heard us scream. What did it matter? To shed a tear or release a whimper at any time throughout this ritual meant a further beating to nullify our weakness. I cried only in private. Mostly I cried for Lewis, who, no matter how hard he tried, could never get anything higher than a 'C' for handwriting and physical education.

Fear dominated every day of my childhood. Fear and the dog shit covering the yard were the smells of my youth. I cannot remember any time when fear did not lurk over my shoulder. Fear seeped through every window, rose up from each shiny floorboard and spilled through the dead cracks in our walls. It hovered over our beds while we were sleeping.

My dearest Aunty Ten tried her best to ease our pain. It was all she could do when report time came to stay at our house for as long as possible to delay the beatings. It comforted me to know that there was another Vietnamese adult in this world who thought that my father's actions were cruel and unacceptable: 'They are only children, for Christ's sake.' Her kindness only made matters worse – elongating our agonising wait, our nerves singed to the flashpoint. Eventually the time would come for her to leave. 'I'm so sorry, honey, I must go … I'm so sorry.'

It made no difference to my father what time my aunty left. He was a patient man, and especially good at playing this game. As soon as Aunty Ten walked out the front door, my father, with the enthusiastic glare of an executioner, would cock his head once in our direction. We knew what we had to do. The regular beatings ensured that I eventually brought home straight 'A's and secured a permanent position in the top three students of my grade – a habit I kept for every one of my dreary school years.

By the time we reached high school, the canings stopped and a new punishment was introduced: public humiliation. While our friends were going out, discovering life and having fun, my father forbade us to go anywhere. He installed deadlocks on every major door of our house: front door, back door, living-room door, dining-room door and bedroom doors. It would have been impossible for a thief to penetrate, let alone for any child to escape. Our lives consisted of school, restaurant, sanctioned activities and home. He tolerated nothing else. My father controlled every hour of our day and when any situation fell out of his control, we suffered the full force of his anger.

I can still recall the stench of my fear when I stepped onto the wrong train going home from school one day. It was overcast – the claustrophobic clouds had already descended with an air of nervous anxiety. In a flutter of lateness, I had mistakenly caught the express train at Liverpool station. It shot past Cabramatta and didn't stop until half an hour later at Town Hall. Distressed and severely panicked at the thought of having to explain the lateness to my father, I carelessly jumped onto the first train I saw heading back. Unfortunately, it was the 'all stops' peak-hour train, delivering me back to Cabramatta another two hours later. Walking to the restaurant that evening to face my father was like losing control behind a car wheel – I was heading at full speed into a brick wall and there was no way of stopping. All I could do was grit my teeth, clench my fists and brace myself for the impact.

My parents didn't want to know about my version of events, accusing me instead of secretly meeting with the phantom boyfriend they had concocted in their heads. My father confirmed my fear with three clean punches to my face, followed by his usual torrent of poisonous words: 'You'll grow up and amount to nothing more than a common whore!'

He made sure his friends were watching.

*

My father fled Vietnam to escape the oppression of the communist regime. It is ironic that we in turn have had to escape the tyranny of his rule to find freedom for ourselves. With the help of a close friend and the support of my brothers, I ran away from home as soon as I was old enough and immediately went into hiding. My brothers, who always knew my whereabouts, warned me by phone if my father or any of his henchmen came close to finding me. He had spread the word that there could be only two reasons for my leaving: one, that I had become a drug addict too ashamed to face the world; or two, that I had fallen pregnant to the phantom boyfriend. These conclusions were so typical of his nature. He had never attempted to get to know or understand his children. What assumptions he did come up with were based on anger and venom in his heart. I do not know which fact is sadder.

That morning, I packed a lone suitcase, said goodbye to my brothers and walked out the tired front door. Leroy, only five years old at the time, pleaded with me to stay. 'If you leave me, Sis, I will get a knife and stab myself in the stomach!' Poor Leroy: how confused he must have felt to be abandoned by his sister.

With the courage of soldiers, my brothers ventured to the restaurant to face the firing line. They presented my father with the farewell letter I had written: a soft, compassionate letter outlining all the reasons I had to leave. My brothers told my father that they had 'found' the letter after 'discovering' that I had gone.

He hastily read my words and put them in his pocket. He ordered my brothers to join him at the table. He picked up four square, stainless-steel napkin dispensers and placed them neatly on top of one another. With steel in his voice, he said, 'These represent each one of you.' He pointed to each dispenser as he spoke, resting his finger on the bottom. 'This one is your sister. She is meant to be the foundation for the four of you.' After a long, deliberate pause, his backhand at the ready, he took a sudden violent swing at the bottom dispenser, sending it flying through the air and smashing it against the tiled wall. As the top three dispensers came crashing to the ground, he shouted, 'Instead, she has chosen to wreck the family home!' My brothers tell me that the restaurant was full of customers, and that he digested not one word of my letter. 'She is wrong,' he said, 'to do what she has done.'

Leaving my three brave brothers was the most painful part of running away – leaving them to face the consequences and pick up the pieces once I had gone. Life only got worse for them as the damp vapour of sadness filled every corner of our family home, lingering persistently over their heads, seeping into their clothes and skin. The pain between my mother and father followed them even to the restaurant, like a translucent shadow, leaving an unnatural mist for all to see. If little dialogue existed between them before, even less existed once I had gone. Communication shut down altogether – not out of hatred for one another, but out of despair. 'Every day was like walking on thin ice,' Luke tells me. My brothers' workload grew heavier as they picked up the duties I had left behind. 'Every day we were afraid – afraid of not working hard enough, afraid of letting any chores go amiss, afraid of stepping out of line in any way. We made sure that we did nothing wrong. Dad's wick was constantly on fire.'

My mother suffered the most, Lewis tells me: 'She briefly lost her mind when she lost her only daughter.' She became emaciated, letting grief eat away at her. 'She sighed constantly, wore a permanent frown and never smiled at all.' She became a vegan and vowed not to eat meat until she could see me again. For many Buddhists, vegetarianism is a means of cleansing not only the body, but also the spirit and the mind. It is a way of asking the gods for forgiveness, guidance and strength. It is custom to abstain from meat twice in every lunar calendar month. My mother's tears fell at last, as she prayed every day for my return.

*

After two long years of waiting, my parents emptied of all hope; every ounce of inspiration drained out of them. They finally surrendered to their own sorrow and closed down the family business.

With their livelihoods packed up, they began living a monastic existence, trying the best they knew how to make amends with the three boys still living at home.

For me, life was also about survival. I could not allow myself, not even for one moment, to think about the tremendous shame that I had dumped upon them. The months passed slowly as I moved around to avoid detection. Truly fearing for my life, I hid in a quiet beach suburb in Newcastle, a city north of Sydney – one of the last places anyone would think of looking. But my spirit grew weary of living in fear and my body tired of being on the run. I made up my mind to return to Sydney and finish my degree.

By this time, I had found a new strength. My fear of the future was nothing compared with my fear of the past. Even so, out of habit, I would look over my shoulder everywhere I went. I completed my arts degree in 1995. Looking back, I find it amusing that even years after leaving home, I still felt compelled to inform my father of my academic achievements. Each year, I would cut away my home address and send him my results, to let him know that there were some things I would never forget: 'Aim high, hold strong ambitions for your future. Remember where you came from and above all else, never forget the true value of your freedom.'

This is an edited extract from *Secrets of the Red Lantern* (Murdoch Books, 2007).

You Can't Choose Your Memories

Paul Nguyen

When she was growing up, my mother's parents owned a successful shoe shop in a beautiful, tree-lined part of Saigon. They never refer to it as Ho Chi Minh City, so neither do I. While their lives weren't the most luxurious, my grandparents earned enough money to send my mother to a French Catholic boarding school to get the best education she could. She, however, saw this as proof that she was unloved, sent away by her parents because she wasn't wanted around the house, and she was resentful for it. Her parents weren't physically affectionate: they showed their love through money, by bringing food to the table and giving their four children shelter and education. In return, the children were obliged to do as their parents told them. This is how my mother was raised and this is how she raised me.

My mother, a doctor, is a workaholic. She became the bread-winner of the family when my dad (also a doctor) became sick, which satisfied her need for control but totally defied her idea of a traditional patriarchal family like the one she was raised in. This caused complications all around. When I was in primary school, I went to my godmother's house each afternoon until my mother could pick me up. When I got home, I would watch TV until bed-time because I had done all my homework at my godmother's house. I shared a bed with my mother for the first ten years of my life, but I don't remember us ever just talking. About my day, about her day, about anything. But my godmother talked. She had two kids of her own and I got along with them well.

However, being a child, I didn't understand the concept of tact. I must have conveyed how much I liked being at my godmother's house to my mother, because one day she stopped sending me there. I had to go to her surgery and wait until she finished work for the day. There was only one TV and that was in the waiting room. Years later, when I confronted her about it during one of our many fights, she said that she was jealous. That she was my mother and my godmother was not. I retaliated that I wanted her to spend time with me and ask me about my day, but that she was never around. Most of my life, she never asked me what I'd been up to or about my friends. Her questions were always specific. 'How is your study going?' 'Do you have enough money?' 'What did you learn today?' She said that she was working hard to give me everything I wanted. Money as love. I wanted a mother, not an ATM.

*

I have a very poor memory. I think it comes from years in front of the television, but I can't seem to remember anything clearly before the age of twelve. I worry that when I become senile, I will fondly reminisce about my days growing up on Ramsay Street with Phil, Helen and the rest of my *Neighbours*. However, there are a few things that I remember distinctly, mostly because they weren't individual incidents but recurring facts of my life. My parents hated each other. They only stayed married because it was un-Catholic to divorce. For as long as I can remember, they never slept in the same room, let alone the same bed. I slept in my mother's bed for the first ten years of my life and while we didn't talk much, there was something she used to do on a fairly regular basis: bad-mouth my father. I would be regaled with stories of how my dad had commanded that they weren't having any more kids; how he verbally abused her and treated her badly; how she never loved him and always loved someone else. For some time, I felt anger towards my dad, until I started noticing that it was she who verbally abused him. He never did anything right. He was lazy and inattentive and was contributing nothing to the family. Frequent shouting matches would occur without anyone thinking to send me out of the room.

My father never knew how to deal with me. He never hurt me, never abused me. He never even talked to me much when I was a kid. I have this photo of me on what appears to be my fifth or sixth birthday with a red fire-truck in my hands, sitting on my dad's lap. He looks happy to see that I am happy. I don't remember getting that look when I was growing up. As an adolescent, I remember our family being very regimented, very segregated, almost like a prison. At dinnertime, we would sit in front of the TV, watch *Sale of the Century* and eat. As soon as dinner was over, we would disband to our rooms, shut the doors and never come out until we needed to use the bathroom or leave the next morning.

For years I resented my father's behaviour. Then he started getting sick. He worked less and less at the clinic and that meant that he was home when I was old enough to take the bus home alone. I started spending more time with him. I found out that he spent most of his time in front of the TV too. He had some great classic movies on video. He was a homebody like me. He liked pizza as much as I did. He would take me to my Saturday morning sport games every week without begrudging me for it. We even looked quite similar. I thought to myself, 'This is a man I could love.' And then he died.

It was Boxing Day, 2000. I was fifteen. My mum, as she did every year, dragged me to the Boxing Day sales to buy things we didn't need but should get because they were on sale. It was a long and boring day and we didn't get home until the afternoon. My mother screamed. I ran in. He was lying on the bathroom floor, his pants still down from his attempt to go to the toilet. She yelled, 'Call an ambulance!' I called and talked at light-speed, in a total panic that my father could die while I was out shopping. To this day, I refuse to go to the Boxing Day sales. The ambulance and fire crew came not long after, pulled him out into the bedroom and began trying to resuscitate him. I waited outside and I prayed to God to give me my father back. I apologised to Him for going out shopping and promised that I would be a better person if He would just let my dad live. Thirty minutes later, the ambulance officer came out and told me he was gone.

My first reaction was, stupidly, to hide in my room and to turn on the television. To pretend that it hadn't happened. *Wallace and Gromit* was on. My mum yelled at me for being inappropriate. Over the next few hours, we had to organise the funeral directors and people came over to say goodbye. I was the last to do so. I said to my dad's corpse that I hoped that heaven had good pizza. Afterwards, I was told that I should be strong. I was the man of the house now. You can't tell a child not to mourn for his father. It's cruel. At his funeral, I didn't cry. I walked out of the chapel at the end of the service with his picture in my hand and I cried alone in the parking lot. The bastard videographer tried to film me, but my godfather told him to fuck off. He asked if I was okay. I nodded and he left me alone too. In case you were wondering, I don't believe in God any more.

*

I have many Asian friends from many different nationalities. What amazes me is the uniformity with which all of us were raised, especially the first-generation Asian-Australians. We were all taught to be good boys and girls. Study hard in high school to get into a good course at university. Study some more until you become top of the class. Then you can get the best jobs and earn the most money and buy a house big enough for a family of six, two of them being your parents. Then, once you start working, you can start looking for a partner. Then and only then you can move out of home. He or she must be approved by your parents. Opposite sex only, preferably of the same nationality. Some other Asian nationalities may be acceptable. No white people. My mother frequently told me, when I was a teenager, how awful it would be if I brought home a white girl. Too bad neither of us knew how unlikely that would be.

*

In my early years of university, my mum would ask me whether I had a girlfriend or not. My response was always no, with the diplomatic Asian qualifier that I was 'too busy studying.' She once asked if I was gay. I said no. She replied that she was worried because I spent so much time with my best friend, who had come out a few years previously. She thought it would rub off. We would have this same conversation every few months and the script was always the same. By my fourth year of university, I had reached breaking point.

The day I decided to come out to my mother was just before we were about to go on a holiday to Vietnam with a group of other families. I had been living out of home for three years, which in itself was a supposed statement of defiance against my mother, and I only came home for Sunday-night dinners. This particular Sunday night, I decided that there was no point stalling. These were my words: 'Mum, you know how you've always suspected that I'm gay? Well, you're right. I am gay.' My step-dad, whom Mum had married three years before, was very calm about it. Maybe he felt it wasn't his place to say anything or to try to act like my real dad, but I think that he's just a really good guy. This is a list of things my mother said to me once we got her lying on the couch:

'How could you do this to me?'
'It's not true, you're lying.'
'I knew it, I always knew it.'
'It's my fault. It's all my fault.'
'Is this because your best friend is gay?'
'You knew about it, didn't you?' (pointing at my step-dad with an accusatory finger)

'Why do you want to hurt me so badly?'

'It's just a phase. You're too young to know who you are.'

'Promise me that you'll stay straight until twenty-four, then afterwards you can do whatever you want.'

The next day I came back to do some damage control, having given her time to recover. I came home and tried to talk it out with her, only to be told, 'Today, I wished I was dead. All I wanted to do was kill myself. But you know what kept me alive? My patients. They love me. They need me. You don't. All you want to do is hurt me.' So I stormed out. Since then, we've never discussed my homosexuality. I still hope one day that we can speak about it, but I may be waiting a long time. For my mother, love is expressed in what she does, not what she says. So perhaps I am waiting for the wrong thing.

*

Like any good twenty-something, I have spent much time trying to define myself. This is what I have concluded. I am gay. I'm a gay Vietnamese doctor, the only child of two doctors. I am the son of two refugees who fought for a new perfect life, only to realise that perfection is unachievable no matter what continent you're on. I am culturally bipolar, raised on television and English while being expected to love *Paris by Night* (Vietnam's answer to Eurovision) and to speak fluent Vietnamese.

I am also a collection of memories. Most of my life is a blur – but ask me to quote *The Simpsons* and I become the Rain Man. You can't choose what you remember, be they good memories, trivial ones, or traumatic. What you can do is choose how they affect you. My mother chose to raise me as she did because of her own memories. Though she desired more for me culturally, financially and romantically, she only knew one way to raise a child: the way her parents raised her. I have decided to treat my memories as a warning sign rather than as a guidebook. One day, I hope to have children of my own. I pray that the memories they keep of me are fond ones. Then again, who knows? Maybe all they'll remember is a senile old man talking about how he was friends with Billy and Anne back when they were still *Neighbours*. But at least they'll be laughing.

These Are the Photographs We Take

Emily J. Sun

1.

Your skin sticks to the sweaty plastic seat.

A red-faced tramp sits opposite you.

His grin reveals a mouthful of neglected ochre teeth and on his face sit oversized plastic blue-framed glasses that shield his ant-like eyes from the world. It's the eyes that remind you of the village idiot Lita left you for.

'I have chest pains,' the tramp explains. 'Maybe I smoke too much.'

He grins and you grin back.

Sitting next to him is a man who looks like your father. You never knew your father until last week and by then it was all too late. He never apologised for leaving you, your mother and your sister Sam for a woman he hardly knew. He left you for that other woman because she had a Green Card, the winning lottery ticket for anyone not rich or politically important enough to leave Vietnam. During his two-hour visit last week he told you that one of your American half-brothers had just started his internship at UCLA's prestigious San Fernando Valley medical program and the other was a pre-med student at the same university. You changed the subject. There was no point in knowing any more of his life. You would never see him again.

The man, who is not your father, is a sick man. His body is hunched over and his hoarse laboured breathing scrapes against the still air.

The village idiot returns and offers you a cigarette.

'You look a lot like my brother,' he says.

A woman, who is only the size of a young girl, walks around the room with a large canvas bag, almost twice her size, slung over her shoulders. You did not notice her before and as she looks directly at you, you notice that sorrow has carved too many a grief line upon her once beautiful face. She has something to say to you, but continues to walk around the room with her eyes downcast. Each step is a deliberate placement as her feet instinctively try to form an arch that does not exist.

She mutters under her breath, 'Fifty-eight, fifty-seven, fifty-six, fifty-five ...'

The village idiot tramp sits closer to you.

'I'm a gambler ...' he says. 'I lost thirty thousand in a week. Couldn't pay my debts. Had to run away from the moneylenders. But I told them my mother is sick ... My mother is dead ... She never smoked ... She was very tall and had very pale skin. Very beautiful. Agent Orange. Bloody Americans. We should have killed them all ...'

You ask him for a lighter.

But he says that that you cannot light a cigarette without oxygen.

... forty-seven, forty-six, forty-five, forty-four ...

'When did you get here?' he asks.

You shrug your shoulders.

'Cigarette?'

You take another one and make your way out of the room. There must be a lighter or oxygen somewhere here.

2.

As you walk down the corridor you think that you must be in the city's main hospital because you remember walking along a similar corridor when your sister Sam accidentally cut her finger on the rusty and jagged lid of a baked bean can. But this is not the same corridor because there are no windows here, only a long corkboard on which there are layers upon layers of leaflets.

Volunteers Wanted, See Jesus,
Save Your Soul, Space for Rent

You think how great it would have been to leave home. You were sick of sharing a bathroom with Sam, who always spent at least an hour in the morning washing and blow-drying her hair. She always complained about her hair and threatened to put it through the chemical bonding process so that it would sit flat and limp against her head. Why did all the Asian girls want their hair to be straighter and smoother? Lita was different. She had naturally straight and beautiful long hair, like a model straight out of a shampoo commercial. She went through phases throughout high school, dying it blonde, orange, teal and pink, but it was always silky, smooth and black in the in-between stages. Lita. Oh Lita. You wonder where she is now, but the more you think about her, the more you feel as if an elephant is suspended over your sternum and you need a cigarette to smoke out this feeling.

You walk until you reach a sliding door on the other side of which you see a pit of butchered buildings. The wiring on one of the remaining grey concrete blocks sticks out like sinews from a freshly severed limb. The remaining window frame is like a mouth agape; a witness to the carnage. You try to step outside but a strong gale-force wind howls, hurls debris in your direction and pins you back behind the door.

There is not a living soul in this place.

3.

An unfamiliar room.

You assume it is four-walled, but you cannot be sure because the fluorescent lights flicker on and off. The only certainty is that you are the only person in this room and your cigarette is still unlit. You are hungry. You cannot remember the last time you ate. You miss the village idiot and his ochre teeth, you miss the man who looks like your father and you miss the laundry woman. Loneliness is the ache in your chest.

It is not always about Lita.

This place reminds you of the time you were seven and were left all alone in a very cold room at the airport on your way to Australia. You were with your mother and Sam, except her name was Trinh back then. They took your mother and Sam away from you because little boys had to wait in another room. You were only wearing your favourite yellow shorts and a Hello Kitty singlet. That woman who was left to keep an eye on you asked you if you were a little boy or a little girl. Little goose bumps rose from your skin and you started to cry. But then she gave you an ice-cream and a plastic construction set. These are not such unpleasant memories, are they now?

You could have ended up anywhere really. You wanted to go to America because your father was there, but your mother said that there were too many guns in America, Canada was too cold, France was too French and England was too English. Anyway, you already had cousins in Australia and your mother heard that no one really cared about Australia. It was a peaceful place tucked away in the furthermost corner of the world.

4.

You look up to the ceiling and see that the fluorescent light panes form a zebra crossing. The room appears a lot larger than you first thought. Do you see the three blue doors at the far end of the room? They look like the classroom doors of your primary school. You could barely speak English when you first started there. Thank goodness for Ronald who lived next door. He stood in his backyard and you stood in yours as you spoke gobbledygook to him and he spoke English back at you. Finally one day you were both speaking English. You didn't go to the same school as Ronald. His parents wanted more for him so they sent him to a private school in a better area, but you played with him after school until his family moved to be closer to his school. Your mother wanted to move too but she could not afford it. It was difficult making ends meet back then. She was grateful for the social security. This is a country that cared about everyone – even the refugees who had no right to be there. She worked at home sewing clothes for a local T-shirt company. She was paid less than fifteen dollars for each bag of T-shirts – which worked out to be around twenty cents a shirt. She was grateful for this work because she was paid cash-in-hand and had time to pick you up from school, cook you dinner and put you to bed. ·

But you hated that she had time for you. You hated it when she walked up to the classroom door and peered in through the small window like an institution inmate. The other kids laughed at her. You knew why they laughed at her and you wanted to laugh at her wild hair and mismatched colours too. They laughed at you for the same reason. You told her not to pick you up from school. You told your teacher she could not speak English so they would not ask her to do canteen duty. You hid her from the world.

Things changed for you when Jenny Prosser, the Aboriginal girl with the golden flax hair, came to the school. They said that she was almost beautiful with her tan skin and green eyes.

What a pity about the rest of the face and her drunken half-caste mother. You were happy when Jenny came to the school because it made the others forget about you. The 'Boong', the 'Abo', the 'Monkey'. They laughed at her when she pissed her pants. This was the funniest incident the class had witnessed and they forgot that the week before you had turned up to school in pink tracksuit bottoms. At least you were clean. Jenny was never clean. She was always late for school and smelt like rabbit shit. Jenny's mum was far more embarrassing than your mother. You did not want to laugh at Jenny because you knew how she felt, but you did not want the other kids to laugh at you either. What if they made you marry Jenny? You always secretly hoped that they would involve you in a game of 'Paralyse' – a tag game where the person who was 'it' touched Jenny and then tried to pass her disease on to anyone they 'caught'. You wanted to be contaminated but they never asked you to play.

5.

You walk through one of the blue doors and are greeted by the familiar aroma of freshly ground coffee. There are men and women dressed up in black business suits. Your mother said she would buy a suit for you after the ... or maybe she would put you in the suit you wore to your high school graduation dinner. Remember the speech you made when you won the citizenship award for tutoring kids at the homework centre?

You were popular in high school. You won a scholarship to a Catholic school. It was a general academic scholarship but you wanted to be an artist. For some reason everyone gravitated towards you. It wasn't just the Vietnamese kids, even though there were quite a few of them at this school. Maybe Catholics were nicer people because they believed in Jesus and Jesus told them they had to love one another and treat others the way they wanted to be treated. Maybe they were nice to you because you were a foreigner and Jesus was a foreigner too.

Throughout high school you believed that there were better

306

times ahead. When you were three, a Chinese fortune-teller, your mother's co-worker at the factory, told you that you were born on the emperor's right hand and were destined for great things if you made it past your mid-twenties. At the time you had every reason to believe that you would live to at least your seventies. With hindsight, your seventeenth year was the best year of your life. That year you had all the potential in the world. You were on your way to becoming the super Asian that everyone thought you would be and your mother had left the Chinaman stepfather who had spent every cent that either of them made. That year, you met Lita Liu.

Even now, here in this place, you think about her.

Lita was spunky. You knew it from the moment you met her in chemistry class. It wasn't just because she had blonde hair, wore purple contact lenses, listened to the Stone Temple Pilots, smoked pot and headed the drama club. The first thing you said to her was 'Are you from Singapore?' and she stopped talking to you for a week. She forgave you and you became friends. You found out she was something crazy like fifth-generation Australian-Chinese. Her ancestors came to the country before they put in laws to stop Chinese people from entering. She said that there must have been some serious in-breeding in her family because after five generations she was still a 'full blood' Chinese.

Lita sat next to you in English and chemistry. She wasn't at school half the time so you let her copy your notes and helped her catch up with assignments. You didn't have much to do with her outside the classroom because she was always with the drama kids in the arts centre and you were always goofing around in the common room with Ronald and the boys. You asked her to the school ball but she already had a boyfriend by then. She did however ask you to dance with her at the graduation dinner. She rested her head on your shoulder and you swayed with her for two minutes.

Lita. It was always about Lita. You were such a fool to believe that she wanted you.

What would a girl like Lita do with a guy like you?

6.

Just when you feel that you are invisible, an overfed child stands in front of you. He reminds you of a Shar Pei dog.

'I would pick the strawberry marshmallow one,' he says and giggles maniacally as he points to the vending machine behind you.

There are so many questions you want to ask him because children are purveyors of truth.

'Why are you here, little brother?'

He throws his head back and continues laughing.

'Do you want me to buy one for you? Do you know the way out of here?'

The child walks up to the machine and points to the chocolate bar. He tells you to eat it. You sink your teeth into the sweet sponge-like marshmallow and the overfed child continues laughing at you. You expect to grow taller, smaller or fade away, but nothing happens. You reassure yourself that life is, or was, nothing but a series of random events. You follow the child as he toddles away from you, because it's what people do when they find themselves in this situation. The child predictably disappears into the darkness. Your feet begin to hurt and that feeling returns to your chest. A set of wooden stairs appears before you. It gets easier after the first step.

7.

The stairs lead to the kitchen of Happy Emperor Garden. This is where you got your first and last job as a waiter and barman. It's the busy lunchtime hour but no one is eating. You search for the manager Coco and her boyfriend Jet. You do not recognise anyone in this place, but you are convinced that it is the Happy Emperor because the towel-warmer is in the far left-hand corner of the main dining room and the two goldfish are in the round bowl next to the lobster tank.

Coco is the daughter of the business migrant who owns this restaurant. Jet is a refugee, just like you. Jet was already twelve years old when he came to Australia, but his mother told the authorities he was only eight. Just like you, Jet was eight years old when he first spoke English. But unlike you, he still sounded like he was from somewhere else and he hated high school because he was bullied mercilessly. You said it happened to you too. It happens to anyone who is different. He said he did not mind being called a 'gook,' because he was one, or a 'Ching Chong Chinaman,' because his father was one, but he hated it when the kids called him 'nigger' because of his dark skin.

Later on Jet would join a gang that went out on weekends looking for black people to beat up. He said that if he hadn't beaten them up, they would have beaten him up. In his neck of the woods, the 'blacks' hated the 'gooks', the 'whites' hated both the 'blacks' and the 'gooks' and everyone just wanted to be white; except they couldn't be, so they sometimes ganged up with the 'blacks' to beat up the white kids. It was too complex a Venn diagram for you, but then again you played footy.

Jet told you that when he was sixteen years old, he witnessed a car full of Asian students rear-end a truck. It wasn't even his problem, but when he saw the truck driver walk up to the students and go on about 'Fucking Asian drivers' Jet got out of his car, pulled his knife out and stabbed one of the guys in the stomach. The other guy was too shocked to retaliate. Jet said it sounded like the air was being let out of the guy. Jet had many more stories like this one and you were his adoring audience.

He treated you like a brother and got you as many shifts as you wanted at the restaurant. You got into the finance and law degree that you were aiming for, but halfway through the finance component you realised there were not enough hours in the day for both work and study. So you cut down on both and picked up an elective from the art department. You were in no rush to be a corporate lawyer or sell bonds on Wall Street.

One day, in the year after the year you should have graduated from your first degree, your mother told you that Mrs Huynh's son, not the doctor but the dental surgeon, had purchased his first house. He was still living at home, rent free, so he was able to accumulate rental income until he got married. Your mother said that she wanted Sam to study medicine because there are always sick people in the world to heal. Sam said she would probably end up studying medicine, not because she wanted to but because she could and also, she was sick of living in a small apartment where you could smell the cigarette smoke from the next apartment.

You told Jet about wanting to be an artist but needing a real job so that you can move everyone away from the small apartment with paper-thin walls. Jet encouraged you to finish your degree and said that you had all the time in the world to draw pictures later on. You asked him for more shifts and he said that he could get you some work from his other boss – tax-free of course.

So your pay cheque at the restaurant increased even though you were working fewer shifts. Jet started taking you out to meet his friends. He called you his little brother and you called him big brother. Soon his friends were calling you little brother as well. You played cards with them, went fishing with them and you helped them get their 'goods' out into the community. You continued with your studies and you were able to give your mother half your pay cheque every week. She asked you once where you got the money from and you told her that you had sold one of your paintings.

That was then. This is now. It's time to move on. You cannot wallow in these memories forever.

Lita.

She came into the restaurant one lunchtime with a friend of hers. You recognised her straight away even though it had been years since you left school. Both she and her friend were dressed in black suits. Her friend looked like a librarian but Lita looked as if she had stepped off the catwalk.

'It's been too long,' she said when you showed her to her table.

You had no idea you were so close. 'The deep fried dishes are just a gimmick to get white people into the restaurants. No Chinese person who knows anything about food would eat the fried stuff,' she pointed out to her friend.

She returned to the restaurant the next day, and the one after and the one after that.

On the fifth visit, you offered her complimentary tea.

On the sixth, you asked her where she worked.

On the seventh, you summoned up to courage to ask her for her number.

Jet teased you mercilessly.

'Fine wine, oysters and a dozen red roses,' he said, 'That's how I won Coco over.'

You knew that Lita was nothing like Coco. Coco was someone who thought the Stone Temple Pilots were a Buddhist cult. Coco had chemically bonded hair.

You did not tell Jet that you had never asked anyone out before.

You must have caught up with Lita half-a-dozen times over a month or two. You were not sure whether or not you were dating, seeing each other or just friends catching up. You found out that she was interested in your life, or rather the life you barely remembered, back in Vietnam. She was doing Asian studies at university and had already finished an accounting degree. She took on the second degree to learn an Asian language. She started with Indonesian, moved onto Chinese and was now in her second year of a Japanese course. She said she enjoyed exploring her cultural roots.

You asked her if she enjoyed her field. She said she enjoyed the pay.

You said you were supposed to be in finance or something related to that, but you wanted to be a painter after you finished university.

She was impressed and asked if you had a girlfriend.

You still had not bought her any flowers.

Jet kept reminding you to keep it cool because there was nothing more appealing to a girl than an aloof and disinterested man. He had even worked out an exponential equation for this phenomenon.

But you couldn't play it cool.

When you found out that she had been saving up to buy the Shisheido lipgloss range if it was ever released in Australia, you immediately ordered it for her on the company's Japanese website. You gave her your new mobile phone, when you saw that hers was the size of a brick. On a walk through the CBD, she pointed to the second balcony of an office building and professed her love of the pink roses that hung from the wrought-iron balustrade. That night, you climbed up there and clipped all the rose buds for her.

How could Lita not have known you were in love with her?

8.
The tramp finds you standing by the empty fish-tank.

'What are you doing here?' he asks, as if you knew where you were supposed to be.

You look at your now limp cigarette.

'There's not much time left,' he says, 'I was told to keep an eye on you but you ran off.

We have to get back.'

He ushers you out onto the bustling street.

'Back where?' you ask.

The people here walk with a purpose and everyone is where they should be.

The tramp, now dressed in a crisp pale blue shirt and beige trousers, hails you a cab.

'You were supposed to wait in that room until I got the go-ahead to show you,' he says.

'Show me what?'

'You're not supposed to be by yourself at this time. There's too much here for anyone to process alone. The laundry woman has been here as long as I have but she hasn't quite figured out what's happened. The old man who was sitting next to you in the waiting room thinks he's back at the hospital even though his children showed him his coffin ten minutes before he arrived here.'

He bundles you into the taxi.

'We need to hurry. The flight is at 8:52, terminal two. You'll need some money for the rooftop swimming pool.'

'I was here wasn't I?' you ask. 'These are the last …'

He pushes you into the taxi before jumping in himself.

You know the rest of your story.

From the taxi you see ordinary people walking, talking, shopping. You see traffic lights, department stores, corner stores, monorails and small patches of grass. There is life on every square inch of this concrete jungle.

'They can't see us, you know,' he says. 'This was before and there's nothing you can change about it.'

9.

The idea to leave the country was Jet's. He saw how miserable you were after it happened. You didn't tell him the whole story, but Jet understood. 'You can't trust the banana girls,' he said.

He was right. Did you misread the signs?

After all she was the one who asked you out that night to see a movie at the outdoor cinema, an Italian film about a group of twenty-something misfits. She was the one who leant against your shoulder and reached for your hand. Afterwards, she suggested a moonlight walk on the beach and it was there that you told her you had been in love with her since high school.

She kissed you and you kissed back.

In that moment you believed that you had reached an epiphany, a turning point, enlightenment, nirvana. You wondered how many other lips she had kissed.

She dropped you back home. You said you would call her and you did. You called her first thing in the morning and left a sheepish message about how much you had enjoyed yourself last night. Maybe you could do it again soon. No you didn't mean do it. You called again to apologise for leaving such a clumsy message. You said you were busy with other things anyway so you had no time to meet up this week, but your phone was on 24/7 only because you were waiting for another call. You texted, just in case she ran out of calling credit, but she did not respond. You emailed her. She did not reply.

Jet knew what was happening. It happened to him once before except it was a Dutch girl. She wasn't really Dutch but her grandparents were born there. You told him it wasn't like that. Lita was just a friend and one thing lead to another. Anyway, Lita was Asian.

Jet didn't want to break the news to you, but he knew the type. Lita was the sort of girl who felt she was too good for her own kind.

You didn't believe him the first week, or the second. But he was right. She finally replied to one of your emails and apologised for her behaviour. She said that she loved you – but only as a brother and had confused these feelings with love. It was so obvious, really, because you looked exactly like her cousin. She added, by the way, she had started seeing someone from work and perhaps you could all meet up. He was a corporate lawyer, but like you had an interest in art.

You cried, you slept and your body started aching. You started sleeping in until lunchtime. You were a fool to think that a refugee boy like you could have had a girl like Lita.

You would have slept forever if it were not for Jet. He was sick of seeing you walking around like an empty shell.

Nothing Jet said made you feel any better. He said that girls were all the same. They rip your heart out and feed it to the dogs. He had his heart broken when he was your age and vowed never to love again. Jet knew how you were feeling, but you were no good to him at the restaurant and the brothers were getting a bit sick of your self-indulgence.

Then he offered you an escape. He had some overseas business to attend to but was too busy with the restaurant. He wanted to spend more time with Coco because he wasn't getting any younger. He said it was a safe job and that the brothers would take care of all expenses. You could even check into one of the expensive hotels near the four floors of whores. It was the perfect chance for you to forget about Lita. The world was full of girls who looked like Lita. All you had to do was pick up a little parcel from the rooftop swimming pool at the airport on your return trip.

You spent your first day in a cinema complex as you tried to escape the damp heat that slowed your brain. You ordered room-service breakfast but ate lunch and dinner at the hawker stalls. You tried to order something different every day because you were not sure when you'd eat such good food again. You discovered that you had a penchant for *dhosas*, hot chicken porridge and green coconut juice. You thought about Lita and even sent her a postcard.

Your last moments of freedom are a blur to you now. You called Sam before you went to meet the man on the rooftop pool. The man was wearing lime-green shorts as Jet said he would be. He discreetly left you the key to his locker, where you found a package that you quickly shoved into your backpack. You wanted to swim but there was so little time, so you smoked an extra-long duty-free cigarette by the pool before an attendant told you to go to the viewing deck. You were on that deck for so long that you had to run to catch your plane. As you rushed through the gates, the alarms went off. They searched your body only to find an imitation Rolex. Then they insisted they search all your bags. It must have been the Cheshire cat. When they found Jet's special package, you banged your head against the wall in hope that your skull would split open and your brain splatter across the interview room. You knew that there would be no second chances. There was nothing special about you. You were so unremarkable.

Sam was going to pick you up at the airport, but the next time you would see her was behind Perspex glass. You never held her hand again.

10.

You tell the tramp to stop the taxi.

But he says that past is set in concrete. There is nothing you can do about it now. He's just here to make sure you stay here.

'Believe me,' he says 'It was a shock to me too.'

You look down and see wooden panelling.

Your nails are still growing.

The taxi plunges into darkness and you are falling through the air.

Five, four, three, two...

1.

Your skin sticks to the sweaty seat.

Homecoming

My China

Kylie Kwong

As a 29th-generation Kwong, I have long dreamt of visiting the Kwong ancestral village in China, where my great-grandfather Kwong Sue Duk was born in 1853. A dedicated practitioner of Traditional Chinese Medicine, Kwong Sue Duk was lured to Australia in 1875 by the promise of gold. Over the years he travelled many times between China and Australia as he forged business connections and secured a future for his family. His descendants now number around 1200 and span five generations, and I am honoured to be a part of what is possibly the largest Chinese family tree in Australia. Today I am returning to the clan village, the first family member to visit our ancestral home in ninety years.

Wong Nai Hang, Kwong Sue Duk's home village, lies in the countryside outside Toishan, a big and modern city in Guangdong province, about three hours' drive southwest from Guangzhou. *Wong Nai Hang* translates as 'Yellow Mud Ditch,' a reflection of the village's fertile soil, but it's also known a little more auspiciously as 'The Good Luck and Peace Village.'

I am being driven down a dirt road through the fields towards Wong Nai Hang, a scattered group of elderly, square-sided houses up ahead, all shaded by huge old trees. I get out and begin walking along the white-pebbled track leading to the Kwong family's ancestral village – the feeling is primal. I find out later that the path was pebbled in my honour.

As I make my way through the village, it buzzes with life: mottled chickens peck at the ground, twitchy-eared dogs sniff the air and stare at us; farmers steer water buffalo through the lush, green rice paddies; worn and weathered wooden wheelbarrows lie by the side of the fields; ducks glide through the murky waters, and waddle in and out of their coops; and pigs run wild and generally make a nuisance of themselves. Some of the villagers, clad in thin polyester floral-patterned shirts and knee-length pants, stand in the doorways of their houses, looking on and wondering what all the commotion is about.

When I finally arrive at the top of a small hill, there stands Kwong Sue Duk's home – I can't believe it! Over 130 years old, infused with tradition and ritual, the house is built of mud bricks and wooden beams, and earthy, musty smells permeate the air. The building comes from a China I have only ever seen before on the television screen or in books. A patina of dark brownish-black and deep sea-green mould covers the narrow, densely layered bricks – I run my fingers over the walls, hoping to 'feel' a little bit of my great-grandfather's spirit. Old wooden lids and baskets sit in what must once have been the living room but is now a safe haven for chickens. On the wall is the Kwong family seal – I am overwhelmed by the feeling that I really belong somewhere. I am thrilled; my heart is pounding with emotion, and I cannot recall the last time I smiled this much.

Warned of my visit in advance, a group of villagers is waiting for me and within a few moments we are talking through an interpreter as if we have known each other forever – they treat me like I am their child, their sister, their aunt. With their high-pitched vocal tone and rather blunt, down-to-earth manner, Chinese people can be quite a noisy bunch … and at this moment I don't know who is louder, the chooks or the villagers! I'm surrounded by a lot of squawking as I am affectionately dragged toward the porch of my great-grandfather's house, in preparation for the ritual of thanks to my ancestors.

The ancestor shrine is inside Kwong Sue Duk's house. A wobbly old card table holds bowls filled with food: a white-cooked chicken, still with head, neck and feet; one unpeeled orange; a juicy, fat strip of roasted pork, complete with crackling; and small bowls variously filled with tomatoes, stir-fried potatoes, and some cauliflower cooked with salted radish. It occurs to me that, even in the context of ceremonies, the Chinese are *always* thinking of balance and harmony of flavour, texture and ingredient. One of my relatives is saying something to me in Chinese, and is becoming more and more insistent. After a lot of kerfuffle, I work out that tradition demands I add a sweet to the platter of food for good luck – and to impart sweetness to the afterlife. I look around desperately at my friends and we all rummage through our bags until, finally, a mint is retrieved … phew!

Three tiny plastic red cups, similar to ones you might find in a doll's house, are placed in a row in front of the food, along with three sets of matching chopsticks. Another relative pours wine into the three cups and then lights a wad of joss sticks, which are a wonderful magenta colour with camel-coloured tips – exactly the same as the ones our family used to light at Rookwood Cemetery in Sydney. Following instructions, I hold the incense between my palms and bow forward three times. I then pour the wine, one cup at a time, onto the ground in front of the table; the cups are promptly refilled and repositioned, before the ritual is repeated. Next I light a wad of paper money, which is left to burn itself out on the ground, and bow a final three times.

To complete the ritual, we all stand back as a box of red firecrackers is lit, and everyone shrieks and runs for cover as they let off an almighty bang and a blinding cloud of smoke. The Chinese enjoyment of noise, fuss, big crowds, bright lights and loud colours is all to do with driving away bad luck and evil spirits; silence, gloom and white are always associated with loneliness and death.

The ritual is over, and it's time to move outside Kwong Sue Duk's home to a perch overlooking the fields, where I'm going to cook lunch for the crowd of villagers and relatives around me. There could be no better spot to do it than here, in the middle of a rice paddy in rural China. My translator tells me that, in fact, very few Kwongs still live in the village today, but one of them – who I immediately think of as an 'uncle' – stokes the fire for me, and I have to do a double-take because he looks so much like my eldest brother, Paul.

We had scoured the local markets that morning for the freshest vegetables, including yellow garlic chives, wonderfully crunchy lotus roots and shiny purple eggplants; live baby fish and snappy little crabs; large red chillies and small green chillies … I make up the recipes as I go along. I am on such a high, I don't know who to smile at next. As the flames roar into life under what seems like the world's biggest and hottest wok, and with the temperature climbing as the sun rises in the sky, it is sultry and smoky. In the background are timeless scenes of paddy fields tended by workers wearing traditional bamboo hats, while closer to me old men sit around the fire flashing gold-toothed smiles and smoking rather interesting-looking cigarettes.

The village women are enchanting. Although we first met just hours ago, I feel as if we have known each other for years, and we easily slip into this incredibly harmonious and efficient 'working bee.' Squatting on their haunches, three of the women wash and wipe dishes, while the fourth goes up and down the path to the well, filling and carrying two pails on each trip.

These villagers are very fit: they live simply, eat only fresh food and, as farmers, work very hard in tune with the seasons. Despite having so few of those essentials we take for granted (there's no piped gas, running water or electricity in the village), they have such spirit – their eyes dance, they laugh all the time, they are responsive and seem to live in the moment ... I say to myself, *This is what living is all about.*

As I cook over an open flame in this remote village, I feel so at home. My mind begins to wander. *So this is where the old man came from, this is what his family life was all about. What incredible courage on his part, firstly to want for more than this simple existence and, secondly, to venture out of this corner of the world and sail to far-away Australia.*

A million questions come to mind – how I wish that Kwong Sue Duk was here right now to answer them. I would ask him what prompted him to embark on such a momentous journey; what was going through his mind and what lay in his soul at the time; I want to know where he got his pioneering spirit from, and I wonder whether my sense of adventure can be traced back to him.

What inspired a 25-year-old man to leave all he had ever known? I would give almost anything to have had just one conversation with my great-grandfather about his thoughts, his feelings, his passions, his views ... I never even got the chance to meet my grandfathers: by the time I was born, both had already passed on. I always felt sad about this when I was growing up as I had heard so much about them: my maternal grandfather Goong Goong's famous homemade pickles, my paternal grandfather's excellent musical talent. If only Kwong Sue Duk could be with us – I feel sure that he would be thrilled to see all of us connecting and living our lives in the same enthusiastic fashion as he lived his own. I guess he is here in spirit ...

*

Sadly, the time comes to pack up and leave. Our farewells are accompanied by much hugging, and as we walk down the track to the bus, one of the villagers roars up beside me on his motorbike. Looking at me with a cheeky smile, he points to me and then back to his bike. The next thing I know I am perched on the back of his Suzuki, charging through the village at quite a speed. I laugh helplessly as we pass a blur of houses, chook pens, pig pens and duck ponds, with the rest of the villagers waving and cheering us on.

As our bus pulls out, we wave goodbye and drive at a snail's pace over my beloved white-pebbled track. I fall back in my seat, smiling and speechless. I can't wait to call my family in Australia and tell them of my experiences – of the path freshly pebbled for my visit, of my uncle's wok and, especially, I can't wait to tell them how deliriously happy I feel to be a part of this enchanting, extraordinary and energetic family.

This is an edited extract from *My China* by Kylie Kwong (Penguin Books, 2007).

The Face in the Mirror

Blossom Beeby

When I was a child, my mother would amuse herself with stories of how I'd come into the world. Perhaps I had arrived on the front lawn in a spaceship, or had been sent to do the cleaning. In the late eighties, people were not accustomed to seeing white parents with a smiley Asian kid in tow. Curious ones would ask my parents why they had a 'Chinese daughter,' and I think my mother liked the idea of shocking them with unexpected responses. It was kind of a secret joke between us.

323

There are of course some truths that my mother shared about my arrival. When I was born on the first of February in 1984, the temperature was thirteen degrees below zero. It was in a city in the south of Korea called 'Pusan.' These are two things I have always known about my birth. For a long time, though, I'd pronounced the '-san' part of Pusan in a hard, Australian-sounding way, to rhyme with the word 'can.' It should have been a softer 'sa*h*n.' My parents gave me the middle name 'Soo Jeong,' which in Korean means 'crystal' and was my first name when I was a baby in Korea. These details were hard-wired into my brain: interesting morsels to satisfy curious people, but static and scripted, with little current meaning.

Parents who acquired 'Made in Korea' babies in the 1980s received scant care instructions. Don't treat delicately. Allow to integrate. Take special care not to acknowledge Asian-ness. My parents heeded the tag, I think. Asian adoptees often talk about their experiences with mirrors. To many of us they have a sad significance. Inside we identified with the Caucasian people who made up our families. If we closed our eyes and imagined ourselves, we would see rosy white kids. When we looked at our faces in the mirror, though, foreigners would appear. I internalised my Asian face, but it didn't mean that I liked it. I just accepted it.

My mother had bought a large coffee-table book with beautiful images of Korea inside. There were tranquil countryside landscapes and serene images of cherry blossoms falling on courtyards. In one of these, there was an elderly woman, hunched over and gazing at the camera. I was repulsed by her brown wrinkledness. I thought about becoming like this in my old age. I genuinely believed that with the progression of time in Australia, I would eventually evolve into a fully-fledged Caucasian and would never have to face the possibility of being a shrivelled-up old Asian woman.

For much of my childhood, my Asian-ness was pushed to a crevice in the back of my mind. My friends were white, my family was white, my world was white. We lived in tolerant, white neighbourhoods. In both my primary and high schools, I was the only Asian kid in my year. The characters I read about in books and watched on television and in movies were white. All my conceptions of beauty were white, and I wondered if boys would ever find me attractive. To me, Asian people were not attractive and were in no way sexual beings.

It was quite easy to forget I was Asian when everyone around me was white, but there were occasions when the facade wasn't entirely effective. Asian people scared me silly. When I was a kid, South-East Asian guys with long, centre-parted hair used to squat, cigarettes in hand, in Adelaide's Rundle Mall. They would look around listlessly and talk amongst themselves. If I ever walked through that part of the mall with my dad, I would stare at the ground and subtly urge him to walk faster. I don't know what I was fearful of. Perhaps if I'd acknowledged that these people existed, I would have had to look in the mirror again.

I spent many summers flipping through my grandmother's trashy weekly gossip magazines. One day I came across an advertisement for pantyhose. The ad featured an Asian woman standing in a boxing ring. She had glistening black hair and was wearing a figure-hugging red dress with a split all the way up her leg. She was wearing a pair of sheer, black pantyhose and impossibly high stilettos. Heavily made-up to look smouldering, her facial expression was confident, if a little smug. She was beautiful and she gave me a glimmer of a hope.

In the latter years of high school, I began a rebellion of sorts. I started going to nightclubs with my best friend, who was half Ghanaian and had grown up mostly with a white English mother. We were both a little culturally confused and suddenly found places where there were a lot of people who looked like us. There were Asians, Arabs, Africans, Indians and every ethnicity in between: the white kids were the minority. It was a cultural hodge-podge and a comfort zone I'd never known before. I felt at ease asserting my ethnicity among the throngs of other black-haired people who gathered in those dark, smoky venues. It was the first time I'd felt comfortable being an Asian, around other Asians. It may have been a very seedy way of achieving it and not one to be advocated in adoptive parenting handbooks, but I was finally kind of glad to be Asian.

I had fully acknowledged my Asian-ness and was proud of it. I met more Asians and felt comfortable around them. I would ask their nationality and they would ask mine. As with the facts about my birth, the response 'Korean' became automated. But if you'd asked, I couldn't have told you one thing about Korea. I didn't feel I needed to delve any deeper.

My university boyfriend was a Japanese-Australian. He determined very quickly that I actually was Korean. He was sensitive and genuinely wanted me to learn about the country. Being proud, I couldn't tell him that I was scared. So I went along with it.

He took me to the Korean food stand in Chinatown. I ordered a generic chicken dish and sat down with it in trepidation. He told me to try the kimchi, Korea's national dish. I shoved it in my mouth and chewed. It was a nerve-wracking experience. I wonder now if he detected that. 'Not bad,' was all I could muster.

From then on, I threw my fears aside and learnt all I could about Korea. Maybe it was the mystical healing properties of the kimchi. Smells of sesame oil and fermented cabbage and soybean paste brought me a certain comfort and epicurean happiness. I ventured timidly into the one Korean grocery store in Adelaide to buy bulgogi and ramyeon and anything else I recognised.

One day, while waiting for a lecture, I noticed a small flyer offering Korean language lessons in exchange for help with English conversation. I hastily ripped off a tab and stashed it in my wallet. I called the number that night and spoke with a young Korean woman. We met up the following weekend and over potato wedges, with sour cream and sweet-chilli sauce, I began to learn my first Korean words.

My tutor began teaching me the basics of the Korean alphabet. To me, written Korean looked like someone had thrown down sticks and circles on a page. But I learned quickly and was soon able to make out the sounds they represented. I returned to Chinatown one weekend and stared at the sticks and circles: 엄마 김밥. They began looking less like meaningless shapes and more like words that I could actually read and say. It was like I had cracked a special code. My tutor was extremely patient and encouraged me. She told me my pronunciation was excellent and attributed this to my Korean tongue. I smirked and accepted the compliment.

The small snippets of information that I had always spat out on cue about my history now began to have significance. I had my university change my records so that my middle name – my Korean name, Soo Jeong – would appear on all my documents. I would sit and write my Korean name over and over in Hangeul: I could be 전수정 or Blossom Beeby. I began to think of my Korean name as the one connection between myself and Korea and my birth mother. I met people who had been to Pusan. They had stories of how Pusan people are tough, Pusan women have distinctive faces, the men are terse and uncompassionate and everyone speaks in a dialect that to outsiders gives the impression that they are yelling at each other. I wondered if I had inherited any of these characteristics.

I scoured my university library for books about Korea. To my dismay, there was scant contemporary material. The few books I could find, much like the country itself, were jammed between numerous tomes about its more glorious and fascinating neighbours, Japan and China. I was dissatisfied and hungry for more.

I decided that I wanted to see Korea. I won a scholarship to a language summer-school in Seoul. This would be the first time I had left Australia since arriving as a baby. I was wrapped up in anticipation and expectations.

I left Adelaide and stopped over in Kuala Lumpur. At the boarding gate in KL, it became increasingly clear that the flight was to be boarded exclusively by middle-aged Korean men in golf gear, Korean women with perms wearing visors and bum bags, and me. A man approached and asked me a question in Korean. I froze, turned bright red and shook my head. I was overcome with paralysing fear. I'd never been surrounded by Koreans before and they thought I was one of them. I was an imposter or somehow incomplete.

But I made it to Seoul. A bustling, smelly and baffling city. It was a fantastic summer. Surprisingly, there were no feelings of 'coming home' or 'finally belonging.' I just wanted to explore, eat, drink, party and in the process, throw away the scholarship. I was no longer fearful or anxious about Koreans. Puzzled and fascinated definitely, but the KL boarding gate feelings have never come back to me.

I was very lucky on that trip. I had approached my adoption

agency and asked them to begin a search for my birth family. They called me about eight weeks later. My birth mother was alive and wanted to meet me. The social worker happily announced that she would be travelling up to Seoul the next day by train from a country town in a southern province.

When I met my birth mother, she confirmed the reasons I had imagined for my relinquishment. I looked at her face and could immediately see myself. It was like her eyes, nose and cheekbones had been imprinted on my face. I asked how she had chosen my name. She hadn't. She'd handed me to the social worker the day I was born and had no say in the name I was given. This shook my comforting idea that my mother had given me my name in love.

I was able to travel to Pusan. With the help of my adoption agency and the local police, I located the building where I was born. In the eighties it had been a maternity home, where unwed mothers could have their illegitimate children in secrecy. Now it was a worn building. The top storeys were occupied by shifty looking offices with metal doors and deadlocks. The floors were cold cement. The thought crossed my mind that the map was wrong or that the policeman had made a mistake. This was not where I had imagined arriving into the world.

The adoption agency had printed out a map to help me find the building. I examined it and noticed that in the vicinity there were a lot of landmarks with the name Soo Jeong. I realised that my name had been given to me arbitrarily by a social worker with very little creativity. My heart sunk a little.

Slowly, it dawned on me that those little snippets out of which I had created Korean Blossom still had little real meaning. I had thought I had a foundation – a name, a place, a date and a temperature. But what did it all mean? Now that I'd learnt that those facts were so unromantic and inconsequential, I wasn't sure.

I have spent many hours contemplating what might have been had I grown up in Korea. It is a cyclical process and I am no closer to a conclusion. Had I stayed, most certainly I could never have had the opportunities that I have had in Australia. I might not have grown up with a loving and stable family. I would not enjoy the open and critical thinking that Australian education seems to encourage. But for each of these factors, another question opens up, sending my mind on another adventure. For all of Korea's shortcomings, I have never felt such social cohesion and an almost familial insularity. As frustrating as it was, I miss that about Korea and I wonder what it would have been like to grow up knowing only that world.

I cannot know how my life might have unravelled had I lived it in Korea. I can't pretend to understand Korean society as though it were my own. But I do feel as though I stand on a kind of cusp, looking in. Material circumstances pushed my life to where it is now, but they might have pushed it in a very different direction. I might have had a life with my Korean family, in their dusty country town on the beautiful southern coast of Korea. I might have grown up with values and a language and temperament that matched my face.

I have come a long way since I was a little girl who recoiled at the image of a wrinkled Korean woman – now I know her as *Halmoni*, or Grandmother. It has taken some time for the different bits of me to fit comfortably, and I am sure they will continue to realign and I will continue to question. For now, I think questioning is good. It seems to makes things clearer.

Baked Beans and Burnt Toast

Jacqui Larkin

The plane slaloms around the buildings, which seem to reach up to grab us. We're in a concrete jungle of chaos and neon when surely we should be above it. I don't know what keeps a jumbo jet in the air – something vague about low pressure and wind-flow over the wings I think I once read somewhere – but as our plane undertakes what is essentially a triple twist with pike, it seems as though the same rules don't apply in Asia. The sick-bags are in short supply as we are buffeted around the sky. I don't know if the laws of physics apply here, but it's clear that the noise pollution laws are also a little lax. Surely the sound of a 747 screaming past your apartment window would require more than double-glazing to keep out.

One more sharp, gravity-defying turn and we are thumped unceremoniously onto the tarmac at Kai Tak airport.

'Welcome to Hong Kong,' announces the steward in several dialects, including Engrish. 'We hope you had a pleasant flight.' *A pleasant flight?* That was nothing more than a controlled crash. I search for a hint of sarcasm in the steward's tone, but there's none to be found. I hope they hurry up and finish the new airport out at Lantau Island, because I'm not sure I could go through that again.

Despite the flight attendants' pleas, people are up and out of their seats, rummaging through overhead bins, getting themselves organised long before the plane has come to a halt at the terminal. Anyone who has survived a landing at Kai Tak develops a certain devil-may-care attitude and is not about to be made to sit down by a leering stick-insect in lip-gloss.

I look through my window at the lights of the city and up to the distant Peak. I can't believe that I've come home. Home to a land that I've never even visited until now. Dad was always promising to take us home one day, but a brain aneurism broke that promise in his fiftieth year. So now I'm bringing him home.

I collect my bags and smile at the customs officer when he calls me up to the counter. Not only does he totally fail to return my pleasantries, he actually sneers as he starts flicking through my Australian passport.

'*Simum sic gong Tongwah?*' He doesn't even look me in the eye when he asks me this. I trawl through my memory, hoping to translate, but, try as she might, my *pau-pau* abandoned any hope of my ever speaking Cantonese when I was about four. It would have been worth sixteen further years of practice just to avoid the embarrassment of this moment.

'I'm sorry, I don't understand what ...'

'I said, "DO YOU SPEAK CANTONESE?"' he interrupts in English, as aggressively as only someone who has the authority to order a rectal probe can. He says it slowly and deliberately, as if he's talking to a monkey at the zoo.

'*Noei,*' I reply, feeling shamed into replying in Cantonese, even if it is just a 'No' with a bit of attitude on the end.

The customs officer mumbles something to his colleague in

the next booth and they both have a good laugh at my expense as I feel myself starting to turn crimson.

'Do you speak Cantonese?' the words hang in the air and taunt me. No matter where I am it seems as though I will always be caught in the middle. Lost in that grey zone where the borders blur. I'm East meets West, an ABC, a banana. As I collect my passport and head off towards the taxis and shuttle buses, I'm transported back to my first day in kindergarten.

*

Even I feel like staring at me as we shuffle into class and sit on the floor. The only black head in a sea of blond, brown, sandy and ginger. I stand out like a plate of chicken feet at a sausage sizzle.

'Good morning girls and boys,' says the teacher in that sing-song way that kindy teachers do. 'My name is Mrs Barton. I will be your teacher for the year.'

Mrs Barton starts marking the roll. Everyone sticks their hand up as their name is called and I feel every single eye trained on me when it's my turn.

'Jacqui?' continues Mrs Barton and, for the first time but certainly not the last, I feel myself turning red. She doesn't do a double-take on anyone else's name, so why mine?

'Yes,' I reply.

She looks closer at the roll and adjusts her glasses. 'Jacqui Five-Hundred?'

For a minute I think there must be two Jacquis in kindy.

'No,' I offer tentatively.

'Well is that *you* or isn't it?' she snaps and then holds up the roll so that we can all see, not that any of us can really spell, though I can recognise my own name.

My friend Jo-Ann, who I've known since preschool, puts up her hand. 'It's Soo, Miss. Not Five-Hundred. Her name's Jacqui Soo.'

Mrs Barton looks back at her roll. 'Oh, I see. The administrative staff have put Jacqui Five-Hundred. Well then, Jacqui Soo, your mother needs to write more clearly so that people can read it. Or else get some help with her writing.'

I try to imagine someone having a last name of Five-Hundred

331

but it doesn't make any sense. Unfortunately there's no one after me on the roll so the teacher's focus is still on me.

'Anyway,' she says. 'Welcome girls and boys. You too, Jacqui Soo.' I don't know why she has to keep using both my names. She wouldn't call Jo-Ann 'Jo-Ann Bakoss'; it'd just be 'Jo-Ann.'

'Tell me, Jacqui Soo, DO YOU SPEAK ENGLISH?'

I'm not sure why she's shouting. I *only* speak English. But I just nod because my tongue feels as though it's swelling up in my mouth.

'Does she, Jo-Ann? Does Jacqui Soo speak English?'

'Yes, Miss,' replies Jo-Ann, already revelling in teacher's-pet status.

'If she has any trouble, Jo-Ann, you can always help her.' Then she turns back to me. 'Where are you from, Jacqui?'

'Carlingford,' I reply, because I am. Mrs Barton bursts out laughing and the rest of the class joins her, though they probably don't know what they're laughing at.

'I mean, where are you from originally? We might even be able to look it up in the atlas. Where were you born, Jacqui?'

I look around for some help, but even Jo-Ann looks blank. Is Carlingford even *in* the atlas? 'In a hospital, Miss' I finally reply, and Mrs Barton and the class have another great snort.

'Yes, but WHERE WAS THE HOSPITAL?'

'Oh,' I reply, finally getting with the program. 'In ... Chatswood, I think.'

The smile fades from Mrs Barton's lips. The conversation is over, and she turns abruptly to another student. What's wrong with Chatswood? I wonder.

At lunchtime I sit with the girls and open my lunchbox. It's fried rice with mini spring rolls. Why couldn't I have vegemite or peanut-butter sandwiches like everyone else? Okay, I can't stand vegemite, it makes me want to vomit, but it's hard enough being the only Asian kid in the school – couldn't my lunch at least be anonymous? I feel like crying until I see, or more crucially smell, what Jo-Ann has on her sandwiches. Hungarian people really go in for smelly sausages and fairly soon Jo-Ann and I have a large space all to ourselves, which I secretly hope is because of Jo-Ann's sandwiches and not me.

Jo-Ann and I are playing chasings with some other girls from class when I notice a boy approaching us. He's much older than us, probably even in second grade, and for a while he just stands there staring at me.

'Ching-chong, ching-chong sitting in a tree. Eating chop suey with a flea.'

From that day on I have that stupid taunt stuck in my head. At least he could have come up with a better rhyme. 'Eating chop suey on her knee,' for instance. Or, 'Eating chop suey for tea.' Or maybe even, 'Eating chop suey with glee.' But with a flea? What had the flea got to do with anything? And as for the chop suey, well, I didn't even know what that was.

My teaser's name is Peter Nugent, I learn after he has been dragged off to the administration block and issued with six of the best, and he is a child psychologist's dream. Nowadays he would be diagnosed with ADHD and dosed up to the gills on Ritalin; but back in the early seventies his type were allowed to roam free. They would tear around the playground like the Tasmanian devil in those old cartoons, beating other boys at random, setting fire to girls' skipping ropes while they were mid-skip and taunting anyone who showed up on their radar.

After that, Peter became a regular part of my lunchtime schedule. As soon as we'd finished eating, Jo-Ann and I would play chasings, king pin, elastics, or that strange game that involved inserting a tennis ball in a pair of old stockings and hurling it about like a set of nunchukas, and Peter would turn up and stare at me. Sometimes he would call us names. Jo-Ann was 'baked beans' and I was 'burnt toast.' Baked beans and burnt toast? I never knew what it meant. Still don't. But mostly he just stared.

And then, just when I got curious enough and confident enough to ask him what the baked beans and burnt toast were about, he wasn't there anymore. I don't remember him leaving. Maybe he just exploded or something. All I remember was that part of me missed the attention. He'd become a bit like a stray dog that follows you around all day. You shoo it away, throw rocks at it, ignore it, but it would always be back. And then suddenly, there's just a hole in the air and you realise that it's gone.

As the years went on, I sometimes wondered what happened to

Peter Nugent. How do kids like that adjust to civilian life? Probably left school as soon as he could, did something breathtakingly unskilled on a building site, married the obligatory Sharon, had a couple of kids called Zac and Tiffany; beer, footy, pokies, smokes, meat-raffle at the club. In other words – a walking stereotype with a beer gut.

I don't know why I'm even thinking of Peter Nugent as my taxi driver winds us through the backstreet maze of Kowloon. Perhaps he's just the face – that ugly face – of all those Aussies who've enquired, 'Why don't you go back to where you came from?' down the years.

Well, I'm back now. Back to a place I've never been to before. Happy?

*

A philosopher once said, 'Hong Kong is like a slap in the face that makes you feel good.' Actually, I think it was Chuck Norris, but you could hardly use that as the frontispiece of a novel, now could you? But as my taxi lurches down Nathan Road I can see what he meant. The neon makes my eyes flicker. Customers and sales people spill out onto the street. It's mayhem: everyone seems to be on the make or out for a bargain. I notice cured and shrivelled bits of something or other hanging in shop windows. I check in to my hotel and take the lift up to my room. I don't know which was more tiring – the nine-hour flight, or the drive from the airport. I'm looking forward to a long, luxurious bath, some room service and then a good night's sleep before getting out and discovering home tomorrow.

I sleep so deeply that I may have lapsed into a coma at some point. Breakfast comes with the room, so even though I'm not hungry I make my way down to the restaurant. It's fairly quiet; either everyone is already up and about, or maybe Hong Kong is a nocturnal city.

The head waiter is Anglo (white, skip, westerner, *gweilo*, whatever the correct term is) but he is speaking fluent Cantonese and sharing a joke with a couple of businessmen. When he sees me by myself he excuses himself and makes his way over to me with his coffee pot.

'*Seug sic di ma yeh?*'

'I'm sorry,' I reply tersely. 'I don't speak your language.'

'Beg your pardon,' he says. 'That was very presumptuous of me. It's full buffet, but can I get you a coffee to start with?'

'I think I'll pass on the breakfast. Just a coffee, thanks.'

He pours the steaming coffee into my cup but I'm in such dire need of a caffeine hit that I'm pretty sure I could absorb it through my skin.

'Long flight?' he asks.

'Not so much the flight as the last five minutes of it.'

'Yes, Kai Tak can get a little hairy. Though it is one of the safest airports in the world, apparently.' He continues as I sip my coffee. 'Pilots are so on edge when they come into land, they're wound up like springs. Senses working overtime. Lantau will be finished soon enough, though.'

'Good,' is all I can reply as he tops me up.

'First time in Hong Kong?'

'Is it *that* obvious?'

'You're from Sydney, right?'

I don't want to show him that I'm impressed. 'Do you know my star sign too?'

He ponders this for a moment. 'Sagittarius. Year of the Rat.'

'Well, you're right about the rat.'

'I'm a Sydneysider too,' he acknowledges. 'Working in hospitality, you get to pick accents.'

'Well, you're obviously very busy,' I say, hoping that he'll take the hint. Perhaps he's after a tip? Then I realise that I've been rude. 'So, how did you learn to speak Cantonese?'

'It's a bit of a talking dog thing, isn't it?'

I don't know what he means.

'It's not that the dog talks well,' he continues, 'it's that it talks at all.'

'So?' I press. 'How did you learn? Don't most Westerners here speak English?'

'I grew up in the suburbs,' he says, taking a seat at my table. 'It was all football, meat pies, kangaroos and Holden cars. Just before Sydney went multicultural and got some class about it. Anyway, this little Chinese girl came to the school and I just thought she was so beautiful, so exotic, so not me, that I couldn't take my eyes off her. But of course, like most emotionally retarded eight-year-old boys, the only way I could communicate with her was by calling her names. Pathetic really, but what do you do?'

I look at his name badge. Pete. I feel my jaw slowly starting to drop open.

'Then my parents split up and we moved up the coast with Mum. But the door had been opened for me and I knew there was another world out there beyond the whole football, meat-pie thing. By the end of my teens I knew that I was an egg.'

'An egg?'

'Yeah,' replies Pete. 'If you're a banana, then I'm an egg – white on the outside but yellow in the middle.'

'Oh,' is all I can manage in response.

'As soon as I finished uni,' continues Pete the egg, 'I moved over here and I've been travelling around ever since, though Hong Kong is home.'

Having finished his tale, he stares at me closely. 'Are you okay?' he says. 'You look like you've seen a ghost.'

'I don't feel so good,' I reply. All his talk about bananas and eggs has stirred things up a bit.

'Travel sickness,' says Pete. 'Wait here. I'll be back in a minute.' And with that, he races off towards the kitchen.

I try to breathe but it's not easy. I need some fresh air. I need sea air. As soon as I've finished breakfast I'll catch the Star Ferry to Hong Kong Island, take Dad's ashes over to Repulse Bay and say goodbye. And then ... and then ... well, then I'll go shopping in Stanley Markets, because in a strange way that's what Dad would have wanted. No big ceremonies. No big send-offs. Just his little girl doing something simple, enjoying herself, smiling with the sun on her face, and him watching over her.

'Here,' says Pete, interrupting my thoughts and placing a covered plate in front of me. 'It's an old Irish remedy for when you're feeling queasy. Mum gave it to us whenever we were feeling bad, or sick, or just off.'

I imagine black pudding, boiled cabbage, pints of Guinness mixed into a thick gruel and I know that I'm going to vomit.

I take a deep breath. 'What is it?'

Pete whips the cover off the plate and rather than puke, I smile.

'Works every time,' he says confidently.

'I'm sure it'll help clear things up,' I say, picking up my knife and fork and tucking into my steaming hot plate of baked beans and burnt toast.

Hanoi and Other Homes

Sim Shen

The drive into Hanoi from the airport was disorientating – first the sweeping boulevards of the outskirts of the city, then the gradual pressing in of the characteristically thin and tall Vietnamese houses, then over the Red River and finally into the narrow alleys of the old city. I felt as if I had stepped back into time, and not just any time, but my own past.

If I tried hard, I could pretend that I was seeing my hometown in Malaysia – not the way it is now, another rapidly modernising South-East Asian city; but the way it once was, the way I remembered it as a kid. The little skinny shophouses with second-storey windows from which lines of washing were skewered on poles, slung out over the street to dry. Plastic wrappers, bits of paper, scraps of food and cigarette butts were underfoot. Little stalls on the street displayed the carcasses of roasted meats as they hung from hooks, steaming behind glass. People spat publicly; sometimes in front of themselves, sometimes by the side of the street. Men in singlets squatted on plastic footstools, languidly working away with toothpicks at the remnants of their latest meal. Little boys huddled everywhere there was some space, flicking marbles in the dirt. Hundreds of motorbikes sizzled past at each intersection, horns constantly beeping. A humid heat forced everyone underneath awnings on the sidewalk – and where there were no awnings, women raised their umbrellas against the sun.

Yet this wasn't quite a vision of Kuching in the '70s. The voices chattering at every street corner were only vaguely familiar, but not Hokkien or Teochew or Hakka. The roadside stalls sold beef or chicken pho, not laksa or satays. Internet shops punctuated the spaces between shops selling lanterns and fireworks. Women in traditional *ao dai* breezed past astride their bikes. Every evening the loudspeakers in the old city would start up and begin espousing (I assumed) the virtues of the revolution. And everywhere there were white faces with blond and grey and red and brown hair. And one of these faces belonged to the woman whom I was in love with then.

The intoxication of this new relationship charged our explorations. Together we walked the old city, exploring like children in a room full of new and exotic toys. Our days were filled with new sensations – the bite of every dragon fruit, the smell of roasting meat emanating from the dog restaurants near the Red River, the endless chatter of spruikers and peddlers. Then at night it always seemed that a new city emerged – the rattle of motorbikes was replaced by the gentler pace of people strolling in the evening cool, glad to be rid, for a few hours, of the intense heat of day. The two of us would walk amongst them, with a freedom and exhilaration I had never experienced before. I had a three-month Asialink writing grant to absorb all I could see and hear, and write it all down.

There was something else about that time; a reconciling of the person I had been with the person I had become. I was clutching at almost faded memories of another time and place, though half my mind remained on the home I had left in Adelaide. That year marked the first time I could say that I had lived in Australia longer than I had lived anywhere else in the world. Yet the Vietnamese thought I was Viet Kieu, one of the returned. They often tried to speak Vietnamese to me, and I would have to smile apologetically and reply in English. Yet something of that false role suited me – the exile who had come home to a place that seemed familiar, yet changed forever. But the place I felt I was 'returning' to was not a real place any more – it belonged to the past.

I had moved to Adelaide when I was thirteen; old enough to remember Malaysia, but young enough to be able to unconsciously adopt the voices and mannerisms of the place that I had moved to. Even now my stepchildren laugh when I order in Chinese restaurants and lose my Australian accent – the words flatten out at the ends of sentences and inflexions bend, just a little, to the sing-song nature of an Asian language. I often don't realise it until they point it out to me. That way of speaking still survives like some kind of instinct, even though it's often a year or two between conversations in a Chinese dialect.

*

Up near Sapa, right in the hill regions of northern Vietnam, while hiking an isolated trail at the back of one of the village markets, I came across a man who spoke Mandarin. He wore thongs that flapped noisily with each step he made as he approached, then greeted me as if he knew I would be Chinese all along. I stumbled along in my halting Mandarin, a small handful of half-remembered phrases. I had gone to Mandarin classes reluctantly as a child and those were the memories I was being forced to drag out now; pleases and thank-yous and how-are-yous and courteous forms of address – all the necessities of a well brought-up Chinese boy. It didn't take long to expend the possibilities of the conversation in my faltering Mandarin, so the man said goodbye and walked off with his bamboo pole perched on his shoulder. To be truthful I don't recall what we spoke about, yet I still remember what should have been an inconsequential encounter – someone who should have been a forgotten detail on an overseas trip, now imprinted in my mind.

I worked a few days a week helping my host organisation translate Vietnamese texts into English. Mainly I worked on *The Twinkling Star Khue*, a very famous and well-loved historical novel about a tumultuous period in Vietnam's imperial past. The text had been mangled – translated from Vietnamese to French, then back to Vietnamese (for reasons I never really discovered) and finally into bad English; its journey to me was a ready-made metaphor for Vietnam's recent history. Monks, courtesans and princes drifted in and out of the tale, adding to its otherworldliness. I excised strange French words and grammatical oddities that had survived the initial culling and out of that, something Vietnamese started to re-emerge. But like Vietnam itself, I was never able to bridge the gulf of culture and history because I never spoke the language – I had tried to learn a little Vietnamese before coming, but came to regret not making the time to have proper lessons.

I worked on translating the book in fitful bursts and tried to write poetry in between. There were late nights in Hanoi when I would sit up at 1 or 2 a.m., my insomnia prompting me to stay up at the writing desk that overlooked the little alley where life entered and exited our little hotel. The odd motorbike sizzled past, unburdened by other traffic, and sometimes a cough or sneeze reverberated from a neighbouring building. Occasionally you could hear conversations drifting up from the street – human noises normally drowned out in the cacophony of Hanoi's day-time hustle, but tantalisingly audible now. For a few short hours Hanoi was nearly silent, and I would fantasise that its inhabitants would finally allow some secrets to emerge.

*

I started a lot of poems then, but only a few were ultimately finished. Perhaps I was trying to capture something ephemeral, something that demanded experience rather than analysis or reflection. I still haven't gone back to finish them, and doubt I ever will now, because that love-affair ended after I left Vietnam.

My partner is seven months pregnant now. Like most Australians, she has travelled widely and lived in a number of other countries too. And the child in her will be born here, will always call this country home, the same way that I will somehow always refer to Malaysia as one of my homes. In that spirit, we're going to try and find this baby-to-be a name that is both Chinese and Australian – some fruitful amalgam of both sides of her family. Sometimes I feel her moving inside her mother and she's a puppet moving upon strings that stretch to Malaysia and England and Australia and Finland and everywhere else that her ancestors came from. But perhaps that's not the right analogy, because no one pulls those strings, and we all move of our own accord. We travel and make unexpected trips to places and sometimes we discover surprising connections to other places we thought lost to memory or time or both.

Publication Details

SHALINI AKHIL's 'Destiny' appeared in *Meanjin*, Vol. 63, No. 2, 2004.

KEN CHAU's 'The Early Settlers,' 'The Terrorists' and 'The Family Tree' appeared in *The International Terminal and Other Poems*, ed. Christopher Pollnitz (University of Newcastle, 1988) and in *Otherland*, No. 4, 1998.

TOM CHO's 'Learning English' appeared in *Yen*, June/July 2003.

AMY CHOI's 'The Relative Advantages of Learning My Language' appeared in the *Age*, 13 July 2002.

BON-WAI CHOU's 'The Year of the Rooster' appeared in *Meanjin*, Vol. 66, No. 2, 2007.

CHRISTOPHER CYRILL's novel *The Ganges and Its Tributaries* was published by McPhee-Gribble in 1993.

MATT HUYNH's 'ABC Supermarket' and 'A New Challenger' appeared in *CAB: Collaborative Autobiography* (2007): <www.stickman comics.com>.

JENNY KEE's *A Big Life* was published by Penguin Books in 2006.

KYLIE KWONG's *My China* was published by Penguin Books in 2007.

BENJAMIN LAW's 'Towards Manhood' is based on work that first appeared in *frankie* magazine, December 2005/January 2006. Sections of 'Tourism' first appeared in *frankie* in May/June 2008.

HAIHA LE's 'Gingseng Tea and a Pair of Thongs' appeared in *Cau Noi (The Bridge): An Anthology of Vietnamese-Australian Writing* (Casula Power House, 2004).

Sections of LIAN LOW's 'My First Kiss' were read at the Victorian Arts Centre, June 1996, as part of the Irene Mitchell Short Play Award.

PAULINE NGUYEN's *Secrets of the Red Lantern* was published by Murdoch Books in 2007.

THAO NGUYEN's 'The Water Buffalo' appeared in *Cau Noi (The Bridge): An Anthology of Vietnamese-Australian Writing* (Casula Power House, 2004)

PHILLIP TANG's 'Teenage Dreamers' appeared in *Peril: An Asian Australian Journal*, October 2006: <www.asian-australian.org>.

OANH THI TRAN's 'Conversations with my Parents' appeared in *Halfway Between Ca Mau and Saigon*: <bac-lieu.blogspot.com>.

CHI VU's 'The Lover in the Fish Sauce' appeared in *Cau Noi (The Bridge): An Anthology of Vietnamese-Australian Writing* (Casula Power House, 2004).

Contributors

TANVEER AHMED is a psychiatry registrar, writer, comedian and former television journalist. He sits on the Advertising Standards Board and was chosen by a prime minister's committee as one of 100 future Australian leaders. He co-hosted the Channel 7 game show *National Bingo Night*, on which he played the part of the Bingo Commissioner.

SHALINI AKHIL is a Melbourne-based writer who has dabbled in stand-up comedy. She has had work published in *Meanjin*, *Girls' Night In 4*, the *Sleepers Almanac*, the *Age* and in *Silverfish New Writing 7*. Her first novel, *The Bollywood Beauty*, was published by Penguin Australia. She is currently working on her second.

TONY AYRES wrote and directed the feature film *The Home Song Stories* (2007) and directed *Walking on Water* (2002). He has written and directed numerous television dramas, short films and documentaries.

SUNIL BADAMI studied communications at the University of Technology, Sydney and writing at Goldsmiths College, University of London. He has written for the *Sydney Morning Herald*, *Good Weekend*, the *Australian*, *Meanjin* and others, and his work was included in *Best Australian Stories 2007*. He is completing his first novel.

BLOSSOM BEEBY was born in South Korea and left when she was five months old. She was adopted by a loving family and grew up in Adelaide. She now lives in Sydney and is finishing her law degree.

KEN CHAN was born in Shanghai and grew up in Sydney. He was a diplomat, Administrator of the Cocos (Keeling) Islands, and a member of the Refugee Review Tribunal. In 2006 he received a doctorate from the University of Canberra for his interlinked stories of Chinese family life in Australia.

LILY CHAN's parents were Chinese migrants who settled in Far North Queensland in the 1970s. At seventeen, she moved to Brisbane, where she completed degrees in commerce and arts at the University of Queensland. She now lives in Sydney and works in the financial services industry.

KEN CHAU is an Australian-born Chinese poet based in Melbourne. His poems have been published in Australia, France, the UK and the USA. He is currently seeking a publisher for his collection of poems, *Strawberries for Mr Promise*.

JOO-INN CHEW works in general practice and refugee health in Canberra. She has had stories published in anthologies, and is editing a collection by local GPs. She and her partner are expecting a baby in 2008.

TOM CHO is writing a short-fiction collection that explores the themes of identity and popular culture. This collection, which will be published by Giramondo Publishing, is part of his PhD in professional writing at Deakin University. His stories have been published widely, with recent publications in *HEAT* and the *Best Australian Stories* series.

AMY CHOI is currently working on a travel book and is a contributor to the travel pages of the *Weekend Australian*. She also has a column in the *Age* in which she writes about things she has bought from op shops. She lives in Melbourne with her partner and their two daughters.

JAMES CHONG is a doctor and PhD student. He was born in Kuala Lumpur. When he was six months old, his family relocated to Scotland for eighteen months before moving to Australia. He lives with his wife in Sydney.

BON-WAI CHOU was born in Chicago in 1968 but spent her earliest years in Hong Kong. At the age of seven she moved to Australia with her family. She has an MA in economic history from the University of Melbourne and completed further studies at the Johns Hopkins Centre, Nanjing University. She works for the Australian government.

MEI YEN CHUA is a freelance writer and book indexer and is compiling a cheap food guide to Brisbane for publication in late 2008.

CHRISTOPHER CYRILL was born in Melbourne in 1970. He started publishing his poetry at the age of fourteen and his first novel, *The Ganges and Its Tributaries*, was published by McPhee Gribble in 1993. His second novel, *Hymns for the Drowning*, was published in 1998. He is writing the twelfth draft of his next novel, *Crown and Anchor.*

HOP DAC has worked with the National Young Writers' Festival and Short and Sweet and is a co-founder of Sunday Drivers Press. A collection of his short stories, *Croak & Grist*, was recently published by Paroxysm Press. Born in Vietnam, he was raised in Western Australia, where he studied fine arts, and now lives in Melbourne.

ANH DO is an actor, film producer and stand-up comedian.

KHOA DO is a film-director, screenwriter and teacher. In 2005, he was named Young Australian of the Year.

MIA FRANCIS is a writer based in rural Victoria.

ADITI GOUVERNEL was born in Mumbai and grew up in Canberra. She is currently in the US working on her novel.

LEANNE HALL lives in Melbourne. She works as a children's bookseller by day and studies publishing and editing by night. She has had work published in *Sleepers Almanac*, *Going Down Swinging*, *Best Australian Stories*, *Meanjin* and *Allnighter.*

JOY HOPWOOD was the first regular Asian-Australian presenter on *Play School*. She now runs her own production company, and is also a painter and musician.

MATT HUYNH is a Sydney-based comic creator, artist and freelance illustrator. His comics have been awarded the Ledger Award for best small-press title and best new talent, and he won the 2007 Cut and Paste Digital Design Competition.

JENNY KEE is a fashion designer and artist. Born in Sydney in 1947, her designs have been internationally influential since the 1970s, and her artwork has been exhibited widely.

KYLIE KWONG is a chef, restaurateur, television presenter and author. Born in Sydney into a fourth-generation Australian-Chinese family, she honed her cooking skills in some of Sydney's best restaurants and now runs her own restaurant, Billie Kwong, in Sydney.

KEVIN LAI lives in Sydney. Having studied media and culture at Macquarie University, he has written for various newspapers and magazines across the country. He is now pursuing a career in advertising.

JACQUI LARKIN (née Soo) is a third-generation Australian-born Chinese. She is a university lecturer and psychologist. She is married to writer John Larkin and they have three children.

BENJAMIN LAW is a senior contributor for *frankie* magazine. In 2008 he completed his PhD in screenwriting, which involved developing an original six-part television series called *The New Lows*. He is one of five children, and lives with his boyfriend in Brisbane.

MICHELLE LAW was born in 1990 on the Sunshine Coast in Queensland. She is currently studying for a Bachelor of Creative Writing in Brisbane.

SIMONE LAZAROO won the Western Australian Premier's Award for all three of her novels: *The World Waiting to be Made*, *The Australian Fiancé* and *The Travel Writer*. Her short stories have been anthologised in Australia and England. She was a judge of the regional Commonwealth Writers' Prize in 2006, and lectures at Murdoch University in Perth.

HAIHA LE graduated from the University of Melbourne with a BA in cinema studies and Vietnamese literature, and studied acting at the HB studio in New York. Her acting credits include *Kick* (SBS), *Bed of Roses* (ABC), *The Elephant Princess*, *Macbeth*, *Stingers* and many independent film and theatre projects. She lives in Saigon.

Francis Lee OAM worked as a civil engineer and as a translator before becoming a full-time journalist and broadcaster. Until March 2008 he was the executive producer of the Chinese Cantonese group at SBS radio. He is the founding chairman of the Asian Media Council of Australia, vice-president of the Sydney Chinese Writers' Association and former president of the Australian Chinese Forum of Australia.

Jason Yat-Sen Li is a lawyer and political activist. He now lives in Beijing, where he runs his own business advisory firm.

Glenn Lieu was born in Sydney in 1985. He studied finance and computer science at the University of NSW and now works in IT. In his spare time he writes, plays the guitar and is an avid fan of country and folk music.

Uyen Loewald was born in Hai Duong, Vietnam. In 1962, while a student at Saigon University, she was detained without trial for her political activism. She married American diplomat Klaus Loewald in 1964; they moved to Australia in 1970. She has worked as a chef, a community worker, a teacher and an interpreter, and is the author of the memoir *Child of Vietnam* (1987).

Lian Low has written theatre and spoken-word performance pieces and has performed at events including Tranzlesbian Gendermash, Dykeworld, Flow and Hello Kitty. Her articles have been published online and in print, including in *Arts Hub*, *MCV* and *Peril*.

Xerxes Matza is of Filipino-Turkish descent and lives in Sydney. His work has appeared in the *Spiny Babbler Anthology*, *Campus Review* and *UNSWeetened*. His novel-in-progress, *Gentle Warriors*, is about Filipino comfort women during the Second World War. 'The Embarrassments of the Gods' is not the story of his life.

Diana Nguyen is a Melbourne-based actor. She performed at the 2008 Melbourne Comedy Festival and the 2007 Melbourne Short and Sweet Festival, where she was nominated for Best Actress for *Death by 1000 Cuts*. She works as a community-liaison officer and volunteers with community radio and theatre groups.

PAUL NGUYEN studied at Monash University and is now an intern at a major country hospital in Victoria. He comes from a small Vietnamese family whose members are scattered across Australia, the US and Vietnam. This is his first publication.

PAULINE NGUYEN was born in Saigon in 1973. In 1975 her family fled Vietnam by sea and, after a period in Thailand, arrived in Sydney in 1978. After studying communications at the University of Technology, Sydney, she worked in film and television. She now runs, with her brother and her partner, Sydney's award-winning Red Lantern restaurant.

THAO NGUYEN was born in a refugee camp in Thailand; her family arrived in Australia in 1980. She has co-ordinated community projects in theatre, literature and multi-media, and was a member of the NSW Ethnic Communities Council and of Australia's non-government delegation to the United Nations Committee on the Rights of the Child in Geneva. She now works in Vietnam as an international lawyer.

CINDY PAN is best known for her appearances on television programs including *The Glasshouse*, *Sunrise*, *The Panel* and *Sex Life*. As a doctor, she has over a decade of general practice experience. She is the author of the bestselling *Pandora's Box* (2001), as well as *Playing Hard to Get* (2007), co-authored with Bianca Dye.

HOA PHAM is an award-winning author and the founding editor of *Peril*, an online journal devoted to Asian-Australian issues.

OLIVER PHOMMAVANH is an Australian-Thai writer for children, a primary-school teacher and a stand-up comedian. 'Hot and Spicy' is his first published story. He grew up in western Sydney.

CHIN SHEN is a media and communications student from Melbourne.

SIM SHEN is a 36-year-old general practitioner and poet. Born in Malaysia, he has lived in Adelaide for over twenty years. He has been widely published in Australian and overseas literary journals. His first poetry collection was *City of My Skin* (2001).

ANNETTE SHUN WAH is a writer, broadcaster, producer and actor. A fourth-generation Chinese-Australian, she was born in north Queensland and grew up north of Brisbane.

JOHN SO is the Lord Mayor of Melbourne.

RUDI SOMAN was born in Singapore to Indian parents. When he was six he and his family moved to Australia. He has written for newspapers, magazines and websites. Recently he worked as a script-writer for ABC Asia Pacific and co-created an SBS multimedia project. His first novel, *Brother Nation*, was short-listed for the Varuna Award for Manuscript Development. He lives in Sydney.

EMILY J. SUN has led a peripatetic life but is currently back home in Perth raising her son. A high-school English teacher, she has also worked as a waitress, photographer's assistant, office temp, New York nanny and curriculum writer. Her work has been published in *Wet Ink* and *Island*.

SHAUN TAN is an award-winning author of picture books for older readers.

PHILLIP TANG is an Australian writer with Saigon–Sydney roots. He has worked as an ESL teacher, travel-guide editor and freelance writer. His fiction has appeared in *Westerly*, *Peril* and *Visible Ink*. He is writing his first novel, *The Night We Vanish*, set in Vietnam and Australia, for which he was granted a Varuna Fellowship in 2007.

CAROLINE TRAN presents the Australian music program 'Home and Hosed' on Triple J, the ABC's youth radio network.

OANH THI TRAN was born near Bac Lieu in Vietnam. She came to Australia with most of her large family in 1983, with a twelve-month stopover in a refugee camp in Malaysia. She grew up in Brisbane and is now a lawyer living in the UK.

Simon Tong works in IT and is studying editing and communications part-time at the University of Melbourne. He is the father of a spirited three-year-old girl.

Ivy Tseng lives in western Sydney and is currently studying for the HSC.

Diem Vo was born in Vietnam and migrated to Australia with her family in 1981. She grew up in Melbourne's western suburbs and graduated from RMIT University with a Bachelor of Nursing. She works with mentally disordered offenders at a forensic psychiatric hospital.

Chi Vu was born in Vietnam and arrived in Australia in 1979. Her stories have been published in *Meanjin*, the *Age*, *Refo*, and various anthologies, and her plays have been staged in Melbourne and Sydney. In 2000 she received an Asialink writer's residency to Vietnam, where she wrote the critically acclaimed *Vietnam: a Psychic Guide*.

Ray Wing-Lun has worked as a storeman, fettler, kitchen hand, childcare worker and restaurant manager. He studied education and philosophy and now works as a strategic planner, helping people to do their jobs well. His wife and three sons provide support for his continuing education.

Vanessa Woods is an award-winning journalist and author. She has written three children's books and is the author of the travel memoir *It's Every Monkey for Themselves* (2007), about her experiences chasing wild capuchin monkeys through the Costa Rican jungle. She currently lives in North Carolina.

Quan Yeomans is the lead singer of Brisbane-based rock band Regurgitator.

Acknowledgements

A special thank you to Denise O'Dea of Black Inc. for her invaluable input, support and experience in editing, Chris Feik for his insight as always, Clare Forster for her skilful and generous assistance, Tom Deverall for the perfect cover, Anna Lensky and the staff at Black Inc., Alexander Pung and Alison Pung for their special help and insight, and my family and friends for their love and support.

Above all, thank you to each of our contributors, who have enriched this anthology in so many ways, and our 'Tall Poppies,' who kindly responded to my interview requests. Thank you to all the Asian-Australians who submitted their writing and shared their stories – it was such an honour to read them all.

Alice Pung